Praise for

THE CAPED CRUSADE

One of:

Amazon's Best Books of 2016 • *The Washington Post*'s Notable
Books of 2016 • *Esquire*'s Best Books of 2016 • NPR's Best Books
of 2016 • *Popular Mechanics*' Best Books of 2016

"A roaring getaway car of guilty pleasures—film gossip, comic-book esoterica, hilarious tales of nerd rage. . . . Weldon writes with humor and Day-Glo élan."

—Jennifer Senior, *The New York Times*

"*The Caped Crusade* is a great read for those who are proud Gothamites, those less initiated, and those who flip the switch on the Bat-Signal in order to find themselves. . . . A sharp, deeply knowledgeable and often funny look at the cultural history of Batman and his fandom . . . both a page-turner and a Riddler Trophy."

—*Chicago Tribune*

"Engaging. . . . What Weldon ultimately achieves here is a character and comic-franchise history that is itself flexible enough to become what the reader needs it to be. If you're a Bat-neophyte, this is an accessible introduction; if you're a dyed-in-the-Latex Bat-nerd, this is a colorfully rendered magical history tour redolent with nostalgia."

—*The Washington Post*

"[*The Caped Crusade*] accomplishes what so many supervillains, from the Joker to Bane, have long desired to do: pin down Batman and systematically dissect him. Weldon navigates Batman's history with an expert step . . . a winning mix of humor, and incisive social analysis. Even his footnotes are funny. Under that famous cowl, he sees ugliness, wonder, and the undercurrents of pop culture in all their conflicting glory."

—NPR

"Writing a book about Batman is tricky. He is a cultural icon deeply meaningful to many because his story touches on themes of loss, adversity and perseverance. Also, he is an implausible character who defies laws of physics and common sense every time he swoops on gun-blazing lunatics. Weldon successfully walks the tightrope, showing reverence for the character but keeping it fun."

—Associated Press

"Excellent, insightful. . . . Weldon has crafted that rare jewel: a book of comics analysis that nerds and 'normals' alike can enjoy."

—*Publishers Weekly* (starred review)

"Sprawling in scope, yet written with breezy flair. . . . An enthusiastic, immersive, entertaining guide for both die-hard Batfans and curious onlookers."

—*Kirkus Reviews*

"Simply put, *The Caped Crusade* is the best book I've read this year. . . . Highly addictive reading, with just the right blend of comic book history and nerd culture analysis."

—*Comic Book Herald*

"*The Caped Crusade: Batman and the Rise of Nerd Culture* doesn't read like a history book, and it's not just due to the author's fantastic storytelling. Weldon informs the reader of the history of Batman with a passion that can be found in any tried-and-true Batman fan, and with a level of knowledge I've never encountered before. It is the book that Gotham City deserves, and I can't recommend it enough."

—*ComicsVerse*

"Weldon, a critic for NPR, offers possibly the most erudite and well-researched fanboy manifesto ever."

—*Booklist*

"There's no better time to stop, relax, take a breath and read NPR critic Glen Weldon's history of Batman. . . . Because here, in these entertaining pages, you will discover that nerd rage over the Dark Knight is nothing new."

—*Mashable* (Geek Book of the Week)

"[A] smart, engaging dissection of Batman's pulpy comic-book roots, his rise to campy '60s TV stardom, his takeover of toy shelves and his resurrection as the dark knight of the silver screen."

—*Parade*

"For fans of Gotham's Batman, this is the perfect book to pick up before you head to the movie. . . . Even casual fans will find themselves quickly turning pages to learn more about how our comic heroes affect and even shape our everyday lives."

—*Bookish*

"Anyone familiar with Weldon's frequent NPR appearances will delight in this book's near-perfect translation of his verbal and comedic sensibilities. Its tone is reverent and analytical, acknowledging the absurdities of Batman and celebrating its wondrous appeal in equal measure."

—*DCist*

"Weldon's *The Caped Crusade* is Batman: sometimes hilarious, sometimes frightening, but always intelligent, fascinating, and impossible to put down."

—Tom King, *New York Times* bestselling writer of DC Comics' *Batman*

"If you looked at Glen Weldon's utility belt, you'd find wit, humor, and endless knowledge about Batman. Thankfully he's condensed that utility belt into a book where you will learn the origin, the ups, the downs, and the sideways of one of the most iconic bat-based superheroes of all time."

—Kumail Nanjiani, comedian and star of HBO's *Silicon Valley*

"This is the hero's journey of Batman from a raw idea of a character to a cornerstone of pop culture. Weldon pulls the back the cowl and reveals us—creators, performers and fans—all collaborating to shape a modern myth that bends with the times to endure. Once I started, I kept reading every chance I got."

—Jeff Parker, writer of *Batman '66*

"*The Caped Crusade* is seriously informed, daringly opinionated and endlessly charming. . . . It's not just a book about Batman, its Nerd Culture's origin story."

—Guy Branum, host of *Pop Rocket*

"*The Caped Crusade* is breezy, insightful, and surprisingly moving. Glen Weldon is the illuminating, hilarious writer Batman deserves—and the one we need right now."

—DC Pierson, author of *The Boy Who Couldn't Sleep and Never Had To* and *Crap Kingdom*

ALSO BY GLEN WELDON

Superman: The Unauthorized Biography

THE CAPED CRUSADE

BATMAN AND THE
RISE OF NERD CULTURE

GLEN WELDON

SIMON & SCHUSTER PAPERBACKS
New York   London   Toronto   Sydney   New Delhi

Simon & Schuster Paperbacks
An Imprint of Simon & Schuster, Inc.
1230 Avenue of the Americas
New York, NY 10020

First Simon & Schuster trade paperback edition March 2017

SIMON & SCHUSTER PAPERBACKS and colophon are
registered trademarks of Simon & Schuster, Inc.

For information about special discounts for bulk purchases,
please contact Simon & Schuster Paperback Special Sales at
1-866-506-1949 or business@simonandschuster.com.

The Simon & Schuster Speakers Bureau can bring authors
to your live event. For more information or to book an event, contact
the Simon & Schuster Speakers Bureau at 1-866-248-3049 or visit
our website at www.simonspeakers.com.

Interior design by Lewelin Polanco

3 5 7 9 10 8 6 4

Library of Congress Cataloging-in-Publication Data is available.

ISBN 978-1-4767-5673-8
ISBN 978-1-4767-5674-5 (ebook)

FOR BILL FINGER

CONTENTS

Contents

THE CAPED CRUSADE

THE CAPED
CRUSADE

INTRODUCTION

Batman, Nerd

Over his seven decades of fictive life, the elastic concept of "Batman" has taken on a host of shapes. He started off simply enough, as a murderous, gun-wielding rip-off of the Shadow. Since then he's clocked field time as a time-and-space-hopping gadabout, a Pop Art scoutmaster, a globe-trotting master spy, a gadget-happy criminologist, and a grim, remorseless ninja of the urban night.

No single image defines Batman, because any single image is too small to contain the various layered and at times contradictory meanings we've instilled in him. Since his first appearance, we have projected onto the character our own fears, our preoccupations, our moral imperatives, and have seen in him what we wish to.

It's this limitless capacity for interpretation that sets him apart from his comparatively stolid fellows in spandex. It's why so many different iterations of Batman have managed to escape the nerd enclave of comics to blithely coexist in the cultural consciousness of normals. Anyone can look at Christian Bale's Kevlar-suited, mouth-breathing Batman, croaking his dire threats like an enraged, laryngitic frog, and immediately recognize him as the same character as Adam West's Batusi Batman, out there on the go-go floor, shaking what his dead mama gave him.

They are both equally true, because every thirty years or so Batman cycles from dark to light and back again. Twice before in his seventy-seven-year history, the Dark Knight has given way to the Camp

Crusader, and twice before a small subset of his most ardent fans have risen up in protest to demand that Batman return to his grittier roots. These hard-core enthusiasts accept only the darkest, grimmest, most hypermasculine version of the character imaginable and view any alternate Bat-iteration as somehow suspect, inauthentic, debased, and ssssorta gay.

Adam West's Batman ended one cycle in 1969, and Denny O'Neil and Neal Adams's Batman began the next the following year. Joel Schumacher's Batman ended that second cycle in the mid-nineties; ten years later, Christopher Nolan's Batman began the one in which we now find ourselves.

But this recursive pattern isn't immediately apparent to the casual fan. To the culture at large, it's the mix that matters.

To most people, there is no one Batman, but an endless blurry parade of Batmen, broadly identifiable by a series of core signifiers: millionaire Bruce Wayne, dead parents, bat costume, secret lair, and Gotham City. Precisely how these signifiers combine, and in what idiom—crime noir, gothic melodrama, Boy's Own adventure, spy thriller, broad slapstick, or slick science fiction—remains endlessly, defiantly mutable. It's exactly this protean adaptability (paired with a multinational megaconglomerate's marketing muscle) that has ensured the character's longevity.

That, and his vaunted "relatability."

THE MYTH OF RELATABILITY

"Batman's my guy," a friend and lifelong comics fan told me when I described this book project to him. "No powers, just grit. He's human. He's *relatable.*"

This is an oft-heard refrain among the subset of people who talk and think about superheroes. We were sitting in a diner; our order had just arrived. "You or I," he said, pointing with his French fry at each of us in turn, before dipping it into his milkshake, "could be Batman."

Here's the thing: we really could not.

But we *think* we could.

There is a widespread tendency, among nerds and normals alike, to dismiss the impact of Bruce Wayne's billionaire status on the idea of Batman. But of course that wealth is Batman's true superpower. Its narrative function, in any Batman story, is to turn the flatly impossible into the vaguely plausible. It works, essentially, as magic.

Yet few fans acknowledge that socioeconomic wish fulfillment plays even a small role in the bond they feel with him; many don't even consider his wealth to be a core element of his character.

Which, given that it is only this unimaginable wealth that makes his whole one-man, Chiroptera-themed war on crime possible in the first place, is a) nuts, and b) fascinating. It speaks to the abiding and uniquely American belief that anyone can become obscenely rich if they just . . . *want* to, really hard.

This belief aligns closely with the wildly aspirational and borderline-delusional conviction among even the most indolent of nerds that becoming Batman is an achievable goal, given sit-ups enough and time.

That is the key difference between Batman and many of his other super-cohorts: Superman, after all, represents an ideal we can never achieve, and we know it; that's pretty much the whole point of him.

Yet one unintended and insidious consequence of Batman's humanity is that consciously or not, we are doomed to compare ourselves to him, and we cannot help but find ourselves wanting. In the ad for the fitness regimen, the miracle diet, we are forever the before photo, and he, always, the after.

But of course, there's more than just a few workout DVDs separating us from him. However much Bat-fans profess it, Batman's status as a nonpowered human being is not the true reason they feel such a kinship with the character. There is something lurking deeper in the character's essence that speaks to them. Something coded into his conceptual DNA.

The bond fans feel with him has less to do with the tragedy that formed him—the violent death of his parents—and everything to do with his singular reaction to it.

Which is to say: his oath.

Young Bruce Wayne first swore it back in *Detective Comics* #33 in 1939. He'd been around a while by then, having made his first appearance months earlier in *Detective Comics* #27. It took him seven issues to merit an origin story, albeit one dashed off in a brisk twelve panels.

Having seen his parents gunned down before his eyes, wee Bruce Wayne makes the following vow by candlelight: "And I swear by the spirits of my parents to avenge their deaths by spending the rest of my life warring on all criminals."

This oath is ridiculous on its face, so laughably grandiose and melodramatic that only a kid could make it.

Which is exactly its power.

That oath is a *choice*. An act of will. A deliberate reaction to a shattering injustice. More crucially, it is an act of self-rescue. It's these twenty-four words, after all, that give his life purpose and launch him into an existence entirely devoted to protecting others from the fate that befell him. This is why, for all the character's vaunted darkness, he is now and has always been a creature not of rage but of hope. He believes himself to be an agent of change; he is the living embodiment of the simple, implacably optimistic notion *Never again*.

But in the 1970s, something odd happened to Batman's childhood oath. It entered puberty.

Writers of Batman comics spent the seventies and eighties desperately striving to course-correct for what they saw as the grave disservice done to the character by a late-sixties fad of frothy Pop Art Batmania. In a very real sense, everything about the dark, grim Batman that exists today in the public imagination was born in reaction to—and would not exist without—Adam West's goofy, groovy Caped Crusader.

Many of the changes introduced by the writers of the post-Batmania era were obvious, like sidelining Robin the Boy Wonder and returning Batman to his very earliest incarnation as a lone urban vigilante. But they also took his ceaseless war on criminals (which had remained a part of the character, even in the heyday of his most outlandish interplanetary adventures) and submerged it in a steamy broth of seventies pop psychology. Thus, a crucial element of his backstory long treated as subtext now became the central, driving text in every issue: his childhood vow curdled into psychological obsession.

In the eighties, writers like Frank Miller went even further, amping up Batman's obsession into a study in violent sociopathy.

ENTER THE NERDS

At exactly the same time Batman was becoming an obsessive, a new breed of enthusiast began its rise to prominence. For years they had lurked in the shadowy corners of popular culture, quietly pursuing their niche interests among themselves, keeping their heads down to avoid the inquisitive, judgmental gaze of the wider world.

They called themselves fans, experts, *otaku*. Everyone else, of course, called them nerds.

Nerds had spent decades creating and policing carefully wrought self-identities around their strictly specialized interests: comic books, computers, science fiction, video games, Dungeons & Dragons. What truly united them, however, were not the specific objects of their enthusiasm but the nature of their enthusiasm itself—the all-consuming degree to which they rejected the reflexive irony their peers prized. Instead, these fans blithely surrendered themselves to their passion.

The rise of the Internet would fuel this passion by connecting them to others who shared it. In only a handful of years, their particular species of enthusiasm—"nerding out"—would supplant irony to become the dominant mode in which we engage with each other and with the culture around us.

And it was Batman—Batman the obsessive, Batman the ultimate nerd—who acted as the catalyst for billions of normals to embrace the culture they had once dismissed or rejected. It is Batman whose comics, television shows, and movies continue to serve as gateway drugs to the nerdly life. Because whether it is treated as lofty mission statement or driving obsession, his childhood oath is the thing about this character—far more central than his "relatability"—that resonates deeply with us, ardent Bat-fan and casual moviegoer alike.

COMIC-CON AS MICROCOSM

July 2013. San Diego, California. Comic-Con.

I am a forty-five-year-old man standing in line for a toy Batmobile. And I am not alone.

The line in question begins at the Entertainment Earth booth in the 2300 section of the convention floor, wraps twice around a dining area where families huddle in clots to listlessly chew terrible pizza at one another, doubles back and extends down over the thick blue carpet to bisect no less than twelve aisles, travels past the Small Press Pavilion (whose beardy, be-flanneled residents regard us line-standers warily), and continues on through Webcomics, to reach its terminus somewhere beyond the horizon in the mist-shrouded recesses of the 1100 section, where there be dragons. And dungeons. And mages and paladins, presumably, as I think the 1100 section is Tabletop Gaming.

I have been standing in this line for the past forty-five minutes. I don't know it yet, but I will be standing in it for another hour. When I at last make it to the front, I will too-happily plunk down sixty bucks for a chunk of extruded plastic in the form of a "CON-EXCLUSIVE!" toy Batmobile—the classic version from the late-sixties television show.

Like most nerds my age, my first exposure to Batman didn't come in the form of a comic, but from television. In my case, from reruns of the *Batman* TV show every afternoon at three thirty on channel 29.

By age six I had memorized the schedule of every Philadelphia station, so while other kids spent their after-school time sweatily to-ing and fro-ing in the sunshine, I'd run inside, kneel before the TV, and spend the hours until dinner spinning the UHF dial like a safecracker: *Spider-Man* on channel 17. *The Space Giants* on channel 48. And always, every day, *Batman* on channel 29 at three thirty sharp.

The show is famous for its bifurcated appeal: kids love its bold colors, its fight scenes, its derring-do, while adults appreciate the goofy, po-faced "Holy Priceless Collection of Etruscan Snoods!"–iness of it all.

But that's not the whole story. Because something happens to us nerds *between* childhood and adulthood, as the long, greasy night of our teenaged years settles over us. Our youthful ardor for the show decays into a pitched loathing. "That's not Batman," we begin to insist. "Batman's a *badass*, that show doesn't take Batman *seriously*."

For the last three decades, the American superhero has been trapped in a perpetual age of adolescence, with fans and creators peevishly avowing that these spandex-clad fantasy characters created to entertain children must now be taken seriously, by which they mean they should be mired in joyless nihilism: *badass*.

It was Batman and his fans who brought this benighted era about, and there are hopeful signs that Batman and his fans may soon be responsible for ending it.

For now, however, I am standing in this endless line in hopes of scoring me some of that sweet, sweet Batmobile action. I decided to wait in line for it because waiting in line is, on one level, sort of what Comic-Con is all about. But mostly because I feel for the sixties *Batman* TV series a profound and passionate love.

It's not simply nostalgia, though of course nostalgia is the nutrient agar upon which all of nerd culture grows. No, I love it because of what it represents, what it argues against: the mere existence of Adam West's Batman breezily yet effectively rejects the notion that the only valid Batman is a grim, gritty badass.

This is why I am so heartened to look around me at Comic-Con and see, for the first time, toys and merch based on the 1966 television show, after long decades when it seemed as if DC Comics wished to disavow any trace of it.

The young men ahead of me in line are waiting not for the Batmobile, but for some robot action figure thingy. Yet I hear something familiar in the urgent rush of their voices, and in their adjective choices, like "superior," marked by the telltale overarticulated terminal *r* to which we nerds default in conversation. I see it lighting up their faces as they tick off the names and combat specs of their favorite *kaiju*-whomping fightin' mechs. It's what I saw in my friend's face at the diner as he rhapsodized about how and why being Batman was an achievable goal. Same passion, just dressed up in a different suit. And that's all that Comic-Con is: a whole lot of different suits.

THE WAY WE NERD NOW

It's no longer just nerds like me who love Batman and things like him. The entire cultural context around him has changed. Over the past few decades, "geeking out" has become the new normal, the default mode in which many millions of us engage the world around us. When we love a thing, we love it deeply.

Hobbies have been around forever, kept discreetly in a tidy, out-of-the-way corner of one's day-to-day existence. That's not what I'm talking about.*

Now, spurred by the Internet, which inspires and nurtures niche interests, many millions of us define ourselves by our specific enthusiasms: Foodie! Politics wonk! Wine snob! Music geek! But this is misleading, because the *object* of our enthusiasm isn't what matters. What's important—what we share—is the delirious, all-consuming, and blissfully unself-conscious nature of that passion.

---

* Sports, of course, are the one area of public life where a nerdy obsession is so uniformly embraced by the culture at large that it is not recognized as nerdy, and is even considered a sign of healthy, normal development. That's not the issue here, either.

The passion is not new. But its current cultural ubiquity very much is.

I talk to a couple of San Diego locals, for whom Comic-Con is not the Great Nerd Hajj it is for me, but an annual family tradition in which they've taken part for as long as they remember. To them, dressing up and hitting Comic-Con just comes with the zip code, like Mardi Gras in New Orleans or the Mummers Parade in Philly.

That's how it worked for comedian Scott Aukerman, who grew up in Orange County and has been coming to Comic-Con for decades. I ask him the question I've been asking everyone this year: Why do you think that what we've come to call "nerd culture" has grown so pervasive?

I get lots of different answers, and I've noticed, unsurprisingly, that the answers seem to be a function of one's perspective.

To the comics pros I've talked to, it's simply that the wider world has finally discovered the appeal of comics. The medium of the comic book carried a stigma that acted as a barrier to entry and kept the normals out. But today's cinematic special effects can reproduce comic book action easily, so the joy and wonder of these characters and stories can now be seen and enjoyed by all.

To many of the fans I've talked to, especially those couples who come to Comic-Con in themed costumes with their kids in tow, it's just a family thing. Their parents were/are nerds who instilled in them a love of nerdy pursuits. They love the things that brought them together as a family; it's just that simple: My family had Uno. Theirs has Joss Whedon's *Firefly*.

To the bloggers I've talked to, it's the Internet that changed everything. They were nerdy kids loving the thing they loved for their own reasons, and then one day they found a message board or website that told them they weren't alone. Communities formed, communities that not only accepted them but reinforced their nerdiest behavior traits. They found a home.

All of these answers, and many more, are perfectly correct, of course. Because cultures are messy things that grow and thrive for a host of overlapping reasons. But Aukerman is the first person I talk to who puts the rise of nerd culture in a wider sociopolitical context.

"We were the first generation without a draft," he says matter-of-factly. "We didn't need to worry about life and death, so we channeled all that time and energy into obsessing over this TV show or that comic book."

This blunt theory—let's call it "the Lamest Generation"—is one that hits close to home, as I have spent much of the last few days wondering how Comic-Con's garish gewgaws and ephemeral delights would strike my dour, Welsh-immigrant grandparents, who came of age in the Depression.

That night I imagine the ghost of Norman "Bud" Johnson, who as a boy would wait by the railroad tracks to scavenge lumps of coal that fell from passing trains so he could heat his parents' house.

I see him floating at the foot of my hotel bed, glowering incredulously at the nightstand, where I, his forty-five-year-old male heir, have lovingly placed my new toy Batmobile.

1

Origin and Growing Pains (1939–1949)

Criminals are a superstitious, cowardly lot. So my disguise must be able to strike terror into their hearts. I must be a creature of the night, black, terrible . . . a . . . a . . .

—DETECTIVE COMICS #33 (NOVEMBER 1939)

But out of the sky, spitting death . . . The Batman!

—BATMAN #1 (SPRING 1940)

The very first thing Batman does—and he does it right up at the tippy-top of page 3 of his very first adventure in *Detective Comics* #27, which was dated May 1939 but actually hit newsstands in late March—is strike a pose.

Even then, as he was first set loose upon the four-color world, striking poses was already his thing.

He stands on a rooftop, behind two burglars. The text floating in the night sky above him offers a luridly gleeful introduction that could have been lifted straight from pulp magazines of the day: "As the two men leer over their conquest, they do not notice a third menacing figure standing behind them . . . It is the 'BAT-MAN!'"

Indeed it is. Instantly recognizable as Batman to our modern eyes, if we allow for nearly a century of iconographic shift, he glowers at the thugs with his feet shoulder-width apart, arms folded across his chest.

Despite what those words over his head would have us believe, his carriage does not quite rise to the level of menacing as much as it lends him an air of snitty impatience. He seems a stern and gravely disappointed dad. Standing on a roof. In a Dracula getup.

Said getup seems less familiar to us as we gaze back at it from our contemporary vantage point. His ears are devil's horns, thick and conical—two large carrots sticking out of a snowman—and the angle's wrong. They jut from the sides of his head at forty-five-degree angles like the arms of a ref signaling the extra point, or a Village Person doing the "Y."

The cowl itself is fine, revealing only the nondescript mouth and chin of the man inside it, as we have come to expect. The color scheme checks out, mostly: gray long johns, blue-black trunks, yellow belt—and, bizarrely, purple evening gloves.* The chest insignia is still little more than a black squiggle, but that will change.

The cape is where the real drama of the garment lives: it arcs out and away from his shoulders, hanging above them in vaulting parabolas (clearly there's some underwire involved) that allow the graceful concavities of its deeply scalloped hemline maximum visual impact.

The cape will prove to be a constant, adding an Expressionist punch, a bolus of gothy showbiz. In the hands of his first artists, like Bob Kane, Sheldon Moldoff, and Jerry Robinson, it'll take the form of stiff bat wings or flow like silk, depending on a given story's needs. Later, under Dick Sprang, Win Mortimer, Jim Mooney, and others, it will settle down a bit, save for snapping in the breeze to convey Batman's speed. By the 1970s, Neal Adams, Jim Aparo, and Dick Giordano will overlay a rigorous and unforgiving photorealism onto Batman's universe, yet the cape will remain unfettered to such mundane concerns as physics. It will lengthen and shorten at will or swirl around him like tendrils of malevolent smoke. Later still, stylists like Marshall Rogers and Kelley

---

* The weird gloves wouldn't hang around long, and whenever DC Comics reprints this first appearance, the gloves are recolored to match the cape.

Jones will literally and figuratively stretch the cape and its role in story-telling to dazzling lengths. It will become a major character, a silent but expressive narrator who guides the reader's eye and infuses the action with layers of meaning, evoking a moldering grave shroud, or the leathery wings of a demon, or the fierce and howling winds of Aeolus.

But back on that rooftop in the spring of 1939, facing down two thugs who have just murdered a wealthy businessman and pilfered his safe, dude was basically wearing an umbrella.

The final visual element that clicks into place has less to do with *how* he appears and more to do with *where* he appears. He has carefully interposed himself between the robbers and the full moon, which looms over his right shoulder like it's trying to steal a peek at them.

This imagery—Batman in silhouette against the round yellow circle of the moon—is deeply embedded in the character's narrative DNA. We'll see echoes of it in the Bat-Signal and in the chest insignia that distinguishes the Batman of the sixties. It's a motif that will occur and recur on all manner of Bat-merchandise, from jigsaw puzzles to bath towels; Tim Burton's 1989 *Batman* film will stop its third act dead in its tracks to pay it homage. Batman and the full moon are inextricably linked, and they have been ever since this very first adventure.

RAW ELEMENTS

The building blocks were in place from the start. He was a detective; you couldn't miss that. The title of the story, not to put too fine a point on it, is "The Case of the Chemical Syndicate," deliberately evoking Poe, Conan Doyle, and dime detective novels. The familiar story beats are plain: After dispatching the two goons on the roof,* the Bat-Man reads the contract they lifted from the wealthy man's safe, pieces together the

---

* By KO'ing the first and tossing the other off the mansion's roof without a backward glance.

nefarious plot behind the murder, and makes for the head villain's lair to confront the mastermind behind this grisly business.

This first outing also establishes the Bat-Man as a skilled martial artist, or at least an effective bruiser. In writer Bill Finger's prose, as in the pulp magazines he loved, no noun would think to be seen in public without a modifying adjective on its arm; thus we are informed that our hero's headlocks are "deadly," his right crosses "terrific," his heaves "mighty," his tackles "flying." We witness him deliver a powerful sock to the jaw of the chief bad guy,* which sends the poor schmuck tumbling backward through a guardrail and into a waiting tank of acid.

Here at the start, this freshly minted, antiheroic hero's vigilantism takes a particularly ruthless and frequently deadly form. The story's opening panels reveal that "this fellow they call the 'Bat-Man'" has been active in his as-yet-unnamed city long enough to attract the ire of Police Commissioner Gordon.

As for the Bat-Man's attitude toward his own violent actions, or any hint of what first set him down this grim road, this first adventure offers no clue. Old-School Bat-Man is a laconic cuss, a creature of action, not words. It'll take a few more issues for us to earn even a glimpse of our hero in repose. It will take even longer for the advent of thought balloons to make us privy to his inner monologue.

So we know only what we see: the Bat-Man punching a villain over a railing to his agonizing death and commenting to a nearby hostage, "A fitting end to his kind."

This homicide proves only the beginning of his murderous spree. In just the first year of his existence Batman will send some twenty-four men, two vampires, a pack of werewolves, and several giant mutants to their ultimate ends, occasionally at the business end of a gun. Eventually—after the tyke in the pixie boots shows up to lighten the tone—Batman will find himself resorting to deadly force less often, and will

---

* SFX: "Sock!"

ultimately reject the use of firearms outright. For now, though, he's a remorseless killer.

The final element is the story's last-panel revelation that the Bat-Man is secretly wealthy young socialite Bruce Wayne.

The notion of a masked vigilante with a secret identity was certainly not new. Neither, in a time when the country was still climbing shakily to its feet after the Great Depression, were light entertainments that revolved around the lives of the young, beautiful, and very rich. It was the era of *The Thin Man, Topper, Private Lives,* and *Anything Goes.* Millions of Americans passed long, happy hours in theaters watching the adventures of gadabouts in smoking jackets and sylphs in organza gowns, trading barbs and champagne toasts against a backdrop of unimaginable luxury.

And even though the quaint drawing room whodunit was passing out of vogue, supplanted by the pulpy urban noir of hard-boiled detective yarns, a fascination with the upper crust lingered.

In "The Case of the Chemical Syndicate," and indeed in many of these first adventures, it's notable how thoroughly writer Bill Finger grafts the guns-and-gumshoes tropes from pulp magazines like *Argosy, True Detective, Spicy Mystery Stories,* and *Black Mask* onto the rarified world of old-money privilege.

The result is a puzzling alloy indeed: Bored man-about-town Bruce Wayne lives a life of pampered ease and dons his outlandish garb to bust the heads of brutish thugs. Crucially, he does so not to defend the rights of the honest American workingman like the populist hero Superman, but more often to protect his wealthy friends and associates—and their money.

In this first adventure, he settles a dispute between rich rival businessmen over a chemical fortune. In his next, he nabs jewel thieves. Over and over, throughout this first year, he faces down those who would threaten the lives of millionaires to extort their millions from them.

Of course, the wealth of Bruce Wayne, and by extension the social world he inhabits, is a central tenet of the Batman mythology, and one that serves two simultaneous narrative purposes. On a practical level, it's a plot device to explain it all away: the gadgets, the vehicles, the HQ, the vast featureless stretches of leisure time that allow him to pursue his single-minded quest for justice. That quest will ultimately leach into Bruce Wayne's life as well. In the decades to come, writers will transform Wayne from bored socialite to passionate philanthropist who uses his money to fund civic programs that combat crime in ways that do not involve donning tights and punching it.

But the second and more essential storytelling function of his lavish wealth is wish fulfillment. He was birthed at a time of national hardship when the country reveled in escapism. He embodied a glamorous lifestyle free of prosaic concerns like paychecks and debt, foreclosures and defaults.

So that's the Bat-Man, in his first-ever adventure: detective, martial artist, grim vigilante, aristocrat. And so he has remained, through the decades. But in that first appearance, and for most of his first year of existence, he was one more thing as well:

A rip-off.

IN THE CROWDED SHADOW OF THE SHADOW

Batman ripped off the Shadow. This is by no means a controversial assertion; both of his cocreators essentially acknowledged as much in interviews. Indeed, "The Case of the Chemical Syndicate" so closely apes the November 1936 Shadow tale "Partners of Peril" as to seem to modern sensibilities howlingly, and legally, actionable.

The Bat-Man was by no means the only Shadow rip-off stalking his prey in the urban jungle of late-1930s America. Introduced as a mysterious announcer on the *Detective Story Hour* radio program in July of 1930, the Shadow swiftly became the very first multimedia sensation when the public found itself more fascinated by the program's creepy announcer than the stories he introduced. The publishers of *Detective Story Magazine* commissioned a series of Shadow film shorts and tasked writer Walter B. Gibson (under the pen name Maxwell Grant) with churning out tales of a sinister, black-clad crime fighter who worked under the cloak of night to terrorize his victims.

In those print adventures, the Shadow was in fact famous aviator Kent Allard, a master of disguise who availed himself of several different identities, including a successful businessman, a humble janitor, and—most famously—Lamont Cranston, wealthy gadabout.

These pulp adventures gave rise to a wave of mystery-men imitators like the Crimson Avenger, the Green Hornet (both millionaires), and the Phantom Detective (a wealthy socialite who could be summoned from his crime lab by a beacon). *Popular Detective* magazine featured a mysterious figure who donned a hood emblazoned with a black bat to hunt criminals. He called himself the Bat.

In 1937, the Mutual Broadcasting System launched a new program in which the Shadow stepped out of his usual radio role as anthology host to take a central part in the action. The show streamlined the character's already Byzantine pulp continuity to focus on the Lamont Cranston identity. This new radio version (voiced, initially, by Orson Welles) also came with a new superpower: the ability to "cloud men's minds" and render himself invisible, a device that neatly obviated any need to explain to a radio audience just how it was that the Shadow always managed to overhear his victims' nefarious schemes.

The show's opening theme* became a cultural touchstone, saturating the airwaves and imprinting itself upon a generation of listeners.

Thus the Shadow's shadow grew longer still—long enough to inspire two additional imitators in 1939. Both wore cowls and swanned about the rooftops of their respective cities in scalloped capes that resembled the wings of a bat. One, who first appeared in the July 1939 issue of

---

* Strains of Saint-Saëns's *Le Rouet d'Omphale*, Opus 31, accompanied by the character's spine-tingling catchphrase: "Who knows what evil lurks in the hearts of men?"

Black Book Detective, called himself the Black Bat. He hung around until the early fifties. The other, who'd hit newsstands two months earlier in *Detective Comics* #27, proved to have more staying power.

He went by "the Bat-Man."

BECOMING A BAT

Bob Kane created Batman. At least that's what Vin Sullivan, his first editor at National Comics, and later, generations of fans, believed. That was because Kane said so.

In fact, Kane had designed a character that looked nothing like the one he ultimately sold to National. In a bid to create a comic book character that could match the wildly unprecedented success of National's Superman—introduced almost a year before and already a merchandising sensation—Kane had sketched a dutiful knockoff.

To do so, he traced an Alex Raymond drawing from the January 17, 1939, *Flash Gordon* comic strip, which depicted Flash swinging in on a slender rope to rescue his companion from a monster. Kane kept the action pose but drew a new costume on the figure that essentially reversed the color scheme of Superman's outfit—instead of blue tights and red trunks, his guy wore a skintight scarlet leotard and blue-black trunks. Superman wore nothing to disguise his features, so Kane gave his character a domino mask.

The only significant thing that set him apart from Superman— what Kane considered his true magic, and which, he would later tell interviewers, was inspired by a Leonardo da Vinci sketch—was the wings. Kane drew a pair of stiff, black bat wings affixed to the figure's back. It looked dramatic. It had potential, Kane thought, because it was different, but not—if the idea was to appeal to the kids who loved Superman—*too* different.

He scrawled a name below it: "The Bat-Man."

As for the Bat-Man's shtick, who he was and what he did, Kane had some vague thoughts, but he knew a guy who could flesh that stuff out.

Years before, he'd met a kid named Milton "Bill" Finger at a party, and they'd gotten to talking about the comic strips they loved. Kane and Finger began to collaborate on a variety of strips that Kane ended up selling to newspaper syndicates and, ultimately, National Comics, home of Superman. They made an effective team. Finger attacked his work with zeal but lacked social confidence, occupying the periphery of any room he entered. If Kane, who was merely a competent cartoonist, were to enter the same room, he'd plant himself at its center, all back-slapping, glad-handing brio. Drawing was hard work for Kane and always would be, but he was a tireless negotiator; selling came easy to him. So the gigs kept coming.

They had a system. He and Finger would fire ideas back and forth and Finger would write the scripts. Kane would draw them. None of Kane's editors knew that Finger existed, as he signed only "Rob't Kane"—and, later, "Bob Kane"—to the strips he turned in.

So when this Bat-Man idea came around, Kane considered it business as usual: he showed up at Finger's apartment with the sketch and asked for his thoughts.

The young man's reaction was simple: the drawing looked too much like Superman wearing a craft project. The wings seemed ungainly, impractical, even a little silly. Finger proceeded to suggest several changes that introduced the iconographic elements now universally associated with the concept "Batman," changes that effectively transformed Kane's Winged Underwear-Man into a Dark Knight.

First off, it was a guy in red long johns. He didn't look scary enough to merit his name. Finger showed Kane an illustration of a bat in a dictionary and pointed to the distinctive long ears. Lose the wings, Finger said, and replace them with a flowing, scalloped cape that would help convey speed. He'd need gloves, to ensure he didn't leave fingerprints behind. And fix the color scheme—if this was to be a bat man, he'd work at night; he'd blend into the shadows. The crimson tights became a dusky gray, and the cloak and cowl became black—or as near to black as the printing process of the time allowed, which was black with blue highlights.

They didn't bother with supplying him an origin, at first. Superman had a nifty one, but Superman was science fiction, and their Bat-Man would be a two-fisted detective straight out of the pulps; pulp heroes had adventures, not backstories. It took years for readers to learn the true identity of the Shadow, for example, so Batman's secrets could wait. In their place, Finger needed a story that would sell the character. So he swiped one, streamlining Theodore Tinsley's 1936 Shadow yarn "Partners of Peril" to fit within the allotted six pages, and to make room for an even more outré hero.

Kane, for his part, would later cite several other influences on Batman's look, including Zorro (another hero birthed in the pulps) and the 1930 film *The Bat Whispers*, in which a mysterious figure in a hooded costume terrorizes and murders guests at a wealthy estate.

But when it came to the task of penciling and inking that first Bat-Man script, Kane's inspirations were much closer to home. He drew the cover by swiping the same Flash Gordon pose he'd used in his concept sketch and he filled several panels of "The Case of the Chemical Syndicate" with figures he'd traced from a 1938 children's book called *Gang Busters in Action*. He would continue to swipe panel layouts and figures from other sources for the duration of his tenure as Batman's artist—which was significantly shorter than he let his publishers, or the public, know.

OUT OF THE SHADOW(S)

When *Detective* #27 hit the stands, nobody seemed much to care that this outlandish new mystery man owed so much, in both concept and execution, to so many different sources, or that Kane and Finger's attempt to cash in on the Superman craze had birthed a character who was in so many ways the Man of Tomorrow's antithesis.

Superman was a creature of the daylight, burnished in panel after panel by the golden rays of a sunrise straight out of a neosocialist mural.

The Bat-Man haunted the urban shadows, literally and figuratively cloaked in the colors of night. He was a grim, laconic figure of menace. In his first outing, he brought no hopeful reassurance, personified no we're-all-in-this-together promise of a better day and brighter future. Instead, he came steeped in the lurid violence of gangster films and dime novels, a mysterious harbinger of death and destruction.

In other words: the Shadow.

During his first year, the disparate borrowed elements coalesced into the unique and familiar form we now call Batman. It's the raw-element Batman of this one brief year that continues to cast the longest shadow over the character, more than three-quarters of a century later. Because it's to this grim, violent proto-Batman that writer Denny O'Neil would return, in 1970, in his attempt to rescue the character after the television-inspired Batmania fad of the late 1960s had cooled.

Generations of readers that followed would consider O'Neil's take on the character "their" Batman—the one true version—while in effect dismissing the three decades of adventures prior as campy, unserious kid stuff. Here was Batman as a loner and a badass, and it's these two aspects of his character that continue to possess a fundamental appeal to the most vocal segment of his fan base.

O'Neil, along with everyone who has since attempted to reframe, remount, or reinterpret the Batman story, from Frank Miller to Tim Burton to Grant Morrison to Christopher Nolan, has returned, again and again, to the loner, badass Batman of 1939–40. And so must we.

THE BAT-MAN: YEAR ONE

In the Bat-Man's second adventure, in *Detective Comics* #28 (June 1939), Bill Finger didn't deviate much from the formula he'd laid out in the previous issue. The Bat-Man foiled a ring of crooks in James Cagney drag* who possessed the temerity to heist jewels belonging to

---

* Cocked fedoras, pin-striped suits.

"the Vandersmiths" and other wealthy scions of the city. Our antihero pitched another unlucky goon off a roof and extorted a confession from the ringleader by dangling the poor sap out a window—all straight from the playbook of Lamont Cranston's slouch-hatted alter ego, or his many imitators.

But Finger was already trying to find something that would set this character apart. Here, for the first time, the Bat-Man seemed to justify his circus tights by displaying marvelous feats of acrobatics in his pursuit of justice. He hurled himself off skyscrapers to somersault through the air and swung from building to building via a "tough silk rope."

He made for a dashing figure, certainly, but he wasn't yet Batman. For one thing, he'd spent these first two adventures essentially working security—a Pinkerton man in a leotard. For another, he had yet to match wits with a true villain, and even in the pulps, a hero without a nemesis was no hero at all.

Because Finger tended to agonize over his stories and let deadlines blow past him, Kane secretly hired writer Gardner Fox, who pounded out the scripts for the next five issues. Those issues took the character in a new direction, adding showy gothic flourishes that swiftly became part of his permanent makeup. But it remained a period of experimentation, and Fox flirted with several other ideas, including Batman's first supervillain, that didn't quite take.

In *Detective Comics* #29 and #30, for example, the Batman* faced Doctor Karl Hellfern, a forgettable mad scientist straight from central casting (down to the goatee and monocle) who developed a lethal plant pollen† with which he threatened the wealthy of the world. Fox's script skimped on the sleuthing that was Finger's passion but reveled in tricking out our hero with utility belt, gas pellets, and suction-cup gloves

---

* In *Detective Comics* #30 "the Bat-Man" loses the hyphen and the scare quotes, for the most part. He'll go by the Batman from here on out.

† Hell fern, get it?

and knee pads for climbing the sides of buildings. The Batmobile was still two years away, but the Batman's distinctive red roadster got a lot of play, as did his tendency to worry about where to discreetly park it, which remained one of the oddest leitmotifs of Year One Batman.

In squaring off against his first archcriminal, Batman threatened to kill a couple of Doctor Hellfern's (aka Doctor Death's) assistants— and promptly took a bullet to the shoulder. It looked like curtains for our hero, until he managed to make his escape by fishing a gas pellet from his belt, crashing through a window, and swinging to safety on his rope.

It was a clear message: Batman was not Superman. Kane seemed to take a lurid glee in drawing the blood trickling from the entry wound on our downed hero's deltoid. He was human and vulnerable, set apart from us not by uncanny physical strength but by the strength of his will.

The careful reader may have noticed the beginnings of a subtle stylistic shift in this issue. Kane's line work was thicker and more confident, his compositions moodier, lingering over depictions of the Batman using his distinctive, angular silhouette to unsettle evildoers unlucky enough to catch a glimpse. Beginning with this issue Kane shared the art duties with inker Sheldon Moldoff, and it showed.

In the next issue (*Detective Comics* #30, August 1939) Gardner Fox's script gave us our first hint that demons might roil in the unguessed-at depths of our hero's psyche. The story's introductory caption matter-of-factly informed readers that Batman was a "winged figure of vengeance."

Vengeance. It was an odd, conspicuous word choice, and a concept that Superman—even the frequently brutal Golden Age Superman— would piously disdain. It was also a deliberate pivot: in his previous adventures, Batman "fought for righteousness" and spent his nights "righting wrongs and bringing justice"—par for the hero course. But *vengeance*?

That was new, and it underscored the character's ties to the flawed antiheroes of the noir tradition. Readers wouldn't have long to wait to learn exactly why he thirsted for vengeance, to witness the tragedy that formed him and the oath that defined him, in issue #33.

In the meantime, however, *Detective Comics* #31 and #32 saw Fox and Kane (with help from Moldoff) send Batman on his first international adventure. It was an odd one indeed, featuring a Lois Lane–like damsel in need of rescue, a mysterious supervillain called the Monk, hypnotism, a giant ape, werewolves, and vampires. It wasn't unusual for pulp heroes to come up against supernatural foes, but this was a full-bore monster-movie matinee of a tale that took Batman from his home amid the rooftops of New York City* to a gloomy gothic castle in the mountains of Hungary. Along the way, writer Gardner Fox introduced readers to the "Bat-Gyro"† and "a flying baterang [*sic*]—modeled after the Australian bushman's boomerang!"

As befits the subject matter, Kane and Moldoff load up the page with elements borrowed from German Expressionist cinema: long shadows and tangled trees against the moon. The cover image could have come straight from Caligari's cabinet: a lonely castle atop a mist-shrouded mountain, over which the titanic image of Batman looms ominously. It's a tableau of primal, iconic power, and one that has inspired dozens of homages over the decades, in and out of comics.

At this point Batman's adventures were only twelve-page stories in each issue of *Detective Comics*, which contained eleven features in total, including the more prosaic adventures of two-fisted lugs like Speed Saunders, Slam Bradley, and Buck Marshall, Range Detective. Against such bright punch-'em-up yarns, these dark, heavily inked, claustrophobic stories about a guy who hopped around rooftops in devil horns and a cape must have stood out. After this tale, however, with its swoonily melodramatic horror trappings, there could be no mistaking which character was *Detective Comics*' star.

---

* Bill Finger wouldn't coin the name "Gotham City" for another two years.

† A helicopter with wings, also referred to as the Batplane.

But Batman's dalliance with the supernatural proved brief. The very next month, it was back to business as usual, or at least, a switch of genre from horror to science fiction. In November 1939's *Detective Comics* #33, Batman tackles the Dirigible of Doom—an airship armed with a death ray and piloted by a madman with a Napoléon complex. This issue also introduced readers to Bruce Wayne's "secret laboratory"—a precursor to the Batcave—where our hero mixes chemicals to use in his fight against crime.

But *Detective Comics* #33 isn't of interest for its tale of deadly zeppelins or the fact that Batman once again used a gun and fretted about parking.* What earns this issue its prominent place in popular culture history is a two-page introduction written by Bill Finger.

"THE BATMAN AND HOW HE CAME TO BE"

It all happens in twelve panels.

Panel one: a terrified child and his parents are threatened by a gun-toting mugger under a streetlight. Panel twelve: the boy, grown to manhood, crouches on a moonlit rooftop in a bizarre, bat-winged getup. The brief tale that unfolds between those two images, the chronicle of how that boy became this "weird figure of the dark," will prove itself the most powerful story engine in modern history. These twelve panels will be iterated, embellished, deconstructed, and parodied thousands of times through the decades, infiltrating the collective consciousness. To modern eyes, they seem crude, even slapdash, but together they retain a simple intensity.

"Some fifteen years ago," a caption informs us, "Thomas Wayne, his wife, and son, were walking home from a movie." Below those words, on the panels' left-hand side, stand the Waynes: the adults in smart hats, the boy goggle-eyed with fear. On the right, the mugger in

---

* "The car will be safe here where no one can see it!"

a blue newsboy cap, having stepped out from behind a street lamp. "I'll take that necklace you're wearin' lady!" he says, leveling his weapon at Thomas Wayne, who seems to be raising his hands into a fighter's stance.*

The second and final page of Finger and Kane's 1939 origin of Batman is laid out in a simple nine-panel grid. In the first two panels, we watch a weeping young Bruce react to his parents' slaughter as the mugger makes his getaway. But it's the quietly remarkable panel that follows, which occurs at the very middle of this origin story and acts as its pivot point, where everything changes.

In it, young Bruce Wayne kneels beside his bed, hands clasped in prayer, gazing upward. The wall behind him glows in the guttering light of a candle, but the right half of his face is sunk in shadow.

The boy speaks. It's a single sentence, delivered in a breathless rush of pure emotion.

"And I swear by the spirits of my parents to avenge their deaths by spending the rest of my life warring on all criminals."

This is the moment that makes Batman Batman, this solemn oath made by candlelight in a child's lonely bedroom. This vow that transforms inner turmoil into public crusade. Because this considered choice, despite its impossibly grand objective, manages to evince a stealthy pragmatism.

Note the lack of vague ideals and abstract nouns of the sort that vows generally entail: there is no Truth or Justice being sought here, and certainly no civic-minded paean to the American Way. The boy doesn't swear to stop Crime or protect the Innocent. Yes, he vows to avenge his parents' death, but Vengeance per se is not his true goal.

---

* Martha Wayne's necklace will prove an aspect that many storytellers, across all media, will fixate upon whenever they iterate Batman's origin. The fact that the murders occurred as the family was leaving a theater will also provide many stories with their narrative grist.

This oath, which resides at the core of every iteration of Batman that has ever or will ever exist, from pulp antihero to TV buffoon, is much more practical and matter-of-fact. It is a declaration of war.

The enemy combatants? "All criminals."

A lofty goal, surely. But young Bruce understands this. He's prepared to dedicate "the rest of [his] life" to this war, knowing victory is not assured. Victory is not even his objective. Rather it's *the war itself* that he dedicates himself to in that panel. A lifetime of violent opposition. He consigns himself, in this image, to decade after Sisyphean decade locked in perpetual combat.

Or, as his jock older brother in the red boots might put it: to a never-ending battle.

The final sequence of the origin finds the adult Bruce on the cusp of insight. He sits ruminating before the roaring fireplace in his fabulously appointed study. "Dad's estate left me wealthy," he says, as if the smoking jacket didn't tip us off, "I am ready. But first I must have a disguise."

"Criminals," he muses, "are a superstitious, cowardly lot. So my disguise must be able to strike terror into their hearts. I must be a creature of the night, black, terrible . . . a . . . a . . ."

In the next panel, Bruce is startled when "as if in answer, a huge bat flies in the open window!" Kane depicts this creature with its wings extended against the yellow circle of the moon.

"A bat! That's it! It's an omen!" says the man who just seconds before scoffed at the superstitions of criminals. "I shall become a bat!"

In the final panel, Batman stands poised for action on a midnight rooftop, a character unlike any the world had ever seen, a brand-new hero unleashed upon the public.

Except that he wasn't.

Nothing about the character was new. He was simply a combination of tropes from many sources: even his origin story itself was full of swipes.

Kane lifted many of the origin's panels from the children's book *Junior G-Men*, illustrated by Henry Vallely. The tale's concluding image of

Batman springing to action on the rooftop was traced from a drawing of Tarzan by Hal Foster.

It wasn't just Kane: Finger borrowed just as shamelessly. The whole business of Bruce's being inspired by a bat flying in his window was lifted wholesale from a 1934 issue of *Popular Detective.*

As for the oath sworn by young Bruce? The key element of the Batman legend that sets him apart, that defines him as a character and provides the basis for his enduring appeal?

The Phantom had one just like it.

The details were more grisly—instead of a kid swearing by the light of a candle, Lee Falk's jungle hero swore on the skull of his father's murderer, and the wording was both more abstract and more grandiose—"I swear to devote my life to the destruction of piracy, greed, and cruelty, in all their forms"—but the gist, the mission statement, was the same.

So there you have Batman: a crude, four-color slumgullion of borrowed ideas and stolen art. And yet there was something new, legitimately so, in the precise proportions of those ideas and images found in the stories that Finger, Fox, Kane, and Moldoff were grinding out. Those proportions were not yet fixed—and it would take another five months, with the addition of Robin, the Boy Wonder, for the final core element of the character to manifest—but in that bizarre mixture lay a potent, and lasting, appeal.

A DARK KNIGHT, BEFORE THE DAWN

The remainder of Batman's first year of life was fitful and bizarre, as he struggled to coalesce into a clear and consistent character. *Detective Comics* #34, for example, found Fox, Kane, and Moldoff riffing wildly, as Batman went toe-to-toe with an evil French duke in the sewers of Paris. Once again, Fox's script introduced uncanny elements of the sort the more grounded Finger would likely have rejected as grotesque—a mysterious ray that removes faces, a hothouse of flowers that, for reasons never explained, bear the faces of beautiful women. But the writer adhered to two story conditions that marked Batman's earliest adventures: he helped the wealthy, and he killed the bad guy.

Bill Finger returned to script chores with *Detective Comics* #35 (January 1940) and came back with a vengeance, offering a comparatively grounded mystery involving a ruby statue. The story's dramatic opening splash page depicted Batman entering a room with a grimace of determination . . . and carrying a smoking pistol. It was a standalone image, and Batman didn't wield a gun at all in the accompanying story, but it couldn't help but to underscore the character's conceptual roots as a Shadow knockoff, even as he was struggling to become his own hero.

In *Detective Comics* #36 (February 1940) Finger began to nudge Batman out of the Shadow's grim shadow. For the first time, he wisecracked as he mowed down a crowd of thugs* and comforted a hostage.† On the cover, he grinned(!) as he kicked his attacker down a flight of stairs.

Finger also introduced the Batman's second recurring villain, the "scientist, philosopher and criminal genius" Professor Hugo Strange. In an important development, the threat posed by Strange (he creates a thick fog to confound the police while he unleashes a crime wave) affected the entire city, not only the upper echelons of society. And in another significant break from tradition, Batman did not kill Professor Strange but merely subdued him and handed him over to the police. The plan was for Strange to return often, of course, and perhaps even establish himself as Batman's Moriarty. But it was not to be: just two months later, another, even more twisted and diabolical archnemesis shouldered the professor roughly aside.

Kane—joined for the first time by a young Jerry Robinson on inks—brightened the visual atmosphere of the story to match Finger's lighter touch, devoting more attention to the mechanics of the story's

---

* "This, boys, is what they call a perfect strike, on a bowling alley!"

† "Don't be frightened! I'm the Batman!"

set-piece warehouse brawls than to gloomy, Expressionist shadow play.

In *Detective Comics* #37 (March 1940), Finger seems so impatient to adopt a more humorous mood that he opens the story by turning our hero into a hapless tourist: "The Batman, having lost his way on a lonely road, stops before a lone house to ask directions." The story that followed—which our hero would have avoided completely if he carried his AAA TripTik—saw Batman bumbling into a plot involving foreign agents attempting to draw the US into war.

This was Batman in his eleventh month, now all but fully emerged from the shadow of the Shadow: as his adventures flirted with a lighter tone, he shifted from guns-blazing avenger to a detective in the Sherlock Holmes mode. But there was one more change to come, a change that would put any lingering conceptual debt to the Shadow to rest once and for all, a change that altered the hero's idiomatic framework forever.

And that change wore bright green pixie boots.

BOY WONDER

For Bill Finger, it solved a storytelling problem. For Bob Kane, it was a savvy marketing move. For National's editorial director Whitney Ellsworth, it offered up a tidy opportunity to deflect the wrong kind of attention.

The "it" in question was Robin, the Boy Wonder, the first kid sidekick in comics.

Bill Finger was tired of having Batman talk to himself all the time. He was a detective, after all, and that meant he had to walk readers through his deductive process. It wasn't enough, Finger realized, to model a character on Sherlock Holmes if you didn't also supply him a Watson—an audience surrogate—to talk to.

It was Kane who came up with the idea for a wisecracking kid to fight alongside Batman in the role of protégé, a junior version of the hero with whom, he felt confident, "every boy in the world" would identify.

Ellsworth was keeping a wary eye on a growing national unease. In 1939, just a few years after the comic book was born, American kids were devouring almost ten million comics per month, and parents, teachers, and church groups took notice. Their nascent concern would not erupt into a high-profile, government-sanctioned anticomics crusade for years to come, but attacks on the lurid violence and sexual content of comic books were beginning to pop up in newspaper editorials and church bulletins across the country. Sensing this, Ellsworth had expressed some misgivings about Batman's wielding firearms to Finger and Kane on previous occasions; he hoped the advent of a kid sidekick would push the Batman character in a less grim and violent direction.

According to Kane, *Detective*'s editor, Jack Liebowitz, was not convinced, and expressed two very practical objections. One, that Batman in *Detective Comics* was so successful on his own there was no reason to change the formula, and two, that you don't ease the worries of America's parents by sending a young boy in short pants into battle with gun-toting thugs. Finger and Kane agreed that they'd introduce their kid sidekick on a probationary basis.

They came up with a list of possible sidekick names with young artist Jerry Robinson, who was already exerting considerable influence over the look of both Batman and his world, given that he'd taken over the inking of Kane's pencils from Sheldon Moldoff. Kane's pencils employed a flat, boxy approach to anatomy that owed a great deal to Chester Gould's *Dick Tracy*; Robinson's inks imbued the completed page with a richer, fuller, more rounded quality.

Robinson recalled an illustrated Robin Hood storybook he'd loved as a child, with paintings by N. C. Wyeth. He sketched a boy in a boldly colored and vaguely medieval outfit—tunic, shoes, tights—and designed a logo for him in a typeface that approximated Old English script: Robin, the Boy Wonder.

Any kid who picked up a copy of *Detective Comics* #38 (April 1940) could see that things had changed. Forget about the masked moppet jumping out at us in a skimpy red and green outfit. Forget the breathless marketing copy above his head, touting him as "the SENSATIONAL Character Find of 1940 . . . ROBIN, The BOY WONDER."

The really odd, unsettling thing was that Batman was smiling.

Not smirking grimly, not grinning with relish as he visited a fresh act of violence upon some poor, evildoing sap, but beaming up at us beatifically, his chest thrust out like a Little League dad watching his kid sliding home. Everything about this former lone avenger of the dark screamed, suddenly, "That's my boy!"

Inside the cover, the story's opening splash page reproduced it all—the boy, the logo, the beaming Batman—and threw in an introductory scroll full of still more exclamatory promises that bluntly delivered the new character's mission statement:

"The Batman, that amazing, weird figure of night, takes under his protecting mantle an ally in his relentless fight against crime . . . introducing in this issue . . . an exciting new figure whose incredible gymnastic and athletic feats will astound you . . . a laughing, fighting, young daredevil who scoffs at danger like the legendary Robin Hood whose name and spirit he has adopted . . . Robin the Boy Wonder."

The relationship between Batman and Robin—specifically, the homosocial nature of their bond—would go on to fuel decades of knowing winks, sniggering jokes, gay panic, fanboy outrage, and Derridean deconstruction. In just a handful of years from this first appearance, gay innuendo will be used against Batman by one hugely influential and entirely nonfictional child-welfare advocate in a crusade that will come very close to ending our hero, and his entire medium, forever.

And here, at the moment of that relationship's birth, before the very first panel on the very first page of Robin's very first appearance, a lettering error in the introductory text transcribed above elides the space between the two words "an ally," causing that opening passage to instead inform us that Batman "takes under his protecting mantle anally . . ."

So. Yes. Well.

Fraught from the moment of its beginning, the Batman/Robin partnership came factory-installed with subtext both acknowledged and unspoken, subtext that various audiences have always read and interpreted in a host of discrete ways.

"I'M NOT AFRAID"

As introduced in *Detective Comics* #38, the Flying Graysons are a team of circus acrobats consisting of young Dick, his mother, and his father. While performing on the flying trapeze one night, the ropes break, sending Dick's parents plummeting to their deaths. Dick overhears gangsters gloating to the head of the circus that the "accident" wouldn't have happened if he'd paid protection money to Boss Zucco, the mob chieftain who runs the city.

Dick is determined to go to the police when the Batman appears to him, warning the boy that if he does so, Zucco's men will find him and kill him. "I'm going to hide you in my home for a while," he says, because 1940.

Batman quickly notes an affinity between himself and the newly orphaned boy: "My parents too were killed by a criminal. That's why I've devoted my life to exterminate them . . . All right, I'll make you my aid [*sic*]. But I warn you, I lead a perilous life."

"I'm not afraid," says young Dick, unaware of the multiple decades' worth of kidnappings that lie before him.

Next, in a scene that evokes Bruce's oath, Batman and young Dick face one another in the dark before the light of a single candle. Both raise their right hands; Dick lays his left hand on Batman's. We join them just as the Batman finishes a new oath.

". . . and swear that we two will fight together against crime and corruption and never swerve from the path of righteousness!"

"I swear it!" the boy intones.

Then it was off to the races in Finger's forceful, fast-paced style: Dick goes undercover and finds Boss Zucco's hideout; Boss Zucco reveals himself to be a thug cast in the Edward G. Robinson mold;* and after a climactic fight at a construction site, Zucco is convicted of murder, ushering in a new era of Batman comics, in which the villain of the piece ends up behind bars, not six feet under.

The die was cast: for long decades, Robin would remain essentially the chipper, guileless lad he is throughout this first adventure. Created to epitomize 1930s ideals of American boyhood—the kind of cheerful, athletic, and outdoorsy kid who stared out from the cover of *Boys' Life* magazine—he was exactly the kid that his ten-year-old readers believed they would be, if they ever got the chance to fight alongside their hero.

Batman was the guy they might become in ten years, as long as they ate their vegetables, studied hard, and did calisthenics, but being Robin was just a pair of green underpants away. In his adventures they saw their idealized self reflected: brave and determined, good with his fists, great undercover, quick with a quip or a cringeworthy pun, and unfailingly loyal (a trait that would get him in trouble often).

He also just *looked* good, offering a sharp contrast to the mentor standing beside him. If Batman's colors were those of a gloomy winter's night, Robin's were those of a bright spring morning. He popped.

Whatever the reason, it worked: sales of Robin's debut issue doubled that of the previous month's. And in the ensuing vogue for masked mystery men that arose in the months and years that followed, boy sidekicks quickly became a staple accessory: The Sandman had Sandy. Green Arrow had Speedy. The Shield had Rusty. Captain America had Bucky. The Human Torch had Toro. Mr. Scarlet had Pinky. The Shining Knight had Squire. And the Vigilante, wincingly enough, had Stuff, the Chinatown Kid.

They were all cast in Robin's mold, all of them resourceful, plucky, tenacious, wisecracking, and eminently, achingly kidnappable.

---

* "It isn't enough! SEE! You've got to get more money out of our customers! SEE!"

DYNAMIC DUO

Overnight, the ruthless lone vigilante became a doting father figure. His brand changed, too: he swapped a definite article for a second noun and a coordinating conjunction: the Batman was replaced by Batman and Robin.

"Batman and Robin" were now a single entity occupying the same patch of cultural real estate that the Bat-Man had staked out by himself for almost a year. In the public imagination, their names would soon become shorthand for the very concept of a two-person team: Lewis and Clark. Abbot and Costello. Burns and Allen. Batman and Robin.

Adding Robin was no mere cosmetic tweak; it was a fundamental and permanent change that placed Batman in a new role of protector and provider. With that change, the fifth and final essential element of Batman fell at last into place.

Because at his core, Batman is a hero sworn to wage war on criminals. He is a detective. A martial artist. A millionaire.

He is also, finally, a father.

Beginning with Robin in 1940, Batman would assume the mantle of patriarch and guardian of a slowly growing brood of fellow crime fighters. In the decades that followed, men and women, boys and girls, a masked dog, a shirtless were-bat, and one fifth-dimensional imp would join him. To them, he would be mentor, disciplinarian, sensei, father. To him, they would become that for which he most keenly longed, the family that had been ripped from him as a boy.

Superman, Captain Marvel, and other heroes would eventually accrete their own heroic dynasties as well, but Batman got the ball rolling first, and his relationship with Robin would form the central dynamic all such super-families would eventually adopt.

The Boy Wonder came along at an important time and opened up new narrative possibilities. The mere presence of Robin in a given story deepens its impact by supplying Batman with something to care about, over and above any abstract notion of justice. When the boy is imperiled, the stakes increase. When the boy misinterprets Batman's actions (a go-to Silver Age plot device), the melodrama boils over.

For the next thirty years, a grinning, happy-go-lucky Batman and Robin would fight shoulder to shoulder across a variety of media.

Even Robin's eventual departure in 1970 did not and could not dispense with the concept of Batman as father figure. It would remain fundamental to his character, though in the years that followed it grew more symbolic in nature. True, Batman patrolled Gotham City on his own, but Robin (and Batgirl, and others) would put in the occasional appearance—and in the pages of one Batman anthology comic published from 1975 to 1978, their solo stories would intersect; the resulting adventures looked a lot like the high old times of the forties, fifties, and sixties. The name of that anthology, not to put too fine a point on it: *Batman Family*.

The 1980s would see the Batman-Robin relationship undergo a series of shattering setbacks and bifurcations, and in more recent years, Batman's surrogate family has grown larger and more diffuse than ever. But Batman remains squarely at its center, ever the stern, caring, pointy-eared Ward Cleaver.

"Father figure" was the last of Batman's essential elements to manifest, and it is the first aspect to be jettisoned by writers, filmmakers, and television showrunners whenever they wish to tell Batman's tale anew. In a bid to keep the storytelling simple, they strip him of his familial context and take him back to the dark, brooding loner of this very first year.

But Robin always comes back, eventually, in some form, because he must: Robin is half the story. Despite what many fans believe so fervently, the Batman of that very first year isn't truly Batman—not yet. Robin serves to define and delineate Batman, as do Batgirl, Nightwing, Huntress, and the others. Batman's status as the ultimate mentor is a base principle, inasmuch as it speaks directly to who he is: he saves others because, on one terrible night long ago, there was no one to save him.

DROP THE GUN

With the arrival of Robin, the tone of Batman's exploits in *Detective Comics* lightened even more, but it would take the advent of World War II for Batman to move past the grim violence of his earliest outings.

In the spring of 1940, Batman's runaway success earned him his own quarterly published solo series. When it appeared on store shelves, *Batman* #1 (Spring 1940) was only the second comic book ever published to be devoted entirely to a single character.* Each issue contained four different stories written by Bill Finger, penciled by Bob Kane, and inked by Jerry Robinson and George Roussos.†

The premiere issue kicks off with a reprint of Finger's two-page Batman origin from *Detective Comics* #33. It also contains a tale in which Dick goes undercover on a luxury yacht to protect a priceless necklace from getting pilfered by a mysterious woman known as "the Cat"—the first appearance of the seductive villainess who in later appearances will be known as Catwoman. In another adventure, written before Robin's arrival, Batman is back to his old murdery tricks, offing monsters in various grisly ways and, in one astonishing panel, using the Batplane's machine gun to execute two escaping thugs. "Much as I hate to take human life," he rationalizes, "I'm afraid THIS TIME, it's necessary!"

But National didn't agree. According to Finger, the panel in which Batman mows down his enemies from on high led to an editorial crackdown on firearms. "I was called on the carpet by [editorial director] Whit Ellsworth. He said, 'Never let us have Batman [use] a gun again.'"

Despite that controversy, *Batman* #1 is best remembered for the

_____

* Superman, which premiered one year before, had been the first.

† Roussos began with issue #2.

remaining two stories in the issue, in which the Caped Crusader's greatest nemesis makes his debut.

CLOWN PRINCE

It was then-eighteen-year-old Jerry Robinson who came up with the idea for a new and terrifying villain, a chalk-faced mass murderer with a grisly sense of humor. Robinson was taking creative writing courses at Columbia University at the time and offered to write the story introducing his killer clown, whom he called the Joker. Finger and Kane, worried that Robinson would miss the deadline on what would have been his first comic book script, persuaded the young inker to let Finger write the story instead.

The ensuing tale is pure pulpy goodness, and it fits squarely in Finger's whodunit style: a mysterious villain robbed the wealthy of the city and somehow, amid rooms teeming with protective cordons of police officers, managed to dose them with a lethal venom that left them with a "repellent, ghastly grin, the sign of death from THE JOKER!" Readers watched victim after victim die panicked, horrible deaths as the vicious Joker gloated. Despite his misgivings about such violent imagery, Whitney Ellsworth stepped in to make sure Finger and Kane didn't bump the Joker off at story's end as they had planned to do; he knew they'd struck upon a villain who was too good to lose.

Even in this first tale, so much of what will forever define the character was already set in stone—the white face, green hair, and red lips; the impossible rictus grin; the Joker venom; the maniacal laughter; and the riverboat-gambler couture: tails, vest, spats, and hat.

For the first two years after this debut, the Joker would remain a cold-blooded killer, cavalierly slaughtering both innocent victim and criminal colleague alike. Ellsworth believed that while Batman must resist lethal force—and even had him give up his role as vigilante to become an honorary member of the police department in *Batman* #7 (Fall 1941)—it only made sense for the villains to remain villainous, even homicidal.

But after April 1942 (*Detective Comics* #62), the editorial mandate for gentler, brighter, more kid-friendly fare manages to reach even the Harlequin of Hate. The Joker's schemes grow suddenly more baroque: increasingly elaborate jewel heists and ever-more-involved death traps (which never quite manage to live up to the term) abound. Exit Joker the maniacal murderer, enter Joker "the cackling cut-up of the crime world." It wasn't until the 1970s, when stories involving the newly retrenched, badass-loner Batman needed their stakes raised, that Denny O'Neil and Neal Adams reintroduced the Joker as an archnemesis who could be counted on to add a serious body count.

YA GOTTA HAVE A GIMMICK

Throughout his long life in and out of the comics, the Joker has remained the first among equals, the premier and most flamboyant villain in Batman's vast rogues' gallery of grotesques.

Each archvillain he'd face over the course of his first decade came at him with an individualized quirk that grew out of a warped worldview—corny gags, cats, the number two, fear, the mystifying combination of birds and umbrellas. These signifiers helped readers keep them straight, of course, but they also strongly hinted that these criminals were something more than merely crooked: they were twisted. Not merely criminal but crazy.

For the next thirty years of Batman comics, however, their various colorful psychopathologies took a backseat to their larceny: they were crooks with gimmicks. The Joker was no different—a villain whose signature shtick was, ingeniously enough, exactly the sort of jokes and novelties that readers could order from ads in the very comics they were reading: playing cards, joy buzzers, itching powder, X-ray specs.

But when Batman was returned to his loner roots in the 1970s, O'Neil, Adams, and the writers and artists who followed them attempted to imbue the Dark Knight, and his world, with dense psychological underpinnings. Batman grew deeply obsessive, and his archvillains, who for over thirty years had been routinely carted off to Gotham State Penitentiary at the end of each adventure, began to be taken* to someplace never mentioned before: Arkham Hospital.†

As these dark intimations of obsession and sociopathy began to cling to Batman, his villains grew increasingly tormented, riven by a violent and terrifying madness. The Joker most of all. The now-hoary notion that the Joker represents Batman's opposite number didn't really manifest until late in his history. It took until the 1980s—almost half a century—for writers to explicitly posit that the Joker embraces the chaos of insanity and death, while the Batman instead channels his pain into an endless crusade to impose order.

SERIAL ADVENTURER

With the essential elements finally in place, it was time for Finger, Kane, Robinson, and Roussos (along with other uncredited Kane ghost-artists like Win Mortimer, Jack Burnley, and Charles Paris) to set to work building the fictive universe around the Dynamic Duo.

The New York of the Bat-Man's first-year adventures is renamed Gotham City in the early months of 1941, about the same time that Batman's red roadster gains a bat-shaped hood ornament and is first referred to as the "Batmobile." The Bat-Signal makes its first appearance a year later. Slowly, over the course of several years, the abandoned barn in which Batman houses his vehicles evolves into a subterranean cavern accessible from Wayne Manor via a secret stairway, officially earning the name "the Bat Cave"‡ in January 1944.

Lest Bruce Wayne's intimate relationship with his young ward Dick

---

* As of Batman #258, October 1974.

† It takes until 1979 for its name to change to Arkham Asylum for the Criminally Insane.

‡ The concept was cribbed from the 1943 Batman movie serial, as we'll see.

Grayson raise any eyebrows, Alfred the butler took up residence in Wayne Manor in the spring of 1943, a kind of bumbling British twenty-four-hour chaperone. And speaking of totally 100 percent heterosexual, red-blooded straight maleness, Bruce began dating Linda Page (a debutante turned nurse) from 1941 to 1945. Later still, Bruce met news photographer Vicki Vale, whom he proceeded to date sporadically for the next two decades.

Meanwhile, Batman's rogues' gallery swelled with colorfully vile crooks, as the Joker and Catwoman were soon joined by Two-Face, Clayface, the Penguin, the Riddler, and the Mad Hatter.

Batman starred in a third title in 1941; the bimonthly *World's Finest Comics* featured separate tales of the Dynamic Duo and Superman.*

Throughout the Second World War, many covers of *Detective Comics, Batman* (now bimonthly), and *World's Finest* depicted Batman and Robin in star-spangled tableaux that could have been ripped from propaganda posters: riding an American eagle or a battleship's cannons, hawking war bonds, planting a victory garden, etc. But despite this patriotic cover imagery, only a handful of Batman stories published during the war made even oblique mentions of the global conflict. Instead, Batman's focus remained steadily on the mean streets of Gotham City, which, given the editorial edict for sunnier stories, were growing less and less mean with every passing month.

Let Captain America, Major Victory, and other flag-wrapped bruisers take the fight to the Ratzis—Batman and Robin had more than enough to look after on the home front; besides, sales were surging. By 1943 the three titles that featured Batman's adventures were selling a combined three million copies every month and were read by an estimated twenty-four million men, women, and children.

It was the kind of success that sent Batman caroming into other

---

* It would take fourteen years for the heroes to finally meet one another in its pages.

storytelling formats, turning him into a multimedia phenomenon like the Shadow before him. In 1943 Kane left the comics to his ghost-artists and turned his attention to a syndicated newspaper strip called *Batman and Robin*, penciled by Kane, that ran for three years.*

A pilot script for a *Batman and Robin* radio serial was written, turning Dick Grayson's circus-performer parents into FBI agents who were murdered by Nazis. Despite that canny attempt to cater to the patriotic tenor of the times, the radio show was never produced.

In the meantime, on July 16, 1943, Batman debuted on the silver screen with a movie serial, a full five years before the Man of Steel would make the same leap. Columbia produced fifteen episodes of the *Batman* serial, and it became one of the quintessential matinee cliff-hangers of the war era, filled with repetitive fight scenes, cheap costumes (Batman's ears kept going askew, like the guy was dowsing for water), troubling jingoism, and many deeply weird, albeit fun, touches: A radium gun! Japanese soldier-zombies! Death by alligator pit! An experimental airplane! A room with spiked walls that close in on our hero! A mysterious super-weapon!

The *Batman* movie serial departed from the comics in odd ways: to explain why Bruce Wayne hadn't been drafted, it was implied that Batman and Robin worked for the US government. Commissioner Gordon became, for no compelling reason, Captain Arnold.

Cinema houses offered worried wartime Americans a communal, cathartic experience: they watched newsreels to learn about the progress of the war and got their "Keep 'Em Flying!" fervor stoked by Hollywood tales of brave GIs and leathernecks. This may explain why the serial featured an entirely new villain that people—even non–comics readers—could hiss at on sight. Enter the evil Japanese scientist Dr. Tito Daka, who was from Japan, and was also, not for nothing, of Japanese

---

* Charles Paris inked the daily strip; Jack Burnley inked the Sunday installments.

descent, and who had a Japanese accent and who dressed after the Japanese fashion. Because he was Japanese.

But the serial also influenced the comics in small, telling ways. The concept of the "Bat's Cave" appeared there first, months before the comics version, as did the notion, which quickly became canon, that a secret entrance to Batman's lair lies behind a grandfather clock in Bruce Wayne's study.

Bruce's comic-book girlfriend Linda Page got some screen time, as did Alfred the butler. In fact, in Alfred's comic-book appearances following the serial's stint in the nation's movie theaters, artist Jerry Robinson altered the butler's look to more closely resemble actor William Austin.

Batman became one of Columbia's most successful serials to date and touched off a modest boom in tie-in merchandise—decals, paper Batplanes, belt buckles, decoders, etc. Sales were brisk, though the variety of Batman offerings paled in comparison to the bonanza of Superman paraphernalia on store shelves at the time. But then, Superman had a wildly popular radio show that delivered him straight into American living rooms five times a week; Batman didn't.

On February 28, 1945, Batman and Robin put in the first of their many appearances on the *Superman* radio serial. As the years went on, several episodes at a time would be given over to the Dynamic Duo (who, for the purposes of the drama, made their home in Metropolis), which served to give Bud Collyer, the voice of Superman, some much-needed downtime.

In 1949, six years after the *Batman* movie serial had proven a hit, Columbia tried again with a follow-up serial called *Batman and Robin*.

The budget was lower this time around, but the screenwriter made a concerted effort to pay fealty to the comics—now it was Commissioner Gordon who worked closely with the Dynamic Duo, even busting out the Bat-Signal for the first time on-screen, and Bruce's then-girlfriend Vicki Vale played a largish role.

Unfortunately, the whole affair came off as an even lower-rent, amateur-theatricals version of the 1943 serial; sets, props, and costumes evince a handmade quality. When it was finally released to theaters, on May 26, 1949, the heyday of the movie serial had passed; despite its skinflint budget, *Batman and Robin* did not meet the studio's box-office expectations.

TWILIGHT OF THE SUPERHEROES

Bad box office or not, Batman had managed to accomplish in his first decade of life what most of his comic book colleagues never would. Thanks to the newspaper strip, the appearances on the Superman radio show, and the two movie serials, the idea of Batman established a base camp beyond the comics in the wider, noisier world of popular culture.

And that was important, because back in the comics—in super-hero comics, specifically—something was happening. The masked mystery men (and women) who'd flourished during the war years were dying out. The fad for caped crime fighters faded quickly in peacetime, and the few superheroes who remained (Batman, Superman, Wonder Woman—and in backup features, Aquaman and Green Arrow) were getting shouldered aside by Western comics, war comics, crime comics, and romance comics.

Batman's newspaper strip was canceled in 1946, but *Detective Comics, Batman,* and *World's Finest* managed to stay afloat through the end of the decade although sales had plummeted from their wartime heights. As long as a Batman comic remained on the stands, there was the hope that the character might live to get another big break—maybe even, like his colleague Superman was preparing to do, to make the jump to an exciting new medium called television.

All he had to do was hang in there and trust that, month after month, his comics would keep coming out. He had weathered a world war without getting his ears mussed—surely there was nothing on the horizon that might somehow threaten his continued existence, right?

. . . Right?

2

Panic and Aftermath (1948–1964)

At home they lead an idyllic life. They are Bruce Wayne and "Dick" Grayson. Bruce Wayne is described as a "socialite" and the official relationship is that Dick is Bruce's ward. They live in sumptuous quarters, with beautiful flowers in large vases, and have a butler, Alfred. Bruce is sometimes shown in a dressing-gown. As they sit by the fireplace the young boy sometimes worries about his partner . . .
It is like a wish dream of two homosexuals living together.
—FREDRIC WERTHAM, *SEDUCTION OF THE INNOCENT*

If you were casting the part of the evil scientist who would prove the Caped Crusader's deadliest nemesis, you'd likely glance at the headshot of German-born psychiatrist Dr. Fredric Wertham, with his owl-like glasses and severe Prussian features, and think, "Nah, too on-the-nose."

Wertham, who in the 1940s and 1950s campaigned against the corrosive effect he believed comic books were having on the minds and morals of American youth, is reviled in comics circles as a witchfinder general who came close to killing the comics industry with his baseless accusations.

The good doctor's crusade did, in fact, prove hugely successful, and the national scrutiny it brought to the comics industry caused no less than twenty-four publishing houses to shutter their doors and chased scores of writers and artists out of the business for good.

Wertham's remorseless spotlight also forced publishers to strengthen their self-policing efforts. Comics companies had previously adopted a set of moral guidelines dictating what could and could not be depicted in a comic book. These guidelines, called the Comics Code, were only loosely adhered to, however, as they were largely an attempt to prevent the government's stepping in with its own regulations. In the wake of Wertham, however, the industry instituted the much stricter Comics Code Authority; this move proved the death knell for horror and crime titles, and changed superhero comics—and Batman—forever.

But as for the baselessness of Wertham's accusations—especially those about Batman comics—well.

The guy had a point.

DOCTOR DOOM

Wertham was by no means the first public-minded authority figure to accuse comics of fostering juvenile delinquency—the *New York Times,* the *New Republic,* and most famously, Sterling North, literary editor of the *Chicago Daily News,* had been publishing anticomics screeds for years. The genius of Wertham's war on comics was how, and where, he waged it. He fired the first shot in March 1948, with an academic lecture called "The Psychopathology of Comic Books" before the Association for the Advancement of Psychotherapy at the New York Academy of Medicine in Manhattan. He was received politely and professionally. Which is to say: quietly.

Later that same month, however, an article in *Collier's* magazine gave his anticomics argument a national signal boost. From that point on, Wertham took his crusade directly to the American people. No more ivory tower for him, with its little-read academic journals (in which peer-reviewed pages his methodology likely wouldn't have passed muster). Instead, he resolved to exploit the power of the press and reach parents, teachers, church leaders, and legislators over their morning coffee. In May he made his case in an article that appeared in the *Sunday Review of Literature*, which—in his campaign's first real coup—was subsequently reprinted in a periodical found atop millions of toilet tanks in millions of American powder rooms: *Reader's Digest*.

In the public's mind, Wertham's status as a man of medicine earned him a special cachet quite apart from literary critics like Sterling North and lent his argument greater urgency. A spark was lit: he began to speak before parents' groups and professional associations, he wrote more articles in the popular press, and he provided expert testimony before state and community legislatures, which began to introduce bills to curtail or ban the selling of comics. Across the country, fueled by sensationalist headlines like "Boy Shoots Brother to Death in Fight Over Comic Book" and "Comic Book Inspires Boys' Torture of Pal," church groups staged comic book burnings, and civic groups organized efforts that got parents to demand their local shopkeepers stop selling comics to minors.

Beginning in the fall of 1953, a series of teaser ads in *Ladies' Home Journal* touted the upcoming publication of Wertham's opus *Seduction of the Innocent: The Influence of Comic Books on Today's Youth*, an excerpt of which appeared in *Ladies' Home Journal*. In a move that beggared a literary publicist's wildest dreams, the publication of the book in spring of 1954 coincided with Senator Estes Kefauver's inviting Wertham to testify before Congress and take his case to the American public on national television.

In the end, he took more than one case, as *Seduction of the Innocent* contains a litany of indictments: Wertham maintained that comic books hurt literacy by breaking up sentences in word balloons. That they promote violent behavior with gruesome imagery, which he carefully cataloged and reproduced in the book, noting a recurring "injury to the eye motif" in several horror and crime comics. That they warp the emotional health of readers who see a fascistic Superman remaining impervious to harm while gleefully doling out violence to others. That they offer unrealistic and lascivious representations of the female body, and that they deliberately imbue tales about a grown man and a young boy with a "subtle atmosphere of homoeroticism."

The man and boy in question, of course, were Bruce Wayne and Dick Grayson.

COMIC BOOKS: THE CASE AGAINST

Let's stipulate that *Seduction of the Innocent* is a populist polemic, not a work of scholarship. Though marketed by its publishers as a "scientific investigation" and "technical research," the book contains no data. Instead, Wertham employs rhetorical flourishes to string together excerpts from interviews he conducted with young psychiatric patients at the three New York City institutions where he practiced: his own Lafargue Clinic, the Quaker Emergency Service Readjustment Center, and the Mental Hygiene Clinic at Bellevue Hospital. These subjects suffered from a variety of emotional problems such that society classified them as juvenile delinquents, and all of them read comic books. There you have it. QED.

But this was not quite the damning indictment Wertham hoped it was. In the early 1950s, between 80 and 90 percent of American boys and girls read comics. It'd have been hard for Wertham to find a kid who didn't, in or out of the psych ward.

In 2012, Carol L. Tilley, an assistant professor at the Graduate School of Library and Information Science at the University of Illinois, published a paper in the journal *Information & Culture* detailing several ways in which Wertham manipulated his evidence—combining interviews, inflating sample sizes, and deliberately misrepresenting both the statements of his subjects and the comics they read. Modern-day comics fans dutifully seized upon Tilley's work as vindication for the hardworking men and women whose livelihood Wertham's crusade had wrecked. But Tilley was only the latest member of the academic community to question the good doctor's approach. Well before *Seduction of the Innocent* was published, Wertham's fellow scientists were already onto him. New York University professor Frederic M. Thrasher, for one, had lambasted the man's methods in the December 1949 issue of the *Journal of Education and Sociology*, noting that because Wertham's contentions were not supported by research data and consisted of little more than imputation, Wertham's "conjectures [were] prejudiced and worthless."

Outside of academic circles, however, the book was widely hailed. The *New York Times* called it "careful" and lauded its "sober reflections," and the *New Yorker* welcomed it as a "formidable indictment" of the comic book industry.

"A WISH DREAM"

Some of Wertham's accusations stung more than others. That business about a rampant "injury to the eye motif"? That was fair: in the horror comics of the day, a hell of a lot of needles and knives were indeed plunging higgledy-piggledy into hapless corneas. Some of his most damning critiques about the sexualized treatment of women read as if they were written today. And when it came to calling out racist stereotypes and caricatures, Wertham's was a passionate and progressive voice.

As for his specific concerns about Batman and Robin, it's important to separate what Wertham actually wrote from what many people merely believe he did. He never called Batman and Robin gay. He said they might make a kid worry that *he* was.

That's an important difference. As Will Brooker notes in *Batman Unmasked*, Wertham's attitude toward what he referred to as "the subtle atmosphere of homoeroticism" in Batman comics doesn't come off as particularly shrill or intolerant, as many of Wertham's contemporary critics maintain. True, he believed homosexuality and misogyny to be synonymous, but in this he was simply toeing the American Psychiatric Association's party line. He also indulged in some homophobic hand-wringing and stereotyping—but he was, after all, a product of what was one of the most rabidly homophobic times in American history.

He made his national television debut while the McCarthy hearings were still going on—indeed, the Kefauver subcommittee's investigations into the scourge of juvenile delinquency followed the McCarthy model to the letter. And as Senator Joseph McCarthy himself said repeatedly to millions of Americans during the spring and summer of 1954, homosexuals represented a moral cancer that posed a security risk to the United States second only to the Communist Menace. "Better Dead Than Red"? Perhaps, but McCarthy's Senate Subcommittee on Investigations wasn't crazy about lavender, either; the specter of homosexuality was a frequent guest in the Senate's hearing rooms.

Fredric Wertham's book and Senate testimony arrived precisely at a historical moment when, according to historian Chris York, "a cultural emphasis on the nuclear family and a containment approach to both foreign and domestic affairs fueled a homophobic fire" that spread through all levels of society. It took the form of a new and particularly fervid species of paranoia that seized the American mind and effectively conflated Communism, juvenile delinquency, and homosexuality. They were coming for your kids, this sinister troika of terror, to turn them all into Bolshevik chain-smoking pantywaists.

What's remarkable, then, is the degree of restraint Wertham shows in the scant four pages he devotes to Batman and Robin. Especially compared to writers like Gershon Legman, whose self-published 1949 book *Love and Death* includes an exultantly homophobic chapter railing against the "thick necks, ham fists and well-filled jockstraps; the draggy capes and costumes" of superhero comics. Wertham simply asserts that in a culture where homosexuality is "a great taboo," the *fear* of being gay, which he believed images of Batman and Robin could evoke, consciously or not, in young male readers, "may become a source of great mental anguish" that could "raise feelings of doubt, guilt, shame and sexual malorientation."

Wertham had a point. What he didn't appreciate, however, was that it only applied to gay kids.

His assertion reads, to the legions of gay men who, as gay boys, paid maybe a bit more attention to the swell of Robin's bare, muscled calf than their fellows did, like a blunt statement of fact. Doubt? Guilt? Shame? Check, check, check. Sexual malorientation? The feeling that they weren't *right*, somehow? Check plus.

In *Seduction of the Innocent*, Wertham tells of one "young homosexual" who showed him a copy of *Detective Comics* that featured "a picture of 'The Home of Bruce and Dick,' a house beautifully landscaped, warmly lighted and showing the devoted pair side by side, looking out a of a picture window. . . . 'At the age of ten or eleven,' [the boy said,] 'I found my liking, my sexual desires, in comic books. I think I put myself in the position of Robin. I did want to have relations with Batman. . . .'"

It's safe to say that in this, he was an outlier. It is only the rarest, most precociously self-actualized gay kid who ever gets as far as imagining himself getting his freaky pubescent *relations* on with the Caped Crusader. He may admire Batman's arms, and his medicine-ball deltoids, the wide V of his torso, and the perfect quadrants of his abdominal muscles, drawn so square and even they look like the window on a Chiclets box. But for most gay kids, especially in this era of American history, any confusing attraction they may have felt toward Batman stayed exactly that—an interest that seemed to well up from some deep place below the stomach, a blunt, preverbal ache.

Try for a moment to picture that "young homosexual" patient of Wertham's, standing in the doctor's office in a pit-stained T-shirt and dungarees, with an insolent, Brando–in–*The Wild Ones* sneer on his face. He takes a drag of his cigarette and pauses, eyes darting defiantly over Wertham's dour face; he's dangerous, this kid, he's volatile, he's in it for kicks. He fishes out a rolled-up copy of *Detective Comics* from his back pocket. Opens it with a loud snap. (Does Wertham flinch? I like to think he flinches.) He flips to the page he wants. Shows it to Wertham.

And proceeds to positively *gush* about the velvet drapes in the Wayne master bedroom, which are a sort of dusky emerald.

There's just one problem, and it's a damning one: as Carol Tilley points out, that young man didn't exist. Wertham combined the case studies of two young men—who, turns out, were engaged in a relationship with one another. He also deleted the boys' statements that they were far more strongly aroused by Tarzan and the Sub-Mariner than they were by the Dynamic Duo, as that notion didn't fit his thesis.

But their story checks out: Tarzan and the Sub-Mariner, two muscular he-men who paraded through the panels of their books in nothing but a skimpy loincloth and a pair of tiny green swim trunks, respectively, were more important sexual objects to the nascent libidos of two young gay boys than were Batman and Robin.

Whatever inchoate feelings a gay kid of this era might have harbored for the Dynamic Duo likely paled next to the confusion that ensued upon his sighting a shirtless hero like Hawkman or Black Condor.

Even so: Wertham had a point. There *was* something about Batman and Robin.

THIS SPECIAL SUBTEXT

In *Seduction of the Innocent*, Wertham presented individual comics panels out of context to supplement his thesis. Today, that same practice thrives on the Internet, fueling hundreds of Tumblr, Twitter, and Instagram feeds devoted not to arguing against superhero comics but to celebrating their deep and abiding goofiness. For this reason, many of the very same *Batman* and *Detective Comics* panels that originally inspired Wertham's apprehension still pop up on our Facebook pages and alight in our inboxes, forwarded there from well-meaning high school friends with the subject line "OMG Batman Gay LOL!!!!!!"

The story "Ten Nights of Fear!" in *Batman* #84* opens with one such oft-shared panel: Bruce Wayne and Dick Grayson waking up in bed together.

The opening narration, "Morning. And it begins like any other

---

* The cover is dated June 1954 but the issue was actually on newsstands in April—just as Wertham was testifying before the Kefauver subcommittee.

routine morning in the lives of millionaire Bruce Wayne and his ward, Dick Grayson . . . ," informs us that this bed sharing is a frequent practice. As is, we may infer, their shared morning rituals: "A cold shower, a big breakfast!"

Other Tumblr favorites include a panel from *World's Finest* #59 (July 1952) in which Bruce and Dick lie naked next to each other under tanning lamps. In *Batman* #13 (October–November 1942), we find the pair in a rowboat on a city park's pond. Alone. At night.

And it's not just the art, it's the stories. Throughout the forties and fifties, Robin's jealousy—whether its object in a given month was a new potential crime-fighting partner or a new romantic interest for Batman—drove *Batman* and *Detective Comics* plots with metronomic regularity, and writers could be counted upon to milk these situations for every *choke!* and *sob!* they were worth. In addition to their rowboat idyll, *Batman* #13 also features Batman attempting to protect Robin's life by pretending to dissolve their crime-fighting partnership, an act that causes a tearful Robin to hurl himself upon the nearest overstuffed couch.

But cherry-picking such panels and passages, as a gravely concerned Wertham did in 1954 and as multitudinous sniggering Internet wags do today, means willfully misinterpreting what is meant to be a familial bond as a romantic one instead. Which hardly seems fair. After all, if the characters weren't *written* as gay, they're not gay, right?

This question has launched scores of academic papers and hundreds of Web pages, and the answer, of course, is that it doesn't matter.

Over the decades many writers of Batman comics, including Alan Grant, Devin Grayson, Frank Miller, Denny O'Neil, and even Bill Finger, have been asked if they wrote the character as gay. All, unsurprisingly, have said no, though Grayson averred that she can "understand the gay readings." The notable exception is Grant Morrison, who wrote the character in various titles for the better part of thirty years. "Gayness is built into Batman," he told *Playboy* magazine. "Batman is very, very gay. There's just no denying it. Obviously as a fictional character he's intended to be heterosexual, but the basis of the whole concept is utterly gay."

Morrison understands the same essential truth that Wertham did—the one that every ten-year-old gay kid worriedly understands as he gazes at a panel of Batman placing a friendly hand on Robin's shoulder: Intention doesn't matter. Imagery does.

Heterosexuals see themselves reflected in media so consistently and thoroughly that such representations cease to consciously register in their minds as representations. To them, movies are just movies, comics just comics. That's because their innermost selves exist in a state of perpetual autonomic agreement with the outer world as it's commonly depicted. This cognitive equilibrium produces a closed, continuous circuit of reassurance, harmony, a sense of belonging.

But to gay readers, those same representations matter-of-factly assert a vision of the world not only in which they do not belong, but in which they do not exist. Gays have always looked for their reflections in media, seeking that same sense of affinity and belonging, but until very recently, they've failed to see them: the circuit of reassurance is broken. So they patch it with whatever they can find, by looking more deeply. Every exchange, every glance, every touch, is hungrily parsed for something they recognize, for fleeting glimpses of themselves, their desires, and the world they know.

This is an oblique, allusive process; it's not like Batman comics are deliberately encrypted by their makers with coy messages—that's not how subtext works. Rather, Batman is a character who comes factory preinstalled with rich and varied ideas—ideas in which gay men historically find affinities: the constant threat of a secret self's exposure, the cloak of night, a muscular physicality, a homosocial friendship—and, yes, okay, fine, a flair for interior design that includes some pretty rocking velvet drapes that are actually, now that we're looking at them under better light, not dusky emerald but more of a forest green.

Batman is an inkblot; we see in him what we want to—even if we aren't ready to admit it to ourselves.

Unintended visual cues like body language and background detail lend themselves most easily to gay readings, which is one reason comic books have provided particularly fertile ground over the years. It would be one thing to read a prose description of two heroic crime fighters lying naked together under tanning lamps; it is quite another (and an altogether funnier, and gayer, and eminently Tumblr-able) thing to see it drawn on a comics page.

On a practical level, the gay subtext Wertham fretted about in Batman comics stemmed not from Bruce Wayne himself but from his relationship with Dick Grayson. After all, one man sitting before a fireplace in a sumptuous smoking jacket reads "dandy." Two such men reads "New Hope, Pennsylvania."

It's worth noting that although Robin immediately proved wildly popular with readers, doubling sales and ultimately earning a berth for his solo adventures in *Star-Spangled Comics* from 1947 to 1952, the Boy Wonder was not universally loved.

Take, for example, the kid who would grow up to become cartoonist Jules Feiffer, who in 1940, when Robin made his debut, was an eleven-year-old boy squarely in the character's target demographic. "I couldn't stand boy companions," he wrote in his 1965 essay "The Great Comic Book Heroes." "Robin was my own age. One need only look at him to see he could fight better, swing from a rope better, play ball better, eat better and live better . . . He was obviously an A student, the center of every circle, the one picked for greatness in the crowd—God, how I hated him. You can imagine how pleased I was when, years later, I heard he was a fag."

Indeed, Wertham's very public intimations worried Batman's publishers. Would the public see what Wertham and his cadre of swishy juvenile delinquents did? Had the addition of Robin, which had successfully lightened Batman's tone, also lightened his loafers?

WINDS OF CHANGE

In the wake of the Kefauver subcommittee's scrutiny, in September 1954 the comics industry formed the trade group known as the Comics Magazine Association of America, which created the self-regulating Comics

Code Authority to enforce a newly strengthened Comics Code. Crime and horror comics vanished from the shelves; of the 650 comics of all genres on the stands as the Kefauver subcommittee began in 1954, only 250 would still be around by the close of 1955.*

But the new Comics Code's effect on Batman was far less draconian. As noted, a sunnier, family-friendly tone had been introduced long before Wertham, with the debut of Robin back in 1940. During the war years and after, Batman's villains had grown less vile, content to plot elaborate bank heists and challenge Batman to battles of wits. Shadowy noir trappings gave way to flat-out, full-throated adventure pitched squarely at a slightly younger readership of seven-to-ten-year-olds.

Bill Finger, Jack Schiff, and other writers had spent the forties and early fifties building out Batman's world, turning it into a lighter, more whimsical place to live. Penciler Dick Sprang's Gotham City was a sunlit metropolis in which every rooftop featured a billboard with a huge advertising prop. Public exhibitions of comically oversized objects blew through town weekly. If Batman and Robin weren't sprinting across the keyboard of a giant typewriter, they were bringing an enormous bowling pin or towering hardcover book down on the heads of their quarry.

World's Finest Comics #30 (September 1947) ushered in several elements that would come to define the Batman of this era. Firstly, it featured a giant prop, in the form of an enormous copper penny. Said giant penny would go on to become a highly visible addition to the permanent collection in the Batcave's Hall of Trophies. In fact, its presence alongside two other souvenirs—a mechanical dinosaur and a giant Joker card—would visually anchor all future depictions of the Batcave. The story also employs the ridiculous, kid-friendly logic of the era when imprisoned thug Joe Coyne vows, "When I get out, I'll get

---

* This process of culling was greatly intensified by the concurrent rise of television, which in competing for the same eyeballs depressed all comic book sales.

back at coppers—and pennies! I'll fight coppers—with pennies! Every job I pull will involve pennies! MY CRIME SYMBOL WILL BE PENNIES!"

Writers had spent the years leading up to the Kefauver hearings playing to gear-loving kids by constructing entire stories around Batman's gadgets. Via cross sections and exploded diagrams, eager readers got the full technical specs on the contents of his utility belt, a new Batmobile, the Batplane, the Bat-Signal, and the layout of the Batcave.

And although conventional wisdom—including several histories of the Batman character—assert that Batman comics embraced the more whimsical themes of fantasy and science fiction as a direct result of the newly strict Comics Code, a cursory reading reveals that the books had been steadily moving in that direction from the very beginning. After all, Batman had tangled with werewolves, vampires, and death rays even in his very first year.

A scant few months after Robin's arrival, the Dynamic Duo had fought pointy-eared giants on a trip to the fourth dimension and were transported into a book of fairy tales. In 1944 they first met Professor Carter Nichols, a historian-cum-mesmerist who, via his "weird powers of hypnosis," had sent the Dynamic Duo caroming through time on no less than eighteen adventures by the time the Kefauver hearings began ten years later.

It is true, however, that under the aegis of editor Jack Schiff, Batman comics doubled down on the science fiction plots in the post-Wertham era of the late fifties. Crime and violence were out; aliens, robots, monsters, and more than a few alien robot monsters showed up with increasing regularity. Batman rocketed into outer space without a second thought and continued to hop back and forth in time like he was changing subway trains.

But this had less to do with Wertham and the Comics Code and more to do with the prevailing zeitgeist. The Space Age had dawned. The evening news was suddenly full of satellites and test flights, rockets and UFOs. Hollywood had largely abandoned the gangster movies and noir detective yarns that inspired Batman's creation, opting now for creature features starring ray-gun-toting actors in bubble helmets and shoulder hoops. But science fiction was more than agreeable schlock— it had gone respectable, moving out of the pulp magazines and onto the shelves of Shakespeare & Co.: Ray Bradbury had just published *The Martian Chronicles, The Illustrated Man,* and *Fahrenheit 451* in the span of three years. And although kids' space adventure shows like *Captain Video* and *Space Patrol* didn't survive on the television airwaves past the midfifties, they would be replaced in 1959 by a more sophisticated, even auteurist, take on science fiction with the premiere of Rod Serling's *The Twilight Zone.*

The Space Age was the reason that superhero comics, which had gone fallow in the postwar era, were now undergoing a resurgence. In 1956 DC editor Julius Schwartz decided to haul the mothballed fleet of World War II–era superheroes out of retirement. One by one, in the pages of the anthology comic *Showcase,* he introduced these warhorses back into National's superhero universe, keeping their names for trademark reasons—the Flash, the Green Lantern, the Atom, etc.—while encouraging his writers to create brand-new heroes with origins and adventures grounded entirely in science fiction.

The times, and tastes, had changed; Batman had changed with them.

His changes were not simply those of theme and narrative genre. Anyone who remembered the grim, gun-toting, thug-murdering Batman of 1939 could see that he'd become a fundamentally different guy: a grinning, lantern-jawed, wisecracking adventure hero who'd left that emo "creature of the night" shtick far behind. The blue of his cape and cowl bespoke a brighter hue—that of your friendly neighborhood beat cop's uniform. The Expressionist outlandishness of his early appearance was too flamboyant for the era of crew cuts and pleated khakis, and had steadily abraded away; in its place, he now sported a kind of standard-issue, off-the-rack superhero couture, with a cape that went no farther down his back than would the average bath towel. The ears of his mask had grown more modest, unobtrusive, until they became, for all intents and purposes, a matched pair of phrenological bumps.

Batman writer and editor Denny O'Neil dismisses this clean-cut Eisenhower-era version of the character as a "benign scoutmaster." A fair critique, perhaps—but that same epithet serves as an apt descriptor for most depictions of the adult American male in the popular culture of the time. Batman's persona was no different than *Leave It to Beaver*'s Ward Cleaver, *Ozzie and Harriet*'s Ozzie Nelson, *Father Knows Best*'s Jim Anderson, or *My Three Sons*' Steve Douglas—a stiff but kind patriarchal figure bemused by his charges but always ready when needed with a word of sober advice.

That this would become Batman's role in the post-Wertham era makes more sense when you consider his publisher's desire to scrub the character clean of unintended gay intimations. The call went forth to dial back Wertham's "wish dream of two homosexuals living together" by tethering Batman down as the head of an extended and continually growing family who'd fill up Wayne Manor until its every room reverberated with their boisterous and unignorable heteronormativity.

Or at least, that was the idea.

COURSE CORRECTION

The mass influx of new Bat-themed protégés—and the resulting creation of what would come to be known as the "Bat-Family"—wasn't simply a product of reflexive gay panic, of course. It was also still another instance of Batman copying the success of his big brother Superman.

Mort Weisinger, editor of the Superman books, had begun to populate those titles with new supporting characters who—in a novel development—didn't disappear at issue's end but hung around Metropolis for good. The introduction of Krypto the Superdog in March 1955 established a beachhead in the Superman titles, which was followed by the full-scale invasion of a red-caped menagerie: a superpowered cat, horse, bottled city, idiot doppelgänger, clubhouse of teens from the future, girl cousin, and—of course—monkey. The addition of so many new characters made for a new and evolving continuity of gimmicks and conflicts that kids pored over with relish.

Given that Superman's sales continually outpaced Batman's, editor Jack Schiff instructed his writers to follow suit: as in Metropolis, so in Gotham.

First to join the Bat-brood was Bruce Wayne's aunt Agatha, in *Batman* #89 (February 1955). The kindly old biddy, with her tight bun of white hair, spectacles, lace-collar dress, and cameo brooch, served as a one-issue test case: a feminine presence introduced into Bruce and Dick's life to keep a watchful eye on their monkeyshines. But if the intent was to make it more difficult to derive any louche subtext to Batman and Robin's bond, this effect was vastly undercut by the story itself, which sees the Dynamic Duo only grudgingly tolerate Agatha's presence in their boys-only clubhouse. They construct a series of elaborate ruses to distract and deceive her so they can sneak off to be alone together. Aunt Agatha wouldn't stick around, but she served as a prototype for Aunt Harriet, who would arrive to fill Agatha's "dithering matron" slot nine years hence.

In 1955's *Detective Comics* #215 we meet a Benetton ad of Bat-allies from across the globe: the Knight and Squire (England), the Ranger (Australia), the Legionary (Italy), the Gaucho (South America), and the Musketeer (France).

A scant three months after Krypto's first appearance—which was itself inspired by the success of Rin Tin Tin and Lassie—Ace the Bat-Hound made his debut in *Batman* #92 (June 1955).

Next, in *Detective Comics* #233 (July 1956), came "the mysterious and glamorous girl . . . The Batwoman!" Here, at last, was a brassy broad worthy of Batman's love. Heiress Kathy Kane, onetime circus trapeze artist and motorcycle stunt rider, dons a bright yellow bodysuit accessorized with red gloves, boots, cape, and bat-eared masquerade mask to "use [her] skills as Batman does!" proclaiming, "I, too, will fight crime—I'll be a BATWOMAN!"

It has become a widely held conviction among comics historians that Batwoman was specifically introduced to reinforce Batman's heterosexual bona fides. However, over the eight years she spent as Batman's ally, his amorous intentions toward her remained highly ambivalent. In her debut story, he uncovers her secret identity and convinces her to give up her crime-fighting career by mansplaining, "If I found out, crooks could do so, too, eventually!" In her subsequent appearances, he stubbornly resists her advances, lecturing her that crime fighting is "too dangerous for a girl." Like any emotionally unavailable boyfriend, he is not above throwing her the occasional bone, as when, facing their imminent death in an alien dimension in *Batman* #153 (February 1963), he tells her he loves her, only to rescind it once they return safely home: "Well—er— Batwoman—I thought we were going to die—and I wanted to make your last moments happy ones!" he says. Jerk.

Said ambivalence, of course, was simply an outgrowth of the book's faithfulness to its target audience: the seven-to-ten-year-old boys who found girls yucky and any hint of romance boring and gross. There was also this inconvenient truth: everything about Batwoman was presented as so kitschily überfeminine that she could have passed for Batman's fierce drag queen persona. Her shoulder-bag crime-fighting kit contained a powder puff of sneezing powder, a perfume flask of tear gas, a pair of charm-bracelet handcuffs, a lipstick telescope, and an oversized hairnet for snaring evildoers.

Between Batman's constantly rebuffing her and Batwoman's own preternatural fabulousness, any adult readers determined to mine gay readings from these Batman comics would not have found it a particularly difficult process of excavation.

DIMINISHING RETURNS

Bat-whimsy was now in full flourish: the Dynamic Duo met Mogo the Bat-Ape, and Batman himself began to undergo the kind of freakish transformations that typified superhero comics of the time. Either by dint of magic or mysterious "science-rays," individual issues saw the Caped Crusader transmogrified into a Bat-Baby, Bat-Robot, Bat-Genie, Bat-Alien, Bat-Merman, Bat-Mummy, Bat-Phantom, Bat-Giant, Bat–Rip Van Winkle, or Bat-Monster.

All of these furious quick-changes were driven by sweaty desperation. Artist Sheldon Moldoff, who was still ghosting Batman stories for Bob Kane twenty-three years after he'd begun, would later explain this see-what-sticks approach to interviewer Les Daniels by saying, "It was important to make each cover look completely different . . . One of those things must have worked, so they kept trying."

In fact, it wasn't working. A gee-whiz futurist take on storytelling suited Superman perfectly; he was made to whomp giant robots and ride the stylized tail fins of rocket ships. Julius Schwartz's reconstituted science fiction superheroes were going gangbusters in their own comics and over in the new *Justice League of America* team comic. After their postwar sales decline, coupled with Wertham's attacks, superheroes once again proliferated atop the sales charts—in fact, one scrappy comics publisher (which had weathered the stormy comics seas by changing its name from Timely to Atlas to, ultimately, Marvel) was building a shared fictive universe teeming with squabbling superheroes of its own.

But it quickly became clear that the only way to fit Batman into the world of aliens and rocket ships was to take his status as a non-powered human being—the very thing setting him apart—and set it aside. One reason it was so easy to iterate Batman into Bat-Monster and Bat-Baby and all his other cowl-and-cape-wearing mutations was that the character had become a cipher, recognizable only by his design. The cowl and cape were all that defined him; he'd become, in a very real sense, an empty suit.

Kids had noticed. Of all the comics on newsstands since the postwar superhero bust, *Batman* had habitually languished at the bottom of the top ten in sales. *Detective Comics* struggled to stay in the top twenty. Now, despite the superhero renaissance sending new titles surging up the charts, Batman's sales were on the wane.

Older fans, who grew up with Batman, had noticed, too. The first comic book fanzines now appeared on the scene. One of them—*Alter Ego*, founded by Jerry Bails—wasted no time in creating the very first fan awards for the comic book industry, the Alleys. In 1962, the same year that even Harvey Comics' *Hot Stuff the Little Devil* managed to outsell *Detective Comics*, *Batman* was awarded the Alley for Comic Most in Need of Improvement. Anyone could see it: the Caped Crusader was straining to keep up with the times. National publisher Irwin Donenfeld began to wonder if it might be more merciful to put the guy out of his misery.

NEW LOOK

Editor Julius Schwartz had helped engineer the superhero resurgence, and Donenfeld was fond of his handling of *The Flash*, a bold, colorful title that had debuted in 1959. Donenfeld looked at the team behind that comic—John Broome on scripts, Carmine Infantino on pencils, and Joe Giella on inks—and decided to issue an ultimatum. He called Schwartz and Infantino into his office and told them they were taking over the Batman books. If the two men couldn't turn them around in six months, both *Batman* and *Detective Comics* would be canceled.

Schwartz and Infantino were nonplussed. Neither man harbored any particular fondness for the character. Schwartz in particular preferred the pure-ozone flights of science fiction whiz-bangery evinced by heroes like the Flash, Adam Strange, and the Green Lantern; in comparison, Batman's recent flirtations with space adventure seemed hokey, slapdash, and halfhearted. He suspected that Donenfeld's threat to cancel *Batman* was an empty one, given the Caped Crusader's historical number two status in the publisher's firmament of intellectual property. True, his name recognition paled in comparison to Superman's, but at least he'd enjoyed *some* time in the public spotlight beyond the comic book page, unlike the Atom, the Green Lantern, and the rest of the newcomers.

Instead of completely overhauling Batman as DC had done with the Flash and others, the changes Schwartz and Infantino brought to their first issue (*Detective Comics* #327, May 1964) were subtle but hard to miss. Despite their professed love of space opera, both agreed that Batman just seemed more at home in the urban jungle, grounded in reality—or at least, in whatever passed for reality in superhero comic books. That meant no more Bat-Giants, Bat-Babies, Bat-Aliens, or any such freakish (albeit eye-catching) transformations. Ditto the rocket ships and time travel: gone.

They dismissed without severance the extended Bat-Family of Batwoman, Bat-Girl, Bat-Hound, and Bat-Mite. All vanished in an off-panel puff of editorial fiat, with nary a word of explanation. Once again, Batman and Robin were on their own against the world—even faithful, trustworthy old Alfred, a fixture in the Batcave for some twenty-one years now, got crushed by a boulder one month later.

When asked, years later, why Alfred had to die, Julius Schwartz revealed the remarkable extent to which Wertham's innuendoes still hung in the air a full decade after *Seduction of the Innocent* had been remaindered and pulped: "There was a lot of discussion in those days about three males living in Wayne Manor," Schwartz said. "So I had Alfred die in the process of saving Batman's life, and I brought in Aunt Harriet." And so, in addition to the publishing houses he'd shuttered and the livelihoods he'd crushed, Fredric Wertham's anticomics crusade now at last had a body count: Alfred Pennyworth, RIP.

But comics are a visual medium, and it wasn't these various narrative shifts that made *Detective Comics* #327 such a bold and arresting break from nearly three decades of Batman's comic book history. Batman had a new look.

Over the course of almost thirty years, Sheldon Moldoff, Dick Sprang, Lew Sayre Schwartz, and other members of Bob Kane's stable of ghost-artists had struck upon a "classic" look for Batman—one that deliberately finessed the blocky *Dick Tracy* style of square heads jammed atop squat torsos that Kane had brought to the character in those first few years. In the panels of Batman comics, characters didn't interact, they posed at one another, and all action seemed to take place on a single, flat foregrounded plane. Cartoony and stiff, yes, but distinctive.

Infantino's pencils owed less to cartooning and more to commercial illustration—he imbued his figures with a realistic roundedness. He replaced Kane's angular minimalism with an approach both softer and richer in specificity and detail—clothes wrinkled, surfaces had textures, and where classic Batman's mouth had been rendered as an affectless horizontal pen stroke, Infantino's had full, expressive lips set off by frown lines.

Batman's sartorial makeover was technically only a tiny tweak—but a tweak that would be felt around the world. Infantino shrank the size of the black bat insignia on his chest and surrounded it with a round yellow oval. The resulting design deliberately evoked the Bat-Signal and the imagery of Batman silhouetted against the moon. What's more, by encapsulating the emblem inside a yellow field, Infantino transformed it into an eminently reproducible and trademarkable symbol—a logo that in just a few years' time would become a generation's cultural touchstone.

While he was at it, Infantino beefed up Batman's musculature and drew his ears a skosh longer—nothing that would take him back to the antennae-like jobbers of his first appearances, but just enough to impart a hint of early Batman's more sinister mien.

There was a problem, however: Bob Kane had renegotiated his contract in the late forties by insisting that he'd been underage when he'd signed his original contract, a position he argued successfully despite its untruth. The new contract stipulated that he would get paid for producing a certain number of pages every year; they were stuck with him. So Schwartz split the artist duties. Infantino would pencil every other issue of *Detective Comics*, inked by Joe Giella, while Bob Kane—which is to say, Sheldon Moldoff and Kane's other ghost-artists—would pencil *Batman*, inked by Joe Giella.

Moldoff, of course, was quite capable of imitating Infantino's style, just as he'd emulated Kane's. And by having the same inker finish both books, Schwartz ensured that they'd share a consistent aesthetic. This was doubly reinforced by Schwartz's decision to have Infantino and Giella draw the covers of both *Batman* and *Detective Comics*.

Kane wasn't happy—he complained to his editor about Infantino's more realistic style—but he was about to be made markedly less so. Now that Schwartz was editing the Bat-books, he saw no reason to perpetuate the myth that Bob Kane was still writing and drawing all of Batman's adventures. In the first appearance of New Look Batman, he removed Bob Kane's signature from the opening splash page. In the book's letter column, he hyped the next issue by praising "the swell script of Bill Finger, who has written many of the classic Batman tales of the past two decades."

Full creator credits wouldn't appear in the Batman titles for years to come, but Schwartz's seemingly throwaway shout-out was the first indication readers had gotten that anyone besides Bob Kane was responsible for Batman. It wasn't much, yet it changed everything.

Schwartz decreed that the new era of Batman stories had to do more than distance itself from the flights of fancy that marked Jack Schiff's editorial tenure—they were to reassert the core elements of the character that had gotten lost amid all the alien plant tentacles and science-rays.

Over the next few years, Batman returned to his roots as a master sleuth, sussing out clues and piecing together forensic evidence like the caped criminologist he was born to be.

Abandoning science fiction and fantasy themes meant the books' rotating writers—who included Broome and Ed Herron, as well as old salts like Gardner Fox and Bill Finger himself—could welcome back old foes who'd gone missing. In 1963, the Penguin emerged from a seven-year exile, followed in 1965 by the Riddler, who'd been absent from the pages of Batman comics for seventeen years.

The wild popularity of Sean Connery's James Bond films exerted a potent influence on comics in general and on New Look Batman in particular. New gadgets such as a refurbished Bat-Signal and a new Batmobile—a sleek, open-topped, tricked-out sports car—made their debuts. Batman spent more time than ever before struggling to escape from terrifying death traps. July 1964 saw him jetting off to England to investigate the mysterious "Castle with Wall-to-Wall Danger!" And in *Batman* #167 (November 1964) Batman and Robin chase "the Hydra of Crime" through a "book-length spy thriller" that takes them to the Netherlands, Singapore, Greece, Hong Kong, France, and the Swiss Alps, where they infiltrate the villain's underground lair and foil his plot to launch a nuclear missile that will trigger Armageddon.

Back home, New Look Batman's Gotham City grew into a larger and more idiosyncratic metropolis that for the first time evinced a grubby, lived-in character. In comparison, the Gotham of the previous thirty years had seemed like a studio back lot—nothing but ripe-for-plunder banks and jewelry stores had lined its bright, broad, candy-colored streets. New Look Gotham boasted beatnik coffee shops and used-book stores, groovy art galleries and gleaming skyscrapers.

ENTER . . . THE NERDS

There were missteps along the way: in the new creative team's very first issue Batman holds a gun on a group of criminals. Fans took to the letters pages in protest, and Schwartz later, in his autobiography, offered a mea culpa, noting that neither he nor Broome was a student of the character: "When it came to Batman we were the blind leading the blind," he wrote. Mostly, though, the *Batman* readership was intrigued by the changes he'd brought about.

"The character of Batman has always had the potential of becoming the greatest of all comic book heroes," wrote one fan, ". . . because he might be the most believable of all comic book characters. In this issue, all of Batman's possibilities have been realized."

And over in the pages of a mail-order fanzine called *Batmania*, which was launched in 1964 by a Missouri firefighter named Biljo White, the hardest core of Batman's hard-core fan base weighed in on New Look Batman via a poll.

Batmania, together with other early fanzines like *Comic Art* and *Alter*

Ego, offered a new means for fans and collectors to come together to praise, critique, and commiserate over their shared love of comics. Between its covers, at least, comics were not dismissed as disposable and disreputable bits of junk culture; they were stories told with charm and skill. Contributors offered cogent arguments that characters written for children merited thoughtful consideration by adults, by virtue of the themes they tackled and the aesthetics of their design. In *Batmania*'s pages, Batman and his world became a source of furious, nigh-Talmudic dissection.

Julius Schwartz, who at the age of seventeen had himself copublished one of the first science fiction fanzines, knew all of this firsthand and encouraged his readers to network with one another. It was his desire to take part in the ongoing fan conversation that caused him to introduce letter columns to the comics he edited. He made sure to include the full address of each letter writer he published, which enabled devoted readers to correspond with one another on their own. Friendships formed and—on more than one occasion—nerd romance blossomed.

Schwartz was so encouraging of the fanzine community, in fact, that he gave *Batmania* a prominent shout-out in the letter column of *Batman* #169 (January 1965), boosting its sales considerably.

As for that poll: nine out of ten readers of *Batmania* approved of the new Batman's more grounded, Gotham-based-detective direction.

But almost half—40 percent—hated the new costume; even a sartorial adjustment as modest as the one in question earned the enmity of the newly emerging hard-core fan base. We will see this pattern recur with every subsequent tweak and tuck made to the Batman costume across all media.*

It's fitting that the first significant change to the character's established visual iconography coincided with the first stirring of a culture

---

* And if the fans of 1964 were mildly put out by the addition of a yellow oval, that was as nothing compared to the howling fanboy maelstrom that would attend the fateful advent, in 1997, of the Bat-nipple.

of nerdery to complain about it. A reflexive resistance to change, a white-knuckled grip on a deeply personal vision of the "true" Batman, combined with a penchant for expressing it with hyperliterate force, would swiftly become key elements in the hard-core fans' bond with the character.

But at least readers were talking about Batman again. More importantly, they were buying his comics: sales of *Batman* instantly rose 69 percent, while *Detective* saw a more modest surge.

Things were looking up for the character. Solid sales were all that National Comics asked of him, and now once again he was delivering them. Exciting detective adventure stories were all that his fans asked of him, and now he was delivering those as well.

It could easily have gone on like this indefinitely, with Batman safely ensconced back in his historical role as the superhero set's dependable second-stringer: Superman's ever-loyal wingman in comics that were read only by a small but steady subset of the American population.

But in June of 1965, the Playboy Theater in Chicago added to its schedule daily screenings of individual chapters from the 1943 *Batman* movie serial. The showings swiftly became a "happening," attracting sellout crowds of college students and, according to the incredulous theater manager, "even a hard-core of serial buffs who viewed it as an art form." In October, the theater manager spliced all fifteen chapters together as a midnight movie, an event that made national news.

Columbia Pictures, inspired by the glowing media coverage and ticket sales, dug into its film vaults and followed the Playboy Theater's lead. In November, the 248-minute feature *An Evening with Batman and Robin* kicked off a twenty-city national tour in Cleveland. The crowds were huge and enthusiastic, and grew more so with each stop. "In a college town," wrote *Time* magazine, "who today outdraws *Dr. Strangelove*, outclocks *Gone with the Wind*, and breaks all known records for popcorn sales? It's not a bird or a plane but, of all things, Batman."

It was the last thing Schwartz, or Finger, or even Bob Kane himself

would have ever imagined: suddenly, among crowds of hip young ur-
banites, Batman was a sensation.

There was, however, one tiny hitch. A small snag. An asterisk.

Had any of Batman's National Comics caretakers attended a screening of *An Evening with Batman and Robin* for themselves, or if one of
Batmania's passionate contributors had made it into one of Hefner's
Club Rooms, his delight at seeing Batman back on the big screen would
have lasted exactly thirty seconds, at which point it would have been
drowned out by the crowd around him.

Drowned out, specifically, by their hooting. Their catcalls. Their
jeers.

They were . . . *laughing*! What was the world coming to?

Imagine! Of all things!

Laughing . . . at *Batman*!

3

Same Bat-Time . . . (1965-1969)

*The sixties TV show remains anathema to the serious Bat-fan pre-
cisely because it heaps ridicule on the very notion of a serious Batman. Batman revealed the man in the cape as a pompous fool, an
embodiment of superceded ethics, a closet queen. . . . I'm prepared to
admit the validity, for some people, of the swooping eighties vigilante,
so why are they so concerned to trash my sixties camped crusader?
Why do they insist so vehemently that Adam West was a faggy ab-
erration, a blot on the otherwise impeccably butch Bat-landscape?
What ARE they trying to hide?*

—CULTURAL CRITIC ANDY MEDHURST, FROM HIS 1991 ESSAY
"BATMAN, DEVIANCE AND CAMP"

Sometime in late January of 1966, twelve-year-old Charlie "Chuck"
Dixon, a boy with the largest collection of Batman comics in his class—
and who would, in fact, grow up to write Batman comics himself for
more than eleven years—slugged a schoolmate and shoved him into a
coat closet.

The early months of 1966 saw a rise in schoolyard horseplay of a
weirdly specific nature: children staging mock fights, peppering each
whiffed haymaker and uppercut with shouts of "BAM!" "POW!" and
"ZAP!" Trips to the school nurse spiked as well. The National Parent
Teacher Association noticed and cautioned parents that their children

were imitating the violence they watched each week on a new ABC television series called *Batman*.

But most parents already knew. On the night of its January 12 premiere, in fact, half of all American households that were watching television had watched *Batman*. On the following night, when the previous evening's cliff-hanger ending got resolved, almost 60 percent of the nation's TV sets tuned in—numbers not seen since the Beatles' gig on *The Ed Sullivan Show*, two years before.

But the shadow of Wertham lingered. Celebrity psychologist Dr. Joyce Brothers concurred with the PTA, explaining that *Batman* was more dangerous for children than even the most violent Western or crime show, because while kids could only mime gunplay, they could quite easily smack one another around. Child psychologist Eda J. LeShan took to the pages of the *New York Times Magazine* with an article portentously titled "At War with *Batman*" to assail the series' disruptive effect on the American schoolyard. Even the famous Dr. Spock, who'd at first come out in favor of the show, later recanted his praise, saying, "*Batman* is bad for pre-school children. It encourages free expression for violence."

But little Chuck Dixon's pugilistic coatroom outburst wasn't the kind of incident that shrinks were warning parents about that year. Although it had everything to do with the *Batman* television show, it wasn't an instance of a kid imitating what he'd seen on-screen.

He was repudiating it. Violently.

"I took it all very personally that Wednesday night in January when the series premiere broke my heart," Dixon recalls. "That wasn't *my* Batman! Hell, my parents were *laughing* at the show! Laughing at Batman!"

Later, at school, Dixon's friend "proudly showed off his new [Adam West] *Batman* T-shirt. He thought I'd dig the shirt . . . but instead, I saw red. I knocked him into the coat closet."

It was, very possibly, the first recorded instance of nerd-rage.

THE DORK NERD RISES

"The one constant factor through all of the transformations of Batman has been the devotion of his admirers," wrote critic Andy Medhurst in the 1991 essay "Batman, Deviance and Camp." "They will defend him against what they see as negative interpretations, and they carry around in their heads a kind of essence of Batness, a Bat–Platonic Ideal of how Batman should really be."

The phenomenon to which Medhurst refers, which in the years since that essay's publication has only been amplified and calcified by the rise of the Internet, began on the evening of January 12, 1966.

Until *Batman*'s premiere, that virulent strain of devotion—the conviction that one's love of a character entitles one to ownership of it—remained a sentiment in search of an outlet. The comics fanzines teemed with bookish young men and women who had either kept buying the titles they'd loved as kids or returned to them after a pubescent hiatus. What's more, they tended to adopt a historical view of comics, striving to place new adventures in a context of what had gone before. In the process, this small but fervent group was taking the first tentative steps toward assembling the nerd constructs that would come to be known as comics canon and continuity.

In *The Comic Book Heroes*, Gerard Jones distinguishes between these tiny communities of fanzine contributors and the larger groups of young readers who wrote in to comics letter pages: "The new fanzine publishers were adults looking back, with little emotional investment in the present, while [letter column writers] were the opposite, all waiting for the next issue of *Superman* with no sense of comics history."

In these earliest days of comics fanzines, fans had begun to quibble about plot developments and story choices. The New Look Batman had given *Batmania* contributors chewy fodder for disquisition and debate, and they were quick to scold Batman's use of a gun, but the sense of outrage to which Medhurst refers—the fannish need to run to the forensic barricades to assert that one "true" version of Batman exists and decry

some new development as a flagrant contradiction of the character's nature—had not truly been tested. Until the Batusi.

Michael Uslan, who would grow up to executive-produce eight
Batman feature films in the eighties, nineties, and aughts, was a fifteen-
year-old fanboy when the series premiered. His recollections closely
echo those of Dixon, minus the fisticuffs. "I was horrified when I realized that the world was laughing at Batman. Not with him. *At* him."

British talk-show host Jonathan Ross typifies the condescending,
Jack Black–in–*High Fidelity* dismissiveness of the hard-core Bat-fan
when he notes in one graphic novel's preface that if you hold any fondness for the Batman television series, "then maybe you prefer Elvis Pres-
ley's Vegas years or the later Jerry Lewis movies . . ."

In their defense, the 1966 *Batman* series caught fans of the character unprepared and unequipped. The show beamed its way into the
tiny, scattered pockets of gestating nerd culture and, almost overnight,
presented them with something wholly new: a terrifying, up-is-down
reality in which the thing they prized, the thing that set them resolutely
apart, was suddenly hip.

At last, they were no longer alone in their devotion. They were but
small, serious voices in the new and jubilant cacophony of Batmania
sweeping over the world.

God, they *hated* it.

But now at least they had outlets to register that shared displeasure.
There, in the pages of fanzines and at science fiction conventions, they
could condemn the show and the hordes of fresh, fair-weather Batman
fans it bred. They began to shape, for the very first time, the sentiment
that all nerds who followed after them would employ whenever they
found their niche interests embraced by the mass culture:

"You do not appreciate this thing you profess to love in precisely
the same way, to precisely the same extent, and for precisely the same
reasons that I do."

Or, more simply, "You're doing it wrong."

That these loyal readers of Batman comics were horrified by the show when it first premiered is both predictable and surprising. Predictable, because every adaptation of a beloved property inspires outrage in some quarters, and fans of Batman have shown themselves over the years to be particularly given to fulmination. "That's not Batman!" they protest, when of course what they truly mean, like so many twelve-year-old Chuck Dixons, is "That's not *my* Batman!"

The hard-core fans who would later balk at Michael Keaton's diminutive stature or George Clooney's Bat-nipples or Christian Bale's Welshness did so with a strong and clear conception of what their personal Batman looked and felt like. The Batman comics of the seventies and eighties supplied a consistent, specific, and sharply defined idea of their hero that they could hold up to the latest Hollywood Bat-project, so as to find it wanting.

It's striking, then, that 1966 fans of Batman comics reacted so vehemently to his television iteration. Unlike the nerds of the eighties, nineties, and aughts, they did not come to the TV Batman with a strictly defined idea of who the character was. True, just over a year of New Look Batman comics had offered up a relatively grounded Caped Crusader with occasional flare-ups of James Bondism, but the twenty-five years before represented only a wildly inconsistent stew of science fiction fizziness and sunny, standard-issue superheroing. The dark Batman of his first eleven adventures hadn't been glimpsed in nearly three decades by this point.

But of course it wasn't just twelve-year-old kids like Chuck Dixon and Michael Uslan who rejected the Adam West Batman out of a resistance to change and a desire not to see their hero mocked. There were readers of the comics who remembered the grim avenger Batman of 1939 firsthand. They were the kids who'd bought *Detective Comics* #27 at the age of nine and had stuck with the character ever since. They were readers, specifically, like *Batmania* editor Biljo White, who at the age of thirty-six had created a zine to express his own passion for the character and foster that passion in others like him.

They were the true believers who tuned in to the series premiere on

January 12, 1966; they knew one thing about *their* Batman very clearly, and they knew it in their very bones:

He didn't do the goddamn Batusi.

CAMP, RUN AMOK

Several convictions about the *Batman* TV series have hardened over the years into inaccurate but widely held truths.

First: that it was mere parody.

It was not. To create the *Batman* pilot script, writer Lorenzo Semple Jr. took the story "The Remarkable Ruse of the Riddler" from *Batman* #171 (March 1965) and adapted it into the two-part episode "Hi Diddle Riddle/Smack in the Middle."

Except he didn't adapt it. Adaptation is a process of transmuting a story from one medium to another, and it requires skillful attention to the particular set of strengths and weaknesses of both forms involved. A play poorly adapted into a film can feel stiff and stagy; a novel poorly adapted into a television miniseries can sink under the weight of tedious exposition and excessive detail.

Superhero comics offer bright, broad panels exploding with action and color that capture heightened emotion with a sense of terrible urgency. Television is a quieter and more intimate medium that prefers to convey information via conversations in a two-shot—a camera setup wide enough to allow viewers to watch two actors reacting to one another. Superhero comics deliver spectacle, while television thrives on relationships. Had Semple chosen to truly adapt the story of *Batman* #171 to fit the television screen, he could have done so, and turned in a straight-ahead adventure with a pleasant, kid-friendly tone; the result would have looked something very like an episode of *Star Trek*, *Tarzan*, or *Voyage to the Bottom of the Sea*.

But instead of adapting the comic book story, he directly transcribed it, flatly mapping the tropes of superhero comics onto the existing format of a half-hour television series. He took the narrative architecture of a superhero story—costumed archvillains with idiomatic schemes, elaborate death traps and miraculous escapes, sound effects, a Manichean worldview where unspoiled virtue wages an unceasing war with dastardly greed and mischief—and brought all of it over completely intact.

Many now refer to the show as "tongue-in-cheek" or "winking" but it was avowedly neither. It was, every frame of it, serious business. That, in fact, was the whole point.

The abiding irony that hard-core fans decry the show for "not taking Batman seriously" lies in the fact that "taking Batman seriously" was precisely the show's organizing principle. The particular genius of the show's approach, and the key to its mass appeal, was this tonal jujitsu. They reproduced the conventions of the era's one-dimensional Batman comics in three dimensions and asserted them with a species of terrible, poker-faced gravity that producer William Dozier characterized as "like we are going to drop the bomb on Hiroshima." In so doing, they achieved something that television, let alone the culture, had never seen before.

The showrunner's vision was aided considerably by National's steadfast resolve to keep the New Look Batman of the comics so decidedly and unapologetically square. It required a straight-arrow hero who never questioned his motivations or purpose, whose belief in his mission was so absolute it could be taken for granted, a permanent fixture of the show's narrative architecture.

It wasn't parody, exactly. The producers of the show weren't trying to mock or trivialize comic books. They didn't feel they needed to; comics were trivial already. Neither was it satire, as satire comments on something outside itself. The world of the *Batman* television show is entirely hermetic. It references only itself, albeit stylishly. On rare occasions when the series bothers to engage with current affairs, the topic in question gets so enmeshed in, and processed by, the show's unique brand of artifice as to become unrecognizable and toothless: women's liberation becomes the villainous Nora Clavicle's smartly skirt-suited

Ladies' Crime Club; youth unrest becomes Louie the Lilac's zonked-out flower children.

So if it wasn't parody or satire, what was it? The throngs of columnists and critics who wrote about the show in those first months of 1966 had a few ideas. In article after article, even before the show's premiere, one word was picked from the cultural ether and grafted onto *Batman* so assiduously that fifty years later, no discussion of the show now occurs without it: "camp."

Two years before the show debuted, the Susan Sontag essay "Notes on 'Camp'" in the *Partisan Review* had become a literary sensation. Sontag constructed the piece as a series of fifty-eight numbered prose passages—the "notes" of the title—as a means to demonstrate, or at least gesture toward, the oblique and ephemeral nature of the specific sensibility she wished to dissect.

Until Sontag wrote about it, the entire concept of camp had largely kept itself to the salons of the urban cultural elite and the saloons of the gay demimonde. It took Sontag fifty-eight notes merely to evoke it, and many writers have since hurled themselves against walls of prose in an attempt to parse it further into "high camp," "low camp," "intentional camp," and more. But the definition of camp that filtered into the mass sensibility—that is, the one that critics and columnists were trading back and forth in the popular press—lacked the particulars of academia's literary dialectic.

The shorthand phrase most commonly associated with camp in newspapers and magazines of the day was "So bad it's good." But it wasn't unusual for columnists to go a bit further than that, noting that camp objects exhibit an ostentatious but self-aware theatricality. Many paraphrased Sontag by noting that camp places arch quotation marks around everything it touches, and treats the grave as frivolous, and the frivolous as grave.

The *frivolous* (superhero comics) as *grave* (high drama): this was the *Batman* show's mission statement.

In interviews, *Batman* producer William Dozier claimed credit for the show's adoption of a camp aesthetic, though he assiduously avoided calling it that, lest he invoke the term's gay associations. Instead, he resorted to exhaustive circumlocution. "I got the idea to do it so square and so serious and so cliché ridden and so overdone," Dozier said, "and yet with a certain elegance and style . . . it would be so corny and so bad that it would be funny." Writer Lorenzo Semple Jr. maintained it was instead he who struck upon the idea to play it deadly straight.

NA NA NA NA NA NA NA NA NA NA NA NA NA

In 1965, as the Vietnam War continued to escalate, frothy high-concept sitcoms like *My Favorite Martian*, *The Munsters*, *The Addams Family*, and *Gilligan's Island* dominated the TV schedule. Despite the ratings success of its own fantasy-infused half-hour comedy *Bewitched*, however, ABC had sunk into last place.

Executives put out the word they were looking for another high-concept series—something zippy and larger-than-life, maybe a James Bond character or a comic book property. They conducted an audience survey to gauge viewer interest in various comics heroes, and the results came back:

1. Superman
2. Dick Tracy
3. Batman
4. The Green Hornet
5. Little Orphan Annie

Superman was a nonstarter as they couldn't get the rights; a Broadway musical was already being prepped about the Man of Steel and was slated to debut in spring 1966. They got outbid for the rights to Dick Tracy by NBC. That left Batman.

Earlier in the decade, CBS had attempted to develop a straight-ahead Batman kids' show in the style of the old *Adventures of Superman* series, and had gotten so far as to hire lantern-jawed ex-NFL linebacker Mike Henry* to star as the Caped Crusader. But CBS hadn't taken that show into production, and the rights to Batman were once again available.

In March of 1965 producer William Dozier was summoned to the ABC offices in Manhattan and informed they wanted to do a Batman show. "I thought they were crazy," he said later. Even in interviews following the show's runaway success, Dozier's contempt for the medium of comic books never faded. "I bought a dozen comics and felt like a fool as I 'read' them—if that *is* the word—and asked myself, What do I do with *this*? I was used to loftier projects."

Dozier's distaste for comics was, it should be remembered, simply the prevailing societal norm. It should also be remembered that those "loftier projects" to which he refers included *Rod Brown of the Rocket Rangers* and the sitcom *Dennis the Menace*, based on the beloved scamp of the funny pages.

He tapped writer Lorenzo Semple Jr. to try his hand at a pilot script. They originally conceived the show as a series of hour-long episodes, but that didn't last. In interviews, Bob Kane always said it was he who suggested to Dozier dividing the pilot into two parts separated by a cliff-hanger, to evoke the tension of the old movie serials. But then, Bob Kane said lots of things.

The script Semple eventually turned in was ambitious in its scope, tasked with a great deal of world-building. It also introduced six recurring characters even before the opening titles kicked in: Batman/Bruce Wayne, Robin/Dick Grayson, Alfred, Aunt Harriet, Commissioner Gordon, and Chief O'Hara, created for the series. Semple also managed to cram a hell of a lot of plot into its twenty-two-minute running time, including many elements cut and pasted straight from one of the comics Dozier had read upon getting the assignment.

---

* Henry would instead go on to star as the thirteenth film Tarzan in three movies.

In the first half of Semple's pilot, "Hi Diddle Riddle," the Riddler's lawyers serve Batman with a subpoena for false arrest—meaning he will have to reveal his secret identity when he testifies in court. A clue leads the Dynamic Duo to the groovy What a Way to Go-Go nightclub. One drugged orange juice later, Batman staggers to the dance floor to shake his groove thing, even as Robin is kidnapped by the Riddler.

Semple's script then calls for the narrator to urgently intone:

WILL ROBIN ESCAPE?

CAN BATMAN FIND HIM IN TIME?

IS THIS THE GHASTLY END OF OUR DYNAMIC DUO?

ANSWERS . . . TOMORROW NIGHT! SAME TIME, SAME CHANNEL!

ONE HINT—THE WORST IS YET TO COME!

As part two, "Smack in the Middle," opens, Riddler's moll* impersonates the Boy Wonder with a lifelike mask. Batman rescues "Robin" and takes "him" back to the Batcave. Once Molly's true identity is revealed, she meets her doom when she falls into the atomic pile used to power the Batmobile. Batman reunites with the real Robin, and the Caped Crusaders surprise the Riddler and his cronies.† The Riddler escapes, but his gang is captured. There will be no court date for Batman; Bruce Wayne's secret is safe. Credits.

Anyone who read this script could see Semple and Dozier were going for something beyond straight-shooting kiddie fare. Semple selectively boosted the volume on Batman's civic-mindedness. "Watch it, chum," he admonishes the Boy Wonder as the lad prepares to hurl an iron gate recently liberated from a window to the street far below them, "pedestrian safety." All of the dialogue, too, came weighted with a great

---

* The aptly named Molly.

† The screen fills with the "BIFF! BONK!" sound-effect signage that would come to define the series.

and terrible sense of purpose; it would be hard to miss that something odd was going on here:

BATMAN: Precisely, Inspector Basch. The Riddler contrives his plots like artichokes. You have to strip off the spiny leaves to reach the heart.

And, later:

ROBIN: Riddler, you fiend! Don't you know that crime doesn't pay?

Mindful of the television medium's insatiable hunger for catch-phrases, Semple added a characterizing tic to the Boy Wonder's dialogue: "Holy barracuda!" shouts Dick in his very first scene. The "Holy _____!" construction, which would quickly become a staple of the series, was a corny bit of business Semple borrowed from the Tom Swift books he'd loved as a kid.

But the ABC suits lapped it up and dutifully passed the script along to National Comics for review. Mindful that even a middlingly successful national television show about one of their characters stood to boost sales—even one as defiantly off-plumb as this one was shaping up to be—they approved the script without a fuss. They did, however, ask Dozier to revise the scene in which Molly the moll falls to her death; in the original script, a mercilessly taciturn Batman simply watched her slip into the atomic reactor. National insisted that the Caped Crusader instead do everything he could to save her. The change was made: Batman reaches out to Molly, urging her to take his hand. She slips and dies.

BATMAN: Poor, deluded girl. If only she'd let me save her. [*beat*] What a *terrible* way to go-go.

Thus, given the opportunity to balk at what Dozier and Semple intended to do to their number two character, National Comics instead zeroed in on the one instance in the entire script in which Batman's moral compass wavered by even the tiniest humanizing degree. By insisting that he strive and fail to save the "poor, deluded girl," National's feedback effectively made the Batman of the final shooting script seem even more feckless than before.

Bob Kane wrote a letter to Dozier upon hearing that a Batman series was in the works. "It seems," he wrote, "Batman has caught his second wind and is 'red hot' now. Judging from the many articles and unsolicited tributes being paid to us this year, I am sure that [your show] will burn up the TV tubes when my 'cult' of Batman fans tune in."

Of course, that "cult," as he called it, would roundly—and in Chuck Dixon's case, violently—reject the series. But Kane had bigger fish to fry: he wondered why the producers had chosen a decidedly minor villain like the Riddler—who by that point had turned in a whopping total of three separate appearances in the comics over the course of Batman's twenty-five-year history—over the Joker.

"The Joker is by far the better known villain to my fans and is truly the arch-enemy of Batman, such as Dr. Moriarty is to Sherlock Holmes," he wrote. "I can picture him in color, with his chalk white face, green hair and blood-red lips . . . a combination to chill the most ardent mystery lovers."

Dozier knew that "ardent mystery lovers" weren't exactly the show's target demo but tactfully assured Kane that future scripts would feature the Clown Prince of Crime.*

Later, when Kane got his hands on the pilot script, he wrote, "It is not the mysterious and grim Batman I have lived with all these years." It was an astonishing assertion to make, given that Kane's "mysterious and grim" Batman had spent twenty-four of the previous twenty-five years grinning merrily as he pranced across the bright, sun-dappled rooftops

---

* He conspicuously neglected to mention the actor they were looking at for the role.

of Gotham and the roiling foliage of Planet X, and that by 1965, the closest Kane came to Batman comics himself was when he cashed National's checks.

But Kane knew he stood to get a cut of the merchandising, so he struck a conciliatory tone. "I realize your version is an updated 'camp style' that is keeping with today's TV market a la James Bond and [*The Man from*] *U.N.C.L.E.* .... The only suggestion I would like to make is perhaps a combination of the old, mysterious along with the new. . . . When the opportunity in the script affords itself, have a giant shadow silhouette of the Batman cast up on a building or a room, preceding Batman's entrance. . . . Batman should bring his cape up around his face when lurking in dark shadows."

Of course, there would be no dark shadows in the bright, glossy, candy-colored television series, though the producers did eventually indulge Kane with a single shot of Adam West flapping his cape as he throws an entirely nonthreatening Bat-shadow against a wall before making his entrance.

With those concessions out of the way, Dozier had a signed-off script in his hands. But that was simply the blueprint. This thing would only work if he managed to conjure exactly the right tone. Because to create the living comic book he envisioned, he'd have to keep the whole production perpetually teetering on a knife's edge of oxymoronic sensibilities: Grounded artifice. Arch seriousness.

The artifice wouldn't be a problem, at least, given the series' provenance. The Pop Art movement was cresting, and the series' design would ride that cultural wave as far as it would go. Pop Art, after all, fetishized comic books, just as it celebrated anything cartoonish, exaggerated, mass-produced, and slickly commercial. Andy Warhol had made his bones on images of Batman and Superman, and had even produced a surreal live-action film called *Batman Dracula* for his gallery shows in 1963. Roy Lichtenstein was reproducing the panels of romance and war comics on giant canvases that sold for hundreds of thousands of dollars—a fact that rankled the uncredited comics artists from whom he'd so gleefully swiped. If glossy and slick was the flavor of the month, Dozier would serve it up big.

He instructed the production team: on top of the money they'd spent building the enormous Batcave set, a then-unheard-of $800,000, they had a budget of $400,000 to film the pilot. He wanted them thinking comic books: Garish, retina-sizzling colors on the sets, graphics, and costumes. He wanted outsized props and an unforgettable Batmobile.* And—this was important—labels. Every gadget. Every button. Every lever. As in the comics of the day, every Bat-related prop was to sport helpful signage in a sans-serif font clearly legible for the cameras.

TRUE WEST

Some of the lines in Semple's script were just plain funny, as when Batman, in full cape, cowl, leotard, and blue satin trunks, walks into a nightclub and tells the maître d', "No, thanks, I'll sit at the bar. I shouldn't wish to attract attention." Others, however, were dully expositional, as when Batman solves one of the Riddler's puzzles by working through it aloud, with Robin. Whoever got tapped for the role would have to sell the jokes with absolute and unwavering seriousness. "If they see us winking, it's dead," Dozier famously said. But that wasn't enough. He'd have to keep the audience's interest even during the lengthiest information dumps; those talky puzzle-solving scenes needed an actor who could make them pop. In other words, Batman could be square, but he shouldn't be *boring*.

At the end of the casting process, Dozier brought the studio and the network two screen tests. The first starred handsome, square-jawed actor Lyle Waggoner as Bruce Wayne and squeaky-voiced teen Peter Deyell as Dick Grayson. The second starred Adam West—a bit player

---

* A 1955 Ford Futura concept car originally priced at $250,000 that was given a $30,000 Bat-makeover.

who just was coming off a successful turn on a Nestlé commercial as an ersatz James Bond*—as Bruce, and young, athletic actor Burton Gervis (aka Burt Ward) as Dick.

The setup for both tests was the same. Scene one: Dick enters Bruce's study. The two commiserate about Batman's having to testify in court and expose his secret identity. Dick suggests taking another look at the subpoena the Riddler gave them. Could there be a hidden riddle? Scene two: in the Batcave, Batman and Robin find a hidden clue on the document, solve its puzzle, and set out to investigate.

At this writing, both tests are available for screening on YouTube, and they represent a stark study in contrasts.

Until the tests, the producers had favored Waggoner and Deyell. Waggoner was certainly good-looking, with a jawline that could have been rendered with a T-square, and features so even and uncomplicated that he seemed a Bob Kane drawing made flesh. There was also the way he so convincingly filled out the Batman tights. Waggoner was not simply your average, run-of-the-mill, Hollywood-in-the-sixties fit, but actually muscular. Deyell, on the other hand, is more of an acquired taste, with his high-pitched voice and youthful-bordering-on-pubescent mien.

And in performance, Waggoner is . . . fine. Perfectly fine: he's got the soothing baritone required of a studio day player and delivers a straight-ahead, unfussy performance that'd feel perfectly at home on any adventure series of the era. It gets the job done.

But only the *one* job.

Waggoner can read a line like "When our poor housekeeper Mrs. Cooper learns what you've been up to on these supposed fishing trips of ours, I'm afraid the shock could kill her," and have it just . . . lie there. He asserts it flatly, as if the sole purpose of that line is merely to convey the information it contains.

---

* His was a time-delay-fuse of a catchphrase: "Some people will do anything to get rich [*beat*] Quik."

Deyell sells Robin's youth but never quite manages to register the Boy Wonder's requisite zest for crime fighting. Still: a solid, B-minus showing from him.

The West/Ward screen test, however, is something of a slow-burning revelation. Physically, West's features are softer, prettier than Waggoner's, and in the Batman getup he looks simply trim. But his *voice*.

In his 1994 autobiography, West would expound upon the method of his performance. He saw Bruce Wayne as a man who kept his emotions at arm's length, until, as Batman, he found himself engaged in solving a crime. Batman got excited, enthused, even incensed, while Bruce Wayne remained forever placid, uninvolved.

West makes this much plain enough in the screen test, but that's simply the surface performance. The thing that sets West apart is how thoroughly he invests his voice, his body, his entire being into registering the weighty solemnity of his mission. As he delivers each line, his voice slithers through different registers and volumes. He inserts pauses that are not merely pregnant but two weeks overdue. Those pauses were of course a deliberate choice—he wanted the viewer to see Batman's intellectual processes, the way he thought through a puzzle and excitedly seized upon the answer. The Batman cowl occluded his facial expressions, so the work he would have done with his eyebrows got shunted to his waggling index finger and to that snaky, sinuous voice.

Where Waggoner gives us a Bruce exasperated at the notion of his secret identity being revealed—"In the ashcan! Up the chute! It's too terrible to face!"—West, on the other hand, goes full-bore Olivier on the lines, whispering and shouting in turn, and breaking them up with languorous caesurae: "In the ashcan. [*beat*] UP! THE! CHUTE! It's [*beat*] tooterribletoface."

What strikes you today, watching West's very first pass at what would become the performance he'd never escape, is that it's not *safe*. We can see how thoroughly he's submerged into the role; he's not breaking off a piece of himself to stand apart and roll his eyes at each "Holy barracuda!" There's a risky and willfully unalloyed passion to both his

Bruce and his Batman. His Bruce is the part of the duck visible above the water, serene and circumspect, his Batman the furiously paddling feet.

As for Ward, he commands our attention the moment he enters the scene, because he makes his character's youthful drive impossible to miss. His Dick Grayson never walks. Instead, he bounds across a space on the balls of his feet. He delivers his lines with simple, athletic gusto. If they lack the twelve-tone complexity of West's every utterance, that's fine: athletic gusto is all the part really demands.

Based on their exceptional screen test, Dozier hired West and Ward. The rest of the permanent cast rounded out quickly. Nattily mustached British actor Alan Napier as Alfred the butler. Tremolo-voiced Madge Blake as dithering Aunt Harriet. Jowly veteran character actor Stafford Repp as Irish cop Chief O'Hara. And Old Hollywood staple Neil Hamilton, a revelation as Commissioner Gordon. Hamilton would prove the only actor in the permanent cast capable of giving West a run for his money when it came to selling the scripts' turgid, po-faced pronouncements, such as "Penguin, Joker, Riddler . . . and Catwoman, too. The sum of the angles of that rectangle is too MONSTROUS to contemplate."

The last member of the permanent cast hired was the series' stentorian narrator, a part deliberately written to evoke the old movie serials' melodramatic voice-over. Several actors tried out but failed to nail the specific sensibility Dozier had in mind, so he gave the part to an actor he knew could handle the job: himself. Dozier read his lines with outsized emotion that registered each exclamation point, as if shouting to be heard over the chimes of doom themselves. To stoke a sense of urgency, he'd pummel words into submission, stretching them beyond recognition and picking individual syllables to lean in on: "MEEEEEAAAN-WHIIIIIILE, behiiiiind the faCAAAAAADE of this INnocent-seeming BOOKstoooore . . ."

In an unusual move, ABC green-lit the show and ordered sixteen more two-part episodes before the pilot had finished shooting. The original plan was to produce and release a feature film that would pave the way for the series launch in September of 1966, but ABC's 1965 fall season was in the process of tanking hard. Out of desperation the network decided to launch a spate of new shows as midseason replacements in January of 1966. The keystone of this approach—dubbed "The Second Season!"—was *Batman*.

The decision meant that the originally scheduled nine months' worth of promotion and licensing would have to get squeezed into a handful of weeks. And now arose another unanticipated cause for concern: despite the network's enthusiasm for the series, a test audience had loathed the pilot.

Shows generally needed to earn a grade of sixty-two or higher out of one hundred from test audiences to proceed with production, and the *Batman* pilot scored fifty-two. ABC looked worriedly at the show's $75,000-per-episode budget and ordered more testing. A laugh track didn't help. Neither did extra narration. There was nothing for it: this thing was going to be a gamble and was suddenly on track to becoming the most expensive bomb in the history of the medium.

MANIA

"Television," said William Dozier, "is a merchandising medium, not an entertainment medium."

A cynical philosophy, perhaps, but one that he would ensure the *Batman* series exemplified. In the weeks and months preceding *Batman*'s premiere on January 12, 1966, an unprecedented publicity blitz began. Magazine ads, billboards, television promos, live appearances, and, perhaps most famously, the skywritten words "BATMAN IS COMING" over the Rose Bowl on New Year's Day 1966.

The advertising campaign was accompanied by a massive merchandising push that pumped over a thousand different licensed products onto store shelves, from puppets to puzzles to pocket combs, action figures to Aurora model kits, bubble blowers to Bat–candy cigarettes, all bearing the copyright indicia "© National Periodical Publications, 1966." By the time the year was out National would sue five different companies, including Woolworth's, for hawking knockoff Bat-merch.

The night of the series premiere, ABC threw a "cocktail and frug party" at the Manhattan disco Harlow, followed by a viewing party at the nearby York Theater. The crowd of tragically hip artists and gallery owners, which included Andy Warhol, Roy Lichtenstein, and Roddy McDowall, reportedly received the episode coolly but cheered for a Corn Flakes commercial.

The American viewing public, however, ate it up. When the ratings for the first two episodes came in, ABC realized they had a phenomenon on their hands to rival Beatlemania.

The critics, however, were less than enthusiastic. The *New York Times* threw the faintest possible praise its way by declaring that the show represented "a belated extension of the phenomenon of pop art to the television medium" but warned that by that criterion it "might not be adequately bad" compared to shows like *Green Acres*. In a later piece, *Times* columnist Russell Baker used the show as a jumping-off point to wax prolix about the state of American manhood. "As Batman dashes about with flabby stomach* bellying against his sagging union suit, he spouts a stream of heroic cliché culled from every American Superman from Tom Mix to John Wayne. The effect is subversive. We are invited to believe not that the traditional American hero is absurd in the sad existential sense, but that he is simply a fool."

If it's possible to be vigorously apathetic, the *Saturday Evening Post*'s dismissal qualifies: "The pop art fad . . . has made *Batman* almost foolproof. [The show succeeds] because it is television doing what television does best—doing things badly. Batman translated from one junk medium into another is junk squared."

---

* It should be noted that West mostly kept himself in fighting trim. His stunt double, however, sported a noticeable beer gut.

However, it was syndicated columnist Paul Molloy who turned in the review that would prove the most eerily prophetic, saying, "It's a little like a good joke that scores initially but begins to lose its sheen and wit the third time around."

In the weeks and months that followed, Batmania only intensified. Weekly viewing parties popped up in college dorms and swanky nightclub lounges like New York's 21. A San Francisco discotheque renamed itself Wayne Manor with doormen dressed as Cesar Romero's Joker. A throwaway gag from the pilot improvised by Adam West—using hand motions to mime his costume's mask, ears, and gloves while dancing—had inspired a national craze that came to be called "the Batusi."

The fashion industry glommed on to the fad with a *Batman*-inspired designer dress and women's hairstyle. *Life* magazine bumped a planned cover article on the Broadway debut of *It's a Bird . . . It's a Plane . . . It's Superman* for a feature photo spread, "Batman Makes a Mighty Leap into National Popularity."

All of this attention sold toys, T-shirts, bedsheets, and trading cards by the metric ton. In 1966, style guides* did not exist. As a result, the over $70 million in Bat-merchandise that sold in the show's first year alone varied widely in design and quality.

Composer Neal Hefti's one-word† "Batman Theme" got covered by several rock bands. Adam West, Burt Ward, and Frank Gorshin, the series' Riddler, each released pop singles. West appeared in full Batman regalia on the variety show *The Hollywood Palace* to croon the standard "Orange Colored Sky" with new, Bat-themed lyrics, while mock-fighting his comely miniskirted backup singers.

The show's popularity continued to mushroom over the spring months; celebrities clamored for guest-villain shots, so the producers

---

* Portfolios that provide design specifications that instruct license holders how to make precise reproductions of the property they've licensed.

† Two words, if you count "na."

added "window cameos" to the show's formula—brief appearances during scenes that found the Dynamic Duo scaling the walls of buildings.

Bob Kane enjoyed a flush of new celebrity as well and continued to pass himself off as Batman's sole creator. He became a regular guest on the local New York kids' show *Wonderama*, where he would sketch Batman characters in front of a studio audience. In reality, he secretly hired Batman artist Joe Giella to sketch the characters beforehand in a light blue pencil that the television cameras couldn't pick up. Once in the studio, he simply traced Giella's drawings in Magic Marker.

THE FANS SPEAK

The issues of the *Batmania* fanzine that were published before, during, and after the show's premiere read like an extended exercise in communal post-trauma counseling.

The slow-motion car crash begins with *Batmania* #9 (February 1966), the cover of which depicts the Caped Crusader squaring off against the CBS logo. "BATMAN'S GREATEST BATTLE! VS. THE BIG EYE!! GO BATMAN! WE'RE BEHIND YOU!"

And they truly were, at this stage. Editor Biljo White urged readers to tune in to the show and boasted that he and Batman's producers had been in close contact. He quoted an interview with Dozier in which the weirdly tone-deaf producer explains the intended appeal of the show by assuring White the series won't solely be aimed at kids, like the comics. "Comic books aren't done for adults who don't read them, they are done to enthrall youngsters from 8–14." White, a passionate comics collector, let this assertion pass without comment.

The issue also includes flattering profiles of Adam West and Burt Ward. Particularly poignant, given the reckoning that was soon to come, is White's breathless delight over one detail he managed to pry from ABC's PR department: "Can you imagine an animated POW! appearing on the screen when Batman strikes an evil-doer? Well, look for it, 'cause it's supposed to be there . . . We can hardly wait . . . BE WATCHING!"

By the next issue, fans had had some time to process what was unfolding on their television screens, and they were clearly shaken.

Most who wrote in with their reactions found themselves churning through one or more of the five Kübler-Ross grief stages.

Denial: "The show is too tongue-in-cheek for kids . . . and too over-dramatic and juvenile for adults . . . The TV Batman is about as athletic and acrobatic as an over-fed cow, and hardly sacred; the TV Robin is simply too much."

Anger: "I understand the plan was to reach the adult viewers through the 'camp' or 'pop art' appeal. 'Camp' is an overworked and pretentious word belonging to smug writers of the likes such as *Newsweek* and *Time*, who delight in being smug in their editorial ivory towers."

Bargaining: "The show was exactly what Dozier promised it would be. The dialogue, the action, the plotting—all were straight out of comics. Of course there was some exaggeration, but not a great deal was necessary."

Depression: "Frankly, I'm disappointed. What is more important, others are, too."

Acceptance: "Batman played straight just wouldn't make it. That's the romance of being a fan. Batman will be ours again someday, long long after the plastic Batarangs have joined the ersatz coonskin hats in that great surplus warehouse called Yesteryear."

Meanwhile, over in the pages of *Batman* and *Detective Comics*, editor Julius Schwartz had begun to introduce elements from the series: stories now featured sound effects more prominently than before. Two weeks after the show premiered, the *Batman* comic featured the Riddler winking conspiratorially at the reader while Batman and Robin swing into action behind him. The accompanying copy embraced the kitschy TV aesthetic: "SHEESH! The Riddler's BACK! With a NEW BATCH of ZANY PUZZLES to drive the Dynamic Duo BATTY!"

National, banking on the show's success, ordered a one-million-copy print run of *Batman* #179—a number that hadn't been seen since the heyday of comics, back in the 1940s—of which an astonishing 980,000 sold. Sales on both Batman titles doubled; for the first time in his twenty-five-year history, the perennial second-fiddle Caped Crusader was outselling Superman to become the top-selling comics character in the world.

Schwartz cannily and quickly moved to exploit the Caped Crusader's popularity to boost sales of other books. Beginning with the March 1966 issue of *Justice League of America* #43, Batman started taking over the covers of the DC titles he used to share, like *World's Finest* #166 (September 1966), and made random cameos in others, like *Aquaman, Doom Patrol, Metal Men, Blackhawk,* and even the struggling *Adventures of Jerry Lewis.*

The show's sensibility continued to bleed into Batman comics over the course of 1966, a deliberate attempt to cater to the new audience who were picking up the titles expecting campy kicks. More pages were given over to fight scenes, which grew larger, splashier, and noisier. Even story titles shouldered in on the gag: witness *Detective Comics* #352's "Batman's Crime Hunt A-Go-Go!"

In *Detective Comics* #353 (July 1966), Robin the Boy Wonder, for the first time in comics, utters his As-Seen-on-TV catchphrase. Twice, for good measure. Upon seeing priceless jewels he exclaims, "Holy Sparklers!" and in reference to the speed of the Batmobile: "Holy Jets!"

On the cover of *Batman* #183 (August 1966), Schwartz squared the metafictional circle with a cover depicting Batman blowing off an evening's crime fighting by staying in and watching himself on television. In the same issue, Batman gets stuck in sticky netting but manages to wriggle himself free of it by doing the Batusi.

It was all a bit too much for faithful comics nerds. One exasperated reader wrote in to the *Detective Comics* letter column to complain about the "Holy Jets!" business: "Not only is this not particularly inspired dialogue, it is not the sort of thing 'our' Robin says. This is an expression that the 23-year-old teen-ager who plays Robin on TV says."

The griping would continue throughout the show's run and become increasingly pointed. In August of 1966, editor Julius Schwartz, Batman cocreator Bill Finger, writer E. Nelson Bridwell, and artists Gil Kane and Murphy Anderson appeared on a comics panel at the New York Academy Con. The panel consisted of a Q-and-A during which Schwartz was asked some discomfiting questions by hard-core nerds, including some of *Batmania*'s most vociferous contributors.

When the subject of the television show came up, it inspired "muttered comments" from the audience, which Schwartz attempted to deflect by pointing out that National still had influence on the show's story lines. For example, National wouldn't permit the TV Batman to get married, he offered feebly.

This puzzling assertion inspired an audience member to ask when Batwoman would make her return to the pages of Batman comics. Schwartz firmly told them that the character had been consigned to comic book limbo for good and argued that Batwoman had only ever been a Batman knockoff and not a real character in her own right, which reasoning did nothing to endear him to the crowd. He pressed on, promising that plans were in the works to introduce an all-new Batgirl into the comics.

To mollify them further, he offered them a juicy tidbit: Batgirl's secret identity? Commissioner Gordon's daughter.

A write-up of the event in *Batmania* describes what happened next with decorous restraint: "This announcement met with laughter from the Batmanians."

THE FAD FADES

What Schwartz neglected to mention was that the new Batgirl—and her secret identity—hadn't been his idea. They were Bill Dozier's.

Production had wrapped on the show's first season in April 1966, and the very next week they'd begun filming the *Batman* theatrical feature. The idea was to rush the film into movie houses to keep interest alive over the show's summer hiatus. This feat was made possible by the fact that apart from some fancy new vehicles like a Batcopter, Batboat, and Batcycle, filming the movie required no new props or costumes. The turnaround was swift: production wrapped at the end of May, and the film hit theaters on July 30.

The movie took in a modest $1.7 million. Not terrible, considering how much the movie looked and felt like an extended episode of the series, but considerably shy of expectations.

Dozier knew what that augured and prepared to shake things up.

Of the seventeen two-part episodes of the first season, ten had lifted their plots from Batman comics—five from adventures that predated the New Look era. For the show's second season, only three story lines were lifted from the comics.

But the second season was also twice as long as the first, with an order for thirty two-part episodes, or sixty half hours. That meant the show's per-episode budget had to be drastically reduced, and the production team set to work looking for corners to cut. Superimposing the POWS! and ZAPS! over the fight scene footage had proven expensive, so the decision was made to instead insert title-card graphics for each explosive sound effect. The sets became simpler, and reliance on stock footage increased.

The second season premiered on September 7, 1966, and churned on through more guest stars, more window cameos, more death traps, and more "Holy Oleo!"s. The show's rigid structural formula—you could practically set your watch by the timing of the Bat-brawls—appealed to the show's sizable audience of children, who cherished the familiar, metronomic consistency. But their parents wearied of the repetition, and apart from a few stunts that succeeded—an October two-part episode starring Liberace as a fey pianist and his gangster twin brother earned the show its highest ratings yet—viewership slipped precipitously.

To combat this, Bill Dozier asked Schwartz to plant a new character into Batman's comic book adventures—one that he had every intention of importing to the show as soon as he could fit a new, permanent costar into the budget. He knew what he wanted: a young female who could offer girls in the audience a strong role model and the dads a reason to tune in for the non-Catwoman episodes. Having her be Commissioner Gordon's daughter, he reasoned, was a way to make her seem a natural addition to the show's universe, instead of the desperate ploy she actually was.

Schwartz tapped Carmine Infantino to design her costume and writer Gardner Fox to introduce her in *Detective Comics* #359, which landed on newsstands in late November 1966.

By the time *Batman*'s second season ended in March 1967—just over one year after the show debuted—ratings were down so much that drastic measures were called for. The budget, which had already been cut, was now cut again by a third. ABC was still willing to give up one time slot per week for a show whose best days lay behind it, but not two, so the show's formula was rejiggered and the cliff-hangers dropped.

The existing sets of Wayne Manor, the Batcave, and Commissioner Gordon's office remained unchanged, but the budget crunch showed in the villains' lairs, which were now filmed on a black soundstage featuring only a few impressionistic props to indicate a doorway or a window. It was as if the Joker had chosen to hide out in a community theater production of *The Fantasticks*.

The biggest change, however, was the presence of Yvonne Craig as Barbara Gordon/Batgirl. The producers aimed the show's most flattering spotlight on the character, gifting her with a swanky secret room behind Barbara Gordon's apartment, a massive Batcycle (complete with ladylike fringe), and her own groovy surf-music theme song: "Are you a chick who flew in from outer space? / Or are you real with a tender, warm embrace? / Yeeeeah, whose baby are you, Batgiiiiirl, Batgirl?"

Plus, there was the costume, which stirred the hearts of young girls and men of all ages and orientations. In a skintight, sparkly purple outfit accented by yellow cape and belt, Craig looked like she'd been grown in a laboratory saturated with the show's shimmering Pop Art aesthetic.

Her Batgirl was forthright, no-nonsense, and, when the mood hit her, flirtatious. Craig's dance training translated into a combat style composed of high kicks and balletic spins. The producers' intention had been to introduce a fresh, invigorating element to the show, and Craig delivered.

But it wasn't enough. Ratings flatlined; the patient was too far gone.

None of the third season's twenty-six half-hour episodes were drawn from Batman comics, because by now the show's aesthetic had begun to cannibalize itself. The jokes grew broader, the razor's-edge sensibility blunter: the rigor with which the show maintained its tone of arch seriousness slackened into self-indulgent, smirking silliness.

"If they see us winking, it's dead," Dozier had cautioned at the show's launch, but in the end it didn't matter; by the time the final episode of the third season aired in March 1968, very few were still around to see that the show wasn't merely winking, it was mugging.

Incongruously, however, rival network NBC floated the notion of a fourth season. For it to happen, the NBC suits cautioned, the budget would need to be cut further. Halfhearted plans were made to construct episodes around Batman and Batgirl, cutting Robin and Chief O'Hara from the cast. But when NBC learned that the studio had already dismantled the hugely expensive Batcave set, along with the others, the half-formed deal fell through, and *Batman* was over.

Except of course it wasn't: in its just over two years on the air an astonishing 120 episodes of *Batman* had been produced—roughly three times the number other television series would make over the same time period. This ensured that *Batman* would live on in syndicated reruns for decades. There, for several successive generations of American schoolkids, it would assume a role as nerdy gateway drug: a first, dazzling weekday-afternoon introduction to the concept of superheroes in general and Batman in particular.

But the hard-core Bat-fans of the cons, zines, and letter columns were only too happy to see the whole campy caravan, and what they viewed as its cheapening effect on Batman comics, move on. Their disdain for the show would continue to suppurate for decades, only to experience a particularly virulent outbreak in the run-up to Tim Burton's Batman film in 1989. They feared that Burton would look back to the Adam West series for inspiration and "camp it up." The fans' vocal contempt would peak once more, this time with a piquantly homophobic spin, after Joel Schumacher took over the franchise.

But in recent years, as the children who watched *Batman* in reruns throughout the seventies and eighties grew up and began to infiltrate and expand the nerd culture of the nineties and beyond, the once-pervasive fanboy scorn for the show that Medhurst chronicled in 1991 has softened into acceptance and even affection. Even DC Comics, which until very recently discouraged its creators from making even oblique references to the show in its pages, has come around, granting rights for an animated series (*Batman: The Brave and the Bold*) that gleefully embraced the show's sensibility, and even publishing a tie-in comic (*Batman '66*) written and drawn in the series' distinctive style.

COURSE CORRECTION

But that turnaround occurred incrementally, over long decades. In the months immediately after the show went off the air, the makers and readers of Batman comics could not imagine a day when they'd embrace the series that had, in their estimation, transformed their favorite hero into a clown. True, the show had made Batman the number one character in comics for two years straight, but once the show ended in 1968, sales of *Batman* comics once again took their perennial place below those of *Archie* and *Superman*. One year later, the *Batman* comic was barely clinging to the number nine spot; worse, total monthly sales now hovered below where they'd been in the early 1960s, when cancellation loomed.

Another comic, *The Brave and the Bold*, had recently become a team-up book that each month paired Batman with a different member of National's deep bench. The book was edited by Murray Boltinoff, a veteran comics editor who'd overseen the birth of some of National's weirdest, creepiest heroes, like Metamorpho and the Doom Patrol. He'd hired twenty-six-year-old artist Neal Adams to illustrate a story in which Batman meets up with still another eerie hero, the ghost/circus acrobat known as Deadman.

Adams belonged to a new generation of young comics writers and artists who'd grown up with the medium and saw the opportunity to work in it as the realization of a childhood dream. Boltinoff belonged to the cohort of pipe-smoking pros in their fifties and sixties who'd fallen into comics at a young age and dutifully churned out pages for the steady paycheck. After more than thirty years in the business, Boltinoff was no micromanager; he let the passionate kid do what he wanted.

What Adams wanted, tucked away in his relatively out-of-the-way pocket of National's superhero universe, was a quiet revolution. "It just didn't seem to me like the people at DC Comics knew what Batman should be," he told interviewer Michael Eury years later. Like all hardcore fans of the time, he fervently believed that "the TV show had run roughshod over the Batman character . . . It's hard to think of Batman walking around in the daytime in his underwear."

So he slyly set about changing that. He left the plot and pacing of Bob Haney's straight-ahead detective story alone, which saw Batman and Deadman teaming up to track down a hook-handed thug. But he proceeded to alter its mood in small, palpable ways. He began by lengthening Batman's ears slightly and making his cape longer, fuller, more dramatic. Scenes that Haney had written as taking place in broad daylight Adams drew under the inky cloak of night. In subsequent issues, he played with panel layouts and "camera" angles, and further tweaked the Dark Knight's look. If Boltinoff noticed any of these changes, he let them pass.

The fans, however, did not. In their zeal to disavow and dispel any lingering traces of the television series' existence, they seized upon the way Adams's approach to photorealism managed to save room for something sleek and stylized and uncanny. They wrote in to the comics, and to the fanzines, wondering why the "good" Batman was relegated to *The Brave and the Bold*. Soon sales of *The Brave and the Bold* surged ahead of *Detective Comics*—the comic that had launched Batman into the world thirty years before.

Batman editor Julius Schwartz took another look at the dizzying dip in sales and resolved that a course correction was needed—one that went beyond the New Look. It was not a time for cosmetic half measures; no mere wardrobe tweak would rescue the character from the lingering pall that clung to him while Burt Ward's cries of "Holy Priceless Collection of Etruscan Snoods!" still echoed in the cultural memory.

There was another worrisome bit of business. Schwartz understood that sales of *Superman*—along with Superman-related titles like *Action*, *Superboy*, and *Lois Lane*—would outpace Batman's. Neither did he begrudge the fact that two different Archie comics occupied the number one and number five slots in the top ten.*

But what rankled him was the fact that there was a Marvel book in the top ten. For the first time. And not just any Marvel hero, but the most angst-ridden and self-conscious of them all: the Amazing Spider-Man. Suddenly, the wall-crawler was outselling Batman by an average of twenty thousand copies per month.

Schwartz knew what he had to do. What Batman had to do. In the decades to come, countless other creators would copy the tactic Schwartz now employed in what was the first and most influential reboot in the history of comics:

He ditched the brat.

---

* This surge could likely be traced back to the success of that character's CBS animated series.

4

Back to the Shadows (1969–1985)

The O'Neil-Adams collaborations were state-of-the-art for matur-
ing fans who wanted themselves and their passions to be taken seri-
ously . . . These were teenagers who began to insist that comics could
and should be for adults, mostly because they didn't want to let go
of childhood and had to find a new way to sell its pleasures back
to themselves . . . Thus superhero comics began their slow retreat
from the mainstream of popular entertainment to its geek-haunted
margins, where their arcane flavors could be distilled and savored
by solitary, monkish boys and men . . .

—**GRANT MORRISON**

In *Batman* #217 (December 1969), Bruce Wayne and Alfred the butler
step out of the secret Batcave elevator to survey the vastness of the Dark
Knight's subterranean lair: the towering Batcomputer, the state-of-the-
art forensic laboratory, and the Batmobile, which is by now closely
modeled on the vehicle featured on the canceled television series.

Just one page earlier, the two men packed young Dick Grayson in a
cab and sent him off to his new life as a freshman at Hudson University.
It is, Wayne explains to his majordomo, a time to reassess and start over.

"Dick's leaving brought home the stark fact that our private world
has changed!" he says. "We're in grave danger of becoming . . . outmoded! Obsolete dodos of the mod world outside!"

Bruce's assessment, while *really* weirdly put, was not wrong.

With the cancellation of the *Batman* television series, sales of Batman comics had plummeted. But it wasn't just Batman; the entire industry was shrinking. Total reported monthly comics circulation dropped from thirty-six million into the twenties. Several factors contributed: the explosive growth of television over the past decade was steadily siphoning young readers away, and the old distribution model was showing its age. Comics had always been low-price-point, low-markup, comparatively low-selling products, but now their traditional home—the spinner rack at mom-and-pop corner grocery stores—was vanishing. The bright, efficient supermarkets that replaced them were much less willing to devote floor space to items that not only failed to generate profits but also attracted lingering hordes of snot-nosed kids who pawed through the merchandise without buying.

But as comics were losing young readers, the industry managed to hold on to a small but increasingly vocal cohort of hard-core collectors. These were the teens and adults who wrote college dissertations about Spider-Man, who contributed to emergent fanzines, and who wrote in to letter columns. Those who lived in or near larger cities attended any of the handful of comics conventions that had sprung up in the sixties to meet the writers and artists of the characters they loved. Some of them had also begun to collect underground comics they found in head shops or, beginning in the early 1970s, in small bookstores that also sold back issues of Marvel and DC.

This was new: up to that point, you could only fill the gaps in your collection via mail order or at cons. There weren't many of these comics shops—but indeed, there weren't many comics collectors. Charles Overstreet, editor of a much-thumbed annual comics price guide, estimates that the hard-core fan base in 1970 (when the first Overstreet guide was published) numbered, "at best, in the low thousands."

But that was okay, because these hard-core fans did what kids could not—they spent money. Lots of it. They bought and read many titles at once, in their zeal to track the vicissitudes of their favorite characters and story lines. And they invested far more than their spending money in the pursuit, caring deeply enough to begin mapping and policing the fictive universes of these heroes and villains, vigilant for any new piece of information that enriched or—especially—contradicted what had been previously established.

This was comics readership at the end of the 1960s: older than it had been just five years before, more passionate, more knowledgeable, and—most of all—hungry for stories that took superheroes seriously. The *Batman* television show had left them nursing their wounds and seething; they'd seen the wider culture turn its gaze upon the thing they loved and taint it, twist it, mock it. But now, at last, as it had to, that attention had moved on, taking with it the hordes of fair-weather fans.

Wertham's accusations in the fifties still clung to the character, and while the gay panic that would later electrify the fan base in the era of Joel Schumacher's Batman was more muted here, it lurked inside terms like "campy" and "colorful," which the hard-core fans used to describe the television series' influence on the comics.

The readers of those comics knew exactly the kind of Batman they wanted and began to demand it in letter column after letter column. In *Batman* #210 (March 1969), seventeen-year-old Mark Evanier—who would later become a comics writer, historian, and biographer—laid out a kind of exasperated manifesto: "Batman," he wrote, "is a creature of the night. [He] prowls the streets of Gotham and retains an aura of mystery . . . Get the super-hero out, and the detective in!"

It should be noted that this plea for a harder, more serious edge was published in the back of an issue that saw the Dynamic Duo facing off against Catwoman's Feline Furies, a team of villainous, evocatively named vixens that included Florid Flo, Leapin' Lena, Timid Trixie, and Sultry Sarah.

Two months later, another letter writer offered up a more concrete idea on how to take Batman in a darker direction. "The Joker," he explained, "should be brought back as a murderer . . . his laugh should be blood-curdling and eerie."

Again and again they wrote in, their impatience and dissatisfaction growing more heated with each missive: *Not This*, they said. *You're Doing It Wrong.*

Ever since the introduction of the letter column, a faint but steady drumbeat of dissatisfaction had made itself heard. Complaints about plot holes, or artwork, or errors in continuity were commonplace. But this was different. This went to the core of the Batman character. The fans were making it known that they felt National was asleep at the switch and could not be trusted to pilot Batman into the 1970s.

National could have ignored this, or simply put Batman through another largely cosmetic overhaul, as it had with the New Look in 1964. The story of what it did instead, however, is the story of the comics industry's Great Inward Turn. The drastic makeover Batman would now undergo signaled an irrevocable shift in whom comics were made for and why. In the months and years ahead, the industry would abandon the kids' market and come to depend entirely upon hard-core fans and collectors. That process began here.

Because in 1970, Batman changed for good. It was the first, and remains the most dramatic and influential, reboot of any character in the superhero genre. Julius Schwartz had completely overhauled heroes like the Green Lantern and the Flash in the 1950s, but those were essentially new characters, with new identities, costumes, origins, and powers. The 1970 reboot of Batman changed none of those particulars, yet it remade him completely, and did so in a way that would endure for nearly half a century and counting, inspiring successive generations of comics writers, television producers, video game developers, and filmmakers.

If this first great reboot hadn't proceeded exactly as it did, and keyed into something essential and enduring about Batman and his fans in the process, it would have come and gone in a year or two. It would be remembered today as simply another in a series of see-what-sticks gambits on the part of his publisher, a blip in the character's history no more indelible than Zebra Batman.

If not for this reboot, the Batmen of Frank Miller, Tim Burton, Bruce Timm, and Christopher Nolan could not exist.

Not that the wider world would notice what National was doing with Batman, or care much if it did; to them, Batman meant POW! ZAP!, and it would for decades to come. But beginning with *Detective Comics* #395 (January 1970), a few thousand true believers would see something that rocked them to their core, something for which they'd long clamored but couldn't articulate:

A Batman by nerds, for nerds.

A Batman . . . who was one of them.

REBRANDING THE BAT

It began with a mysterious note in the letter column of *Batman* #215 (September 1969). In the note, Julius Schwartz announced that Dick Giordano would be taking over inking chores on the book, and that this was only "a preliminary move in the BIG CHANGE that's coming to the December issue! You'll have to see it to believe it!"

What readers saw, on the cover of *Batman* #217 (December 1969), was Batman storming out of a darkened Batcave and commanding his tearful butler, "Take a last look, Alfred! Then seal up the Batcave . . . FOREVER!"

In an attempt to get some daylight between the book and the television show's much-mocked "stately Wayne Manor" mantra, writer Frank Robbins sent Robin off to college and moved Alfred and Bruce out of the Wayne mansion completely.

A worried Alfred asks Bruce Wayne how they will manage.

"By becoming new," he says, suddenly channeling a brand consultant in full crisis-management mode, "streamlining the operation! By discarding the paraphernalia of the past . . . and functioning with the clothes on our backs . . . the wits in our heads! By reestablishing the trademark of the *old* Batman—to strike new fear into the new breed of gangsterism sweeping the world!"

The two men would now reside in a swank curvilinear penthouse atop the downtown Gotham City skyscraper that housed the Wayne Foundation. "I'll be keeping a closer eye on foundation affairs by day," he tells Alfred, "and 'sockin' it to 'em' by night!"

If the fifty-two-year-old Robbins's ear for dialogue owed too great a debt to *Rowan and Martin's Laugh-In*, he did what was asked of him, with a story that returned Batman to starting position. Once Wayne and Alfred get settled in their new digs, Wayne announces he'll use his foundation to lend financial support to the families of victims of violent crime. "This is where Batman and the Wayne Foundation can start to join forces!"

For thirty years, the Bruce Wayne identity had been little more than a disguise, and the role of idle billionaire playboy was simply a performative feint meant to throw off suspicion. But now Wayne would drop the fop persona and become a crusader for victims' justice.

Before the tale is over, Batman will puzzle through a murder mystery using only his keen criminological instincts and his skills as a master of disguise, adopting various identities to plant false information in the Gotham underworld and flush out the killer. In so doing, just as he first did in *Detective Comics* #29 thirty years before, he will take a bullet to the shoulder. Only this time, instead of perfunctorily patching himself up with a bit of gauze, we get a close-up of his sweating, agonized face as the bullet is removed: "Ow-tch!"

Batman was once again an avenger of the night, engaged in a ceaseless war on those who would visit violence on the innocent. Only now he'd enlisted the Bruce Wayne identity to open up a new front in that war. Where the Batman of 1939–40 had protected Gotham's wealthy establishment against common criminals, the Batman of 1970 would protect the common man against the criminals who made up Gotham's wealthy establishment.

Moreover, he would return to his original role as lone crusader for justice without sidekicks, vehicles, elaborate gadgets, a tricked-out lair, or powers. This Batman was an eminently vulnerable man who could get taken in a fight, or get shot in cold blood, yet still soldier on by dint of his steel-hardened, but entirely human, resolve.

Or, as *Batmania* editor Biljo White excitedly put it in a letter column, this new Dark Knight first glimpsed in *Batman* #217 was "a crimefighter, a character of some realism, not a cardboard fighter of costumed clowns."

Other fans echoed White's enthusiasm, mixing a tincture of wetold-you-so smugness into their cautious optimism that the character would be "returning to the element that he should have been associated with all the time."

That noirish mood was still missing, however. For all the heavy lifting it does to establish the new setting and logistics of Batman's world, Robbins's story plays like a straight-ahead police procedural—serious, yes, and grounded in "some realism," but lacking in atmospherics.

Batman had been changed, but not yet reborn.

HOW TO MAKE (BATMAN) COMICS THE MARVEL WAY

The first time editor Julius Schwartz approached twenty-nine-year-old Dennis "Denny" O'Neil to assign him a Batman story, O'Neil had taken one look at the 1968 state of the Bat-books—still redolent of the television series' bright, bold, overblown style—and begged off. Instead, he'd set to work on *Wonder Woman*, robbing her of her powers and turning her into an international woman of intrigue and karate chops, and on *Green Arrow*, robbing that character of the fortune that had for years made him seem like still another Shadow/Batman knockoff and instilling in him a volatile temper that caused him to rail against social injustice. In neither case did O'Neil take the character "back to basics." Instead, he attempted to assert an affinity between the hero and some contemporary social issue. In Wonder Woman's case: women's liberation. In Green Arrow's: greedy corporate fat cats, racism, police brutality, poverty, pollution, gang violence, drugs—you name it, really.

O'Neil belonged to a new generation who didn't view superhero comics as pure escapist entertainment. The 1960s had seen the public eagerly embracing airy concoctions to distract itself from the grim realities of Vietnam, political assassinations, and youth riots. Television shows like *I Dream of Jeannie*, *My Favorite Martian*, and *Gilligan's Island*—and, yes, *Batman*—provided a dependable service for a society desperate to avoid confronting its own woes and limitations. Yet O'Neil, a journalist by training, knew very well that underground comics like *Zap Comix*, *Bijou Funnies*, and the parody *Wonder Wart-Hog* ("the World's Awfulest-Smelling Super-Hero") tackled some of these harder issues, albeit at a bleary-eyed slant. If an X-rated goof on the superhero idea could comment on what was going on, why couldn't superheroes themselves?

Schwartz approached O'Neil again in 1969, offering him the keys to Batman on a tryout basis. A bold break was needed, and Schwartz decided O'Neil and penciler Neal Adams—whose Batman work in *The Brave and the Bold* the fans had liked a good deal more than Schwartz had himself—was the team to give it a shot.

O'Neil, who'd been born, like Batman, in 1939, had only dim recollections of the few Bill Finger–Bob Kane–Sheldon Moldoff stories that had seen occasional reprinting in the back pages of various Batman titles. He spent an afternoon in the National Comics archives and read the first year of the character's appearances in *Detective Comics*, hoping he'd find something to build on.

"The origin is the engine that drives Batman," he would tell interviewers Roberta E. Pearson and William Uricchio years later. ". . . It's perfect. When the question of changing it came up, I said, 'How you going to improve on this?' It simply, in one incident, explains everything that anybody will ever need to know about the character."

O'Neil focused, as so many of his fellow hard-core nerds had before him, on the panel in *Detective Comics* #33 featuring a crudely rendered young Bruce Wayne kneeling at his bedside by candlelight, intoning his oath. He understood something about it—something that had never been stated, or even obliquely referenced, in the character's thirty-year history, yet that had always been there.

The oath that drives him, O'Neil realized, must become more than mere backstory, more than the pat, lip-service explanation for the costume and the gadgets it had been allowed to become. No, that oath is everything Batman is.

And what he is, O'Neil understood, is obsessed.

Obsession. A concept borrowed from the definitively adult world of psychoanalytic theory that would previously have seemed out of place in the Manichean world of the superhero comic book. For decades, good guys did good because they were good, and bad guys did bad because they were bad. True, heroes had motivations, but comics were about bold action and steel-trap plots, so those motivations were simple and clear: there are wrongs that must be righted. Unquestioned altruism. You couldn't go basing a hero's motivation on anything so hopelessly mundane, frangible, and abstruse as human psychology, as *feelings*.

And yet, as Marvel had shown, you very much could. The Fantastic Four were a hugely dysfunctional superpowered family seething with anger and resentment. The Hulk was a creature of blinding, omnidirectional rage. Spider-Man was a guilt-ridden teenager beset by anxiety, moral ambivalence, and feelings of inadequacy. And what were the X-Men but adolescent feelings of alienation and self-consciousness given flesh, and fur, and feathers?

O'Neil had gotten his start in comics at Marvel with tryout assignments on *Doctor Strange* and *Daredevil*, among others. It was at Marvel in 1961 that Stan Lee, Jack Kirby, and Steve Ditko had first endeavored to create heroes with personalities. What they ended up with were heroes with personality disorders. In the pages of a Marvel book, outsized emotions led characters down paths that had nothing to do with the cause-and-effect logic of story and plot, and everything to do with the larger-than-life demands of melodrama: mistaken identities, withheld information, and love triangles.

It was a marketing strategy, as much as anything else. Lee was the first to identify and target the cohort of older adolescents who responded to heroes whose concerns mirrored their own: girls, money, popularity in school, the abiding conviction that no one understood them.

That was the lesson O'Neil took away as he proceeded to do to Batman what he'd done to Wonder Woman and Green Arrow. But this time, instead of attempting to tie Batman to some contemporary social issue, the affinity he found and asserted was bound up in the relationship Batman had to his readers. Specifically, to those readers who collected and commented and painstakingly cataloged, who pored over back issues and fanzines with a fervent and abiding zeal. O'Neil ensured that these teens and adults would now see in Batman that which they most longed to see: themselves.

Years later, he'd put it more bluntly: "The basic story," he said, "is that he is an obsessed loner."

"Not crazy," he was quick to add, "not psychotic . . . Batman knows who he is and knows what drives him and he chooses not to fight it. He permits his obsession to be the meaning of his life . . ."

This is what O'Neil brought to the character for the first time: he fused the boy who swore that impossible oath in his bedroom together with the man who dressed up like a bat each night to execute it. From that point on, the oath would no longer be simply a plot point. It became a living thing. At night, every night, he kept his oath alive. He did this because he had to. Because he couldn't help it.

He was obsessed.

GOTHIC REVIVAL

O'Neil's resolve to forefront Batman's psychological turmoil is only one reason his work on the character would define Batman for generations. As a writer, his contributions could go some small distance toward establishing the feel he wanted. He could supply the words and dictate the action, but in comics, substance and style are not separate entities. An artist's style shapes our perceptions. In a comic, mood and tone don't emerge slowly over the course of sentences, paragraphs, and chapters, as they do in prose; they're evident at first glance, infused into everything we see: the arrangement of panels, the thickness of lines, the density of detail. We read books, but we *feel* comics.

O'Neil and Adams worked separately, as was and remains commonplace. O'Neil would send the script to Schwartz, Schwartz would pass it along to Adams, and weeks later, O'Neil would see what Adams had done. After that, Dick Giordano would step in to ink Adams's pencils, adding visual weight, texture, and detail.

Their very first collaboration, a story called "The Secret of the Waiting Graves" in January 1970, signaled a marked departure from everything that had gone before.

O'Neil would later call the story "a conscious desire to break out of the *Batman* TV show: to throw in everything and announce to the world, 'Hey, we're not doing camp,'" saying, "We wanted to re-establish Batman not only as the best detective in the world, and the best athlete, but also as a dark and frightening creature—if not supernatural, then close to it, by virtue of his prowess."

"A bleak hillside in central Mexico," reads a caption on the story's opening splash page, ". . . a pair of open graves . . . and the shadow of the dread BATMAN."

The writing sets a moody tone, but the art is what sells it: we are low to the ground, behind Batman, looking past his boots at a pair of open graves, side by side. Far ahead, a bloated moon hangs low in the sky behind a crumbling monastery. We see the edge of Batman's cape snapping in the wind, we see his shadow falling over the twin holes in the earth before him . . . which, given that the moon is in front of us, doesn't make much in the way of sense, but never mind that. It's only the first time Adams leans into the "ism" of his photorealism, bending laws of optics and physics in pursuit of a punchy dramatic effect; it won't be the last.

The ensuing tale, in which Batman confronts a pair of Mexican aristocrats who hide a sinister secret, is as flamboyantly over-the-top as anything readers had seen during the television show's run. Only this time the storytelling mode is not brightened by high-camp theatricality but steeped in a miasma of pure gothic horror. The melodrama flows thick.

Between O'Neil's florid prose and Adams's haunted, hallucinatory panels, the whole thing starts to read like Poe at his most febrile. But there's no denying how great it all looks. And how perfect it feels. Here was a Batman who was actually *spooky*.

O'Neil's decision to begin his tenure by removing Batman from the familiar rooftops of Gotham City was a considered one. He wanted to deposit Batman in an exotic and foreboding locale choked in gothic mystery, as writer Gardner Fox had done with his stories of crumbling castles, slavering werewolves, and gruesome vampires back in 1939. Unlike Fox, however, O'Neil wanted readers to feel Batman's isolation and vulnerability, to share his confusion over a mystery that smacked of the supernatural and thus defied his worldview of deductive logic.

It worked; readers rejoiced: "At long last," one wrote, "the annoying Batjunk is gone, and with it the commercialized, exploited, overexposed Batman of yesterday."

"Overexposed" is a telling epithet, amid this praise; it testifies to the hard-core nerd's lingering resentment of the television show, which had taken Batman out of their hands, given him to the world, and cheapened him. Now, at last, Batman was back where he belonged. With the people who understood him.

As for the kid? Good riddance.

"Robin," the writer continued, "is finally away at college, leaving our nocturnal creature to once again work in the shadows, unhampered by a red-vested teenage compatriot."

Again and again, fans enthusiastically embraced the O'Neil/Adams Batman—but not before rushing to reject the Batman that had Ruined Everything: "Batman the super-noble, super-merciful, super goody-goody caped cornball is dead! But in his place stands . . . The BATMAN! . . . The dark avenger of wrongs, that mysterious shadowy defender of Gotham City!"

The 1970 hard-core fan's ideation of the "true" Batman was shaped and defined in reaction to the television series. Years before Wolverine, the Punisher, Deadpool, or any of comics' now-omnipresent antiheroes would make their debut, and a year before Clint Eastwood's merciless renegade cop Harry Callahan debuted in the film *Dirty Harry*, fans of Batman were already yearning for their hero to reject conventional notions of heroism—traits like nobility, mercy, doing good—and get his hands dirty.

They saw that O'Neil was harking back to that handful of Batman's first adventures, and they hungered for some old-fashioned, pulpy, Shadow-esque justice. What had the television series offered its viewers, they reasoned, but frothy escapist glitz? "Relevance" was the new watchword, after all. Other superheroes were now confronting gang violence, drug addiction, and racism, often finding that their noble ideals and fabulous powers availed them little or not at all. One of the *Batman* television series' stealth themes, after all, had been how ridiculous, how literally laughable, the notion of the hero had become.

But O'Neil didn't, and doesn't, agree that grit was the way to go. "I think that an element of compassion is a necessary part of the hero recipe," he says. "There are lots and lots of people who don't agree with that and they don't agree with it about Batman. . . . It was a personal feeling [that] you cannot have a sociopath and call him a hero."

Not in 1970, anyway. But give it time.

NEW FOES FOR A NEW AGE

Over the next ten years, O'Neil would write the scripts for thirty-two *Batman* comics and thirty-one issues of *Detective Comics*, but only twelve of these would be penciled by Neal Adams, all of them published between 1970 and 1973. Artists like Irv Novick, Bob Brown, Jim Aparo, and Dick Giordano also defined the look of Batman during this era, taking their visual cues from Adams's version. Frank Robbins split the writing duties with O'Neil, and Robbins generally preferred to keep

Batman in Gotham City, tangling with gangsters and crooked business-men; his issues saw an increased focus on Bruce Wayne the man and philanthropist.

Regardless of his artist, O'Neil loaded up his issues with villains and trappings befitting his new, entirely nocturnal Batman: a variety of vengeful ghosts put in frequent appearances. Robbins also enjoyed injecting horror tropes into the books, as when he introduced the Jekyll/Hyde creature Man-Bat* in *Detective Comics* #400 (June 1970). Later still, witches, Satanic covens, werewolves, and vampires entered the mix.

But it was the O'Neil/Adams combination that fired up the letters pages, with its artisanal blend of gothic foreboding and dynamic action.

Schwartz and his writers dialed back the use of the Joker, the Rid-dler, and other classic costumed villains until enough time had passed to cleanse them of the noisome stink of the television show. That meant finding new adversaries for Batman over and above the one-off gang leaders and crime bosses of Gotham, or the sundry supernatural threats that haunted the lonely countryside.

O'Neil introduced the shadowy League of Assassins in *Detective Comics* #405 (December 1970), planting the seed for the ultimate rev-elation of its leader, the fanatical Ra's al Ghul.† Ra's was a foe unlike any Batman had faced: a man possessed of resources more vast than Bruce Wayne's, with a motivation perfectly in tune with the times: restoring the planet's environmental balance—albeit by wiping out the virulent infection known as humanity.

The two men would tangle often, most notably in a globe-trotting four-part story‡ that sees Batman driven to faking Bruce Wayne's death in a plane crash in order to take down Ra's without fear of reprisal. But

---

* Conceived and designed by Neal Adams.

† Translation: "the Demon's Head."

‡ *Batman* #242–45.

when the Caped Crusader finally tracks the criminal mastermind to his Swiss chalet, it seems the Demon's Head has evaded justice: Ra's al Ghul is dead.

It's here O'Neil introduces the Lazarus Pit, a pool of restorative chemicals that renders Ra's essentially immortal—and returns his corpse to life. After a few more Bond-movie action set pieces, including a snowmobile chase and a climactic swordfight, Ra's al Ghul is captured, and his daughter, Talia, saves Batman's life; they share a passionate kiss.

The cover of *Batman* #244 features Ra's al Ghul looming over an unconscious, bare-chested Batman. Adams, for the very first time, depicts the Caped Crusader with a photorealistic torso, complete with chest hair and areolae. The move proved controversial both within and without the National offices, though it would represent only the first time that the fan base would become discomfited by the mere presence of Bat-nipples.

International intrigue now became a mainstay of the Bat-books, particularly in the *Brave and Bold* team-up title, on which Jim Aparo assumed artistic duties with issue #100 (March 1972). Aparo's Batman echoed Adams's, though he tended to turn in a leaner, more angular Caped Crusader with the body of a sprinter, not a gymnast, rendered in a thicker line.

It would still be a while before some of the more whimsical archvillains would be welcomed back, but those classic foes whose sensibility fit with the new emphasis on the gothic and grotesque were the first to return.

After an absence of seventeen years, the gruesome Two-Face turned up in *Batman* #234 (July 1971), his coin-flipping gimmick now more emphatically established as an obsessive fixation. This issue also features a famous panel in which Batman, "numb with astonishment" over a new wrinkle in the case he's working, contorts his features and clenches his fist in abject frustration. Adams's Batman was not the stoic brooder the character would shortly become, but a creature of churning and frequently explosive emotions.

The Joker returned in *Batman* #251 (September 1973) as a leering creature of homicidal caprice, a serial-killing clown who chased away any memories of Cesar Romero's preening makeup-over-the-mustache jackanapes for good. Out with the larceny, in with the lunacy: O'Neil felt strongly that to restore the Joker to his potential as a villain, he needed to return to his roots as a cold-blooded killer. The Joker slaughters four people in this issue alone. He also had to be unpredictable, a physical manifestation of the kind of random act of violence that had birthed the Batman.

This simple conviction resulted in a moment that would shape all representations of the character that came after it: the Joker manages to knock Batman out cold. He stands over the Caped Crusader, preparing to savor his final victory, when realization dawns, and he stays his hand: "No! Without the game that Batman and I have played for so many years, winning is nothing!"

Prior to this appearance, the Joker hadn't taken a life since *Detective Comics* #62, some thirty-one years before, and readers relished his return to murderous mirthfulness. This, one letter-column writer noted, was at long last "the REAL Joker: grotesque, insane, fiendishly brilliant."

The Joker as sadistic chaos, the Batman as merciless order. This mirror-image theme would come to define the two characters' relationship in the comics and across all media for the next forty years.

The new authorial fascination with the twisted psyches behind the villains, and behind Batman himself, combined with increased efforts to fit costumed crusaders into the modern world, and specifically its notions of criminal justice, led O'Neil and Schwartz to create an alternative to Gotham Penitentiary. *Batman* #258 (October 1974) introduced Arkham Hospital, "an asylum which houses the criminally insane."

Back when Batman's rogues' gallery consisted of felonious foes given to jewel heists and art theft, having them cycle endlessly in and out of jail was simply a trope that made more stories possible: Batman doesn't kill, so his foes live to fight another day.

But in the grim new Gotham, O'Neil and Robbins raised the stakes by bringing many of the classic villains back with trails of bodies in their wake. At first, Arkham counted only the Joker and Two-Face among its denizens, but in the decades that followed, as the gothic atmosphere of the Bat-titles thickened, Batman's foes began to evince more extreme forms of psychosis befitting incarceration at Arkham: the Scarecrow, Poison Ivy, and the Riddler, once merely gimmick-besotted recidivists, became twisted and in some cases even tragic figures condemned to haunt Arkham's gloom-soaked corridors between rounds of Bat-pummelings.

To illustrate the full extent to which the killing of his parents continued to obsess the Caped Crusader, O'Neil introduced another location that would become a permanent fixture of Batman's world with *Detective Comics* #457 (March 1976). We learn that one night every year, on the anniversary of his parents' murder, Batman ignores his other duties to exclusively and mercilessly patrol the neighborhood in which that crime took place: a slum once known as Park Row and now called Crime Alley. O'Neil and artist Dick Giordano added a new character to the mix, the kindly social worker Leslie Thompkins, who looked after young Bruce after his parents were slaughtered. The elderly Thompkins still remains in Crime Alley, doing what she can to offer hope to those who reside there.

O'Neil felt it important to introduce a character like Thompkins, who represented the nonviolent response to the same terrible act that birthed the Batman. Stories played with the tension between Batman's and Thompkins's reactions: that of an emotional child, and that of a rational adult.

BATMAN: THE LICENSED PROPERTY

These developments, and many more, added new facets to the character and his relationships for a small but dedicated readership that numbered less than three hundred thousand in 1970 and shrank to roughly half that by the middle of the decade. Superman was once again selling twice as many comics as the Caped Crusader, and now there was a new wrinkle. *The Amazing Spider-Man* had first overtaken *Batman* in sales in 1969, and Ol' Web-Head's surge continued throughout the seventies, until he was consistently outselling *Batman* by more than one hundred thousand copies every month.

But the haunted and increasingly complex Batman of the comics was not the one the rest of the world was seeing. Publishers like National and Marvel were weathering the steady decline in comics readership by licensing their characters' likenesses. In the 1970s, this income began to eclipse money from comics sales as more Batman action figures, games, jigsaw puzzles, play sets, coloring books, and related merchandise appeared on store shelves. On T-shirts, bed-sheets, and glassware, iconography drawn by Carmine Infantino, Jose Luis Garcia-Lopez, and Neal Adams was suddenly everywhere, establishing Batman as an isolated commodity, a logo, a pointy-eared design component wholly separate from his identity as a narrative character.

Filmation had produced a series of animated shorts starring Batman, Robin, and Batgirl for CBS in 1968, which now lived on in syndication on UHF stations across the country. And in 1973, Hanna-Barbera's *Super Friends* became a part of ABC's Saturday-morning lineup, where it would remain through several different program formats and roll calls for more than a decade. Later, they would be joined by *The New Adventures of Batman* on CBS, Filmation's second shot at a Saturday-morning animated Batman series, with Adam West and Burt Ward reprising their sixties roles, and Lennie "Scrappy-Doo" Weinrib voicing kid-friendly interdimensional pest Bat-Mite, whose magic powers wreaked dependable and putatively hilarious havoc.

Ward and West donned the tights once again for two live-action television specials called *Legends of the Superheroes* in 1977. This benighted attempt to recapture the 1966 series' bright humor succeeds only in slathering a thick layer of seventies lounge-lizard smarm over its memory. With a cast featuring Charlie Callas, Ruth Buzzi, Howard Morris, and Jeff Altman, *Legends of the Superheroes* plays like a fever-dream of some comic-book-themed Vegas revue as witnessed by a guest who got some tainted shrimp at the buffet bar.

All of these television adaptations of Batman, which collectively reached an audience numbering in the hundreds of millions, gleefully perpetuated the imagery and sensibility of the 1960s television series. The Batman of *Super Friends*, for example, drove a Batmobile very like the show's distinctive barge on wheels, referred to Robin as his "old chum," and remonstrated with others for littering. He certainly bore no resemblance to the gothic-mystery Caped Crusader of the comics page. Indeed, any fresh-faced tyke sufficiently intrigued by the TV character to pick up an issue of *Batman* would likely have come away hopelessly confused and—if the issue in question featured a Joker killing spree—shaken.

All of this ensured that the sunny do-gooder Batman would never go away and helped entrench him in the character's conceptual mix for good. In the meantime, however, the Batman of the comics soldiered on in comparative anonymity, growing into something altogether darker and more disquieting.

MYRIAD MILESTONES IN THE LIFE OF A MIDDLE-AGED MASKED MANHUNTER

In 1973, Julius Schwartz stepped away from his editing duties on *Detective Comics* for seven issues, during which time comics veteran Archie Goodwin took over as editor and writer. The Wayne Foundation remained a feature of the comics, but Goodwin steadily nudged Bruce Wayne back into his traditional role as a millionaire playboy.

In 1977, Schwartz decided to try out a new art team on a backup story in *Detective Comics*—former architectural student Marshall Rogers on pencils and Neal Adams protégé Terry Austin on inks. When Rogers's highly stylized sense of design was paired with Austin's clean, forceful brushwork, so many readers wrote in with praise that Schwartz had to add a second letters page to accommodate them.*

Later that year, the thirty-year-old writer Steve Englehart left Marvel comics to write for National (which now officially changed its name to DC Comics). Over the previous decade, many writers had bolted National for the "hipper" competition; Englehart was one of very few to make the reverse pilgrimage. He began writing for *Detective Comics* with issue #469 (May 1977) and was two issues into his run when his art team had to bow out of the assignment. Schwartz promoted Austin and Rogers from backup tales to the book's main story, and the six issues that followed are today considered such a high point in the character's history that many fans, then and now, believe the Englehart/Rogers/Austin collaboration represents the definitive Batman.

One reason Bat-nerds adore this run of comics has to do with its unabashed reverence for history; Englehart, like O'Neil before him, lifted language, characters, and imagery straight from 1939 Batman comics, while Rogers set out to "capture the early pulp vibe" by rendering the Bat-silhouette as the legitimately terrifying tool of intimidation it was intended to be.

In *Detective Comics* #474 (December 1977) Englehart even had Batman trade punches with a bad guy across the keyboard of a giant typewriter, in an homage to the lost Gotham City of fifties artist Dick Sprang.

Fans flooded the mailroom with praise for the art, specifically Rogers's depiction of Batman's cape as an extension of his personality. The final two issues of the Englehart/Rogers/Austin collaboration, *Detective Comics* #475 and #476, are now esteemed alongside the greatest Batman stories ever created and would provide the seed for Tim Burton's 1989 feature film.

---

* Schwartz wasn't as impressed, however, pointing out to Rogers that his grasp of architectural detail exceeded his command of basic anatomy, the nuts and bolts of superhero comics.

In the story, the Joker poisons the water supply such that his grinning visage starts to appear on the faces of fish. His crackpot scheme du jour: to force the copyright office to grant him a legal claim, and thus a percentage, on the sale of all Joker-Fish; if they refuse, he will murder the city's bureaucrats until they comply.

The killer clown wastes little time in making good on his threat, offing one copyright clerk with Joker venom, a grisly scene that Englehart accompanies with an extended quote from the Joker's very first kill, back in *Batman* #1 (Spring 1940): "Slowly, his facial muscles pull the dead man's mouth into a repellent, ghastly grin . . . the sign of The Joker!"

Rogers's Joker is not as cartoonishly gaunt as readers were used to seeing, which lends him a chilling verisimilitude. Readers also responded well to the independent Silver St. Cloud, an Englehart creation who became Bruce Wayne's first serious girlfriend in decades and who in no time saw through Batman's disguise because she recognized Bruce Wayne's chin. That was a new one.

Although this run of comics received fulsome praise from fans and a fresh round of accolades from the burgeoning comics industry press, sales of *Detective Comics* slumped further. And that put it, once again, on the chopping block.

Earlier in the decade, in a move to increase its market share, DC had greatly expanded its line of books. Publisher Jenette Kahn dubbed the campaign, which increased the number of pages in every comic and ultimately saw the premiere of fifty-seven new titles, the DC Explosion. But now, three years later, soaring paper and printing costs combined with the economic recession resulted in the wholesale cancellation of thirty-one titles—almost half the books DC put out each month: the DC Implosion.

Plans called for *Detective Comics* to be canceled with issue #480 (November–December 1978). Ultimately, however, this decision was reversed when staffers pointed out that *Detective* was not only the company's flagship book, but it was also now the longest-running comic in the history of the medium. Kahn granted a stay of execution but ordered that *Detective* be merged with the higher-selling *Batman Family*.

In 1979 Julius Schwartz handed editorship of the Bat-titles to twenty-three-year-old wunderkind Paul Levitz. Levitz had grown up on comics. While still in high school, he cowrote and coedited the comics newsletter *Etcetera* with his friend Paul Kupperberg; they later combined it with the long-running *Comic Reader*, an industry news fanzine. He'd freelanced as a writer and assistant editor on several DC books, including *Legion of Super-Heroes*. At age twenty, he became the youngest comics editor in DC's history and the face of the new generation now taking over the industry.

The editors, writers, and artists were getting younger; the audience kept aging.

During this period, thirty-one-year-old writer Len Wein, who'd cocreated *Swamp Thing* at DC and had revamped the X-Men with artist Dave Cockrum at Marvel, scripted many *Batman* stories. Wein introduced the character of Lucius Fox to run the day-to-day dealings of Wayne Enterprises, giving the lily-white Batman books their first black cast member. And under Levitz's urging, Wein tended to pit Batman against the kind of crazy costumed foes that O'Neil and Adams had assiduously avoided.

It was getting easier and easier to find the Caped Crusader stepping out of his "dark avenger" mode as he matched wits with gimmicky criminals like the colorful Crazy Quilt (armed with a mind-control helmet and a rainbow-colored caftan) and Kite-Man (a hang-gliding thief with kite-based weapons). Unconsciously or not, these younger creators steadily infused the new, darker Batman with the whimsical tone of the fifties and early sixties Batman—the comics they'd grown up on. Only a few readers complained—or at least, ended up getting their complaints printed in the back pages of Batman comics, whose sales continued to stagnate.

Meanwhile, Levitz and his writers drafted the first writer's bible on Batman, which laid out every character's backstory, established

Gotham's geography and place names, inventoried the Bat-gadgets, and distilled every major development that had occurred over the character's forty years into a single coherent timeline.

BATMAN BEGINS . . . TO GET GRUMPY

By 1980, mom-and-pop comics shops began springing up to serve the hard-core fan and collector. In these new, cramped, dingy retail spaces, fans found places to come together, compare notes, and debate the finer points of whose butt could get kicked by whom. The virtual haven of the letter column and the fanzine page now took physical space in low-overhead strip malls across the country.

At the same time, publishers realized that these stores, known as the "direct market," provided them with better feedback that allowed them to tailor their print runs more precisely. Miniseries, one-shots, and prestige formats with higher-quality paper stock were now possible—and could be priced higher for the eager collector. DC and Marvel began to concentrate on creating titles for the direct market and gradually abandoned the supermarket checkout aisle to Archie and Jughead.

One title whose runaway success was entirely dependent on the buzz of the direct market was *The New Teen Titans*, written by Marv Wolfman with art by George Perez. Launched in November 1980, *The New Teen Titans* could trace its genesis to an issue of *Batman* in which Robin announces his decision to quit college. After a heated argument between mentor and ward, the Boy Wonder rebels against being kept in Batman's shadow and departs to form his own superhero team. *The New Teen Titans* quickly became DC's number one book, and did so by out-Marveling Marvel with endless reserves of adolescent angst and lots of talk about feelings.

Because what the fans now wanted, here at the dawn of the eighties, was soap opera with face punching. Marvel had spent almost two decades serving that up with pride and had recently perfected the formula with the phenomenal hit that was *Uncanny X-Men*. The idea was to bring your heroes into heated conflict with one another again and again as a means of characterization, a way for them to delineate who they are by stating (loudly and often) what, and whom, they're against. Wolfman and Perez simply copied the Marvel formula and emptied it over *The New Teen Titans* like a cooler of Gatorade over an NFL coach.

That formula leached its way into all of DC's books: suddenly Batman grew still more brooding and severe, even hostile, toward Robin and his fellow heroes. This tendency became more pronounced under the editorship of Dick Giordano, who succeeded Paul Levitz in 1981. Determined to get the perennially sluggish sales of *Detective Comics* on par with those of *Batman*, Giordano tightened the continuity between the books so that a single story line, featuring the same newly glowering, moody, darker-than-ever Dark Knight, now threaded through them both. Even in the pages of *Justice League of America*, he was suddenly bickering with Superman more and more.

It should have worked. In a series of stories written by Gerry Conway, Batman tangled with old foes like Hugo Strange and adopted a dyspeptic mien that was as reminiscent of his 1939 "badass loner" attitude. This was in all respects exactly what the hard-core nerds had long maintained they wanted from "their" Batman, and they were largely appeased. True, they could be counted upon to complain when they deemed the latest villain insufficiently serious,* but Batman was theirs again, and no one was talking about the damn television show anymore.

The problem, however, was that there weren't enough of them. Fewer than ever, in fact: in 1983, sales of *Batman* dropped below one hundred thousand a month for the first time in the book's forty-four-year history. Even with frequent, editorially mandated cameos from DC's better-selling heroes, books like *The New Teen Titans* thrived, while *Batman* was crashing.

---

* Few readers wrote in to offer full-throated praise for the dirigible pirate Colonel Blimp, for example.

Soon after Len Wein took over as editor in late 1982, he oversaw a series of changes intended to shake things up and get the hard-core nerds buzzing about the books as they perused the comics shops' back-issue bins.

In a feat of narrative déjà vu that staked out the real estate between homage and rip-off, readers met a young boy named Jason Todd in *Batman* #357 (March 1983), who is later orphaned when his circus-acrobat parents are (wait for it) killed by a vicious criminal. Years later, Denny O'Neil would defend the decision of Gerry Conway and artist Don Newton to give Jason an origin that hewed so laughably close to Dick's. "Why not?" he said. "[They] were not trying to innovate, they were simply filling a void. The assignment they were given was simple: Provide another Robin. Quickly and with as little fuss as possible."

Meanwhile, over in the pages of *The New Teen Titans*, Dick Grayson gives up the role of Robin to assume a new costume and heroic nom de good guy, Nightwing. In *Batman* #368 (February 1984) he officially hands over the green Speedo and pixie boots to Jason Todd, who becomes, to the surprise of precisely no one, the second Robin.

Here again, at least, was a Dynamic Duo such as hadn't existed since back before the New Look era of the 1960s, with a Boy Wonder who was actually a boy. The old band was back together, albeit with a new bass player. Writer Doug Moench had taken over both *Batman* and *Detective Comics* from Conway and set the books chugging forward, cycling dutifully through all the classic villains and introducing one or two who'd stick around Gotham for the next few decades, like the twisted crime lord known as Black Mask.

Meanwhile, the Batman team-up book *The Brave and the Bold* ended its run after two hundred issues in July 1983, only to be replaced with an all-new title that saw Batman finally quit the Justice League in disgust and form his own superpowered task force. In the pages of *Batman and the Outsiders*, artist Jim Aparo and writer Mike W. Barr combined jet-setting superpowered brawls with pun-based villain design. The super-patriotic team Force of July, for example, featured a mute capable of splitting into duplicate selves, named Silent Majority. They also added one ingredient no mideighties superhero team could do without: bickering.

MIDLIFE CRISIS

Now that he was installed as executive editor, Dick Giordano and his colleagues worried that DC's ever-burgeoning, now-Byzantine story lines—rife with parallel Earths that each featured alternate versions of every hero and villain across different historical eras—were off-putting to new readers. On one such Earth, for example, Bruce Wayne had begun his Batman career in 1939, married Catwoman, and since retired; his daughter, Helena, now patrolled the Gotham rooftops as the Huntress. On another Earth, an evil Batman avatar ruled the world alongside the sinister Crime Syndicate. And so on.

The word came down from on high: change was coming.

Worlds, and heroes, would die. In a twelve-issue crossover "event" miniseries, all the disparate parallel Earths would be collapsed into a single world, with one and only one version of each character left standing, in a shared, uniform timeline. History itself was to be streamlined and all out-of-date or inconvenient characters summarily dispensed with. When it was all over, in the new DC Universe, those characters would *never have existed*.

This wholesale culling of the publisher's character roster, and revision of the established superheroic history, would reverberate through every title for years to come.

What's more, the publisher let it be known that it was seizing this opportunity to completely overhaul its "big three" characters—Superman, Batman, and Wonder Woman.

Batman, for his part, cried out for a fresh coat of paint. He certainly didn't look much like O'Neil and Adams's distinctive gothic detective anymore, or even Englehart and Rogers's stylish Gotham guardian. The influx of gimmicky villains who evoked Batman's mid-1950s goofiness chafed against the editorial edict for a tone of grim, brooding intensity. And the addition of a new Robin so indistinguishable from the old hadn't done much to invigorate the books creatively. If anything, he was looking a bit generic. Familiar. Predictable. Safe.

As for sales, well: only about seventy-five thousand readers were bothering to pick up a copy of *Batman* each month, while *Detective* slid even further down the charts.

The event that was due to bring about the capital-E Earth-shattering metatextual cataclysm was to be called *Crisis on Infinite Earths*. And if he was to survive it, the forty-six-year-old Batman would need to enlist some sharp and uncompromising crisis management, stat.

But it would be okay: Dick Giordano knew a guy.

5

Bat-Noir (1986–1988)

*I knew there was something wrong from the opening pages, which,
among other credits, include "Lynn Varley, Colors and Visual Effects." Come on now, we're talking about a comic book, not the
Sistine Chapel.... The stories are convoluted, difficult to follow and
crammed with far too much text. The drawings offer a grotesquely
muscle-bound Batman and Superman, not the lovable champions
of old. My oldest son, an expert in these matters, has suggested that
the inspiration is not so much the old comic book as rock videos. I
think he's right. If this book is meant for kids, I doubt that they will
be pleased. If it is aimed at adults, they are not the sort I want to
drink with.*

—MORDECHAI RICHLER, REVIEW OF *BATMAN: THE DARK KNIGHT RETURNS*,
NEW YORK TIMES, MAY 3, 1987

In the spring of 1985, at a back table in a nondescript bar and grill on the
ground floor of the building that housed the DC offices, a twenty-eight-
year-old golden boy named Frank Miller sat arguing over deadlines and
plot with DC Comics vice president Dick Giordano.

Fifteen years before, Denny O'Neil and Neal Adams had restarted
Batman. They had plumbed the character's first adventures and doubled down on two aspects they'd found gestating there: the obsession
that drove him, and the swooning gothic excess of his world. Their

Batman, dosed with a tincture of James Bond, looked and felt like nothing else on the shelves, and was precisely targeted to the hardest core of hard-core comics collectors. This Batman-as-obsessed-loner found a sympathetic resonance that shuddered through his nerd fan base and, as far as they were concerned, shook off any last lingering traces of the arch, made-for-TV buffoonery that clung to the character.

Now, fifteen years later, the affinity Batman's readers felt for their hero had never been stronger. On letters pages and in impassioned conversation at comics shops and cons, the relatively small number of fans that remained called him "relatable" and hailed him as a creature of "skills, not powers." To them, he embodied human achievement, not extraterrestrial entitlement. If lately his actual plots seemed a bit rote, his adversaries less than intriguing, they'd still rather have read about him than some obnoxious jock like Superman, for whom everything came easy.

But it wasn't enough. The peevish "My guy's better than your guy" debates that made up the lingua franca of fandom, and inspired fervent affection, were all well and good, but Dick Giordano was looking at the bottom line. Ultimately, the Bat-fans' depth of feeling couldn't make up for the dearth of sales.

The decision to turn inward and cater to the tastes of the adult nerd had gained the comics industry abiding fan fealty but had lost them any access to the wider world. In the years since 1970, comics had effectively walled themselves inside their own cultural ghetto. Comics shops provided a safe haven for collectors and fans but bred an increasingly potent insularity. Outside of the fan base, comics were seen as a hobby practiced by lonely misfits who fetishized the objects of childhood, like the woman who collected china dolls or the grown man who played with toy trains he wouldn't let his kids touch.

Now DC put its faith in the upcoming *Crisis on Infinite Earths* event to tear down the walls of that ghetto—or at least dramatically lower the barrier to entry. When it was all over, they assured themselves, they'd have a clean slate to offer the mass culture and the potential to entice hundreds of thousands of new and lapsed comics readers.

And if that didn't work, Giordano knew that Filmation had come sniffing around with a proposal for a Saturday morning cartoon that saw an elderly Batman tootling around in a cool spaceship.

So at least they had *that* going for them.

"A GOD OF VENGEANCE"

The young comic book writer Frank Miller (who had recently transformed the fourth-tier Marvel book *Daredevil* into an ultraviolent urban-noir sensation) approached Giordano with some plans for what he thought Batman should look like, once the *Crisis on Infinite Earths* event was done and the DC Universe's timeline had been freshly rewritten. Like the Filmation executives, Miller's idea also involved an aging Batman, but no spaceship. And it was definitely not for kids.

Years before, Miller and irascible *Howard the Duck* creator Steve Gerber had pitched Giordano on an imprint called Metropolis Comics that would feature bold new takes on DC's "big three": *Man of Steel* (written by Miller with art by Gerber), *Amazon* (written by Gerber with art by Jim Baikie), and *Dark Knight* (written and drawn by Miller).

Giordano was receptive but informed the duo that DC would be reviewing proposals from many different teams before deciding on a way ahead. Gerber balked at the prospect and withdrew, but Miller knew he was on to something with his Batman idea and held on to his notes. He knew that DC would want it—no, not just want it; *need* it.

"Right now," he sniffed to *The Comics Journal*, "the comics audience obviously consists of children, and adults who like childlike entertainment."

He was interested in neither: instead, he resolved to create a Batman story for those adults who could handle something grander and more challenging than the tidy, recursive morality plays superhero comics represented. The issue, he noted years later, was the genre's lack of any real stakes: "Comics had become drained of the content that would give the heroes any reason to exist. I wanted to give them an edge."

The edge he had in mind was one of uncompromising, even oper-atic violence: the sweeping romance of Zorro grounded in the gritty urban hellscape of Dirty Harry. News of the "Subway Vigilante," who'd shot four unarmed black youths when they'd allegedly tried to rob him on the 2 train in December 1984, filled the New York tabloids for months, inspiring Miller to infuse his story with an extended critique of media culture.

Giordano and Miller spent long afternoons at the restaurant below the DC offices, going over drafts and quibbling over deadlines. Miller had in mind a sustained examination of Batman's tormented psyche, en-visioning a Caped Crusader more merciless than ever, a man not merely driven by his obsession for justice but reveling in it, consumed by it, and ultimately transformed by it. "A god of vengeance," he said.

In his notebook, next to a hasty sketch of Batman in a familiar pose, looming over a hapless criminal the way a mob enforcer might, Miller scrawled an admonishment to himself: "None of this shit—interrogates criminals by scaring the piss out of them, not by roughing them up. If he fights, it's in a way that leaves them too roughed up to talk. Violence must be fierce, quick, surgical when it happens. He DOESN'T threaten, not literally—his presence plays more on guilt and PRIMAL fears than on rough stuff."

Miller knew the *Götterdämmerung*-noir tone he wanted, but the plotting kept hanging him up. Ultimately, after several drafts, Giordano stepped away from the project, and Denny O'Neil took over as editor. DC publisher Jenette Kahn had first wooed Miller to DC by giving him license to tell his future-samurai tale *Ronin* as a stand-alone miniseries on higher-quality paper that allowed him and his colorist (and then-wife) Lynn Varley to incorporate techniques borrowed from Japanese and European comics. A similar deal was struck for what would eventu-ally become known as *Batman: The Dark Knight Returns*.

It was a four-issue miniseries like no American comic before it: higher-quality printing on heavy, glossy paper, which allowed for images to bleed past the page edge and ensured that the subtler hues of Varley's gouaches—the brown haze of a fetid summer night, the pale cathode glow of the television screens Miller used as an electronic Greek chorus—would survive the printing process. A longer page count, with a sturdy, square binding, imbued each issue with a distinctive heft.

And then there were the covers: on the front of *Batman: The Dark Knight Returns* #1, a bolt of lightning cleaves the night sky. The silhouette of a burly figure captured in midleap hangs in the air between us and the streak of electricity. Here, as he will throughout the book, Miller combines a penchant for Wagnerian bombast with a reductionist's eye for form: this is Batman reduced to iconography.

Miller's line work is spare, but his storytelling infrastructure consists of a sixteen-panel grid; the oxymoronic result is a sort of busy minimalism. He controls the pacing of a given page by combining panels or splitting them in two, driving our eye across and down. Occasionally, as we turn the page, he greets us with a full-page image ruthlessly engineered to take our breath away. The late eighties and early nineties would see many comics artists aping Miller's use of the splash page, though few would share his command of it. Miller unleashes it rarely, timed to produce the maximum possible dramatic impact, and always to deliver a wordless, quasireligious exaltation of his subject: Batman exploding onto the scene, suitable for framing.

"THIS SHOULD BE AGONY. BUT . . . I'M BORN AGAIN."

The Dark Knight Returns opens on a fifty-year-old Bruce Wayne, now become the idle, boozy millionaire he once only pretended to be. Ten years before, Robin perished in the line of duty; Wayne blamed himself and retired his Batman identity. In his absence, a ruthlessly violent gang called the Mutants has taken over Gotham City.

Meanwhile, the government has cracked down on all heroes and forced Superman to work covertly for American military interests. But when Wayne suspects a rash of crimes to be the work of his old foe Two-Face, he comes out of retirement to wreak brutal havoc on Gotham's underworld. His reappearance, and the chaos that arises in his wake, brings him to the attention of Superman—and the Joker. After Batman defeats the Mutant leader and confronts the Joker one last time in a carnival's Tunnel of Love, the Mutant gang swears allegiance to Batman. A worried government sends Superman in to end Batman's growing threat, and the Caped Crusader—with the help of several allies, a military exoskeleton, and some synthetic kryptonite—almost succeeds in taking down the Man of Steel but dies of a heart attack before he can deliver the final blow. Of course, said death is simply an elaborate ruse. *The Dark Knight Returns* ends with the resourceful Wayne living on in secret, deep in the Batcave, surrounded by his ex-Mutants as he plots to restore order to the world above not with a costume, but with an army.

It's difficult to overstate the influence *The Dark Knight Returns* has had on comics and the culture that has arisen around them. Writer Grant Morrison calls the book "a tour-de-force that was not only conceptually bold but also tough and unpretentious enough to attract attention beyond its first enthusiastic audience of delirious geeks, who felt that Batman had finally received the truly serious treatment he'd always deserved."

Morrison is right; Bat-nerds ate the book up with rapt delight. The first issue sold through four print runs, which shocked those comics shop owners who had looked at its unusual format—and $2.95 cover price—and bought in cautious numbers.

But it wasn't just Bat-nerds. Articles in mainstream outlets like *Rolling Stone* and the Los Angeles *Herald Examiner*, and especially a widely syndicated Associated Press profile, piqued the interest of non-nerds.

"[DC] scrambled to meet this sudden demand," Miller said at the time, "because it was not an enormous bunch of die-hard comics fans [who each] wanted to have seventeen copies. The demand is brand-new people who are willing to try out comics by coming into shops and buying *Dark Knight*—thousands of them."

The run on the title sparked an internal debate in the DC offices. At first, some staffers—the old-guard comics traditionalists—argued against doing additional print runs, to ensure that issue number one became a rare and highly sought-after collector's item, as a way to reward those loyal fans who'd bought their copies right away.

Cooler, more profit-oriented heads ultimately prevailed.

Nerds also dutifully bought up the *Dark Knight* posters, pins, stickers, and T-shirts that DC licensed and distributed to comics shops. They wrote to DC with fawning praise and lavished the books with glowing reviews in the comics industry trade press.

The fans loved it, as Miller knew they would.

But he hadn't written it for them.

O'Neil and Adams had created their Batman for the hard-core fan and ensured that the reader would see himself—or at least, an idealized version of himself—in Batman's dark visage, his laconic mien, his cold intellect, and, yes, his biceps. Their Batman was an adolescent's vision of American masculinity, and as such administered to the soft and unathletic among his readership a monthly dose of machismo by proxy.

Miller, on the other hand, hadn't concerned himself with the existing fan base. He'd swaggered up to the plate and pointed over the walls of the comics ghetto, out where non-nerds blithely went about their days without sparing a silly notion like Batman a passing moment. Out there, in the world of normals, the word "Batman" did not evoke vivid tales of globe-trotting adventure and twisted clown-faced serial killers or schematic diagrams of the latest Bat-gadget, but only the haziest memories of televised brawls in odd, candy-colored warehouses. Pow. Zap.

Miller set out to engage with, and update, Batman the Idea, not Batman the Character. He structured his story to exploit the cognitive dissonance between his brutal, thuggish Batman and the "Careful, chum. Pedestrian safety!" Adam West Batman that still lingered in the public's mind.

Which is why, despite the repeated assertions of those who've written about the book since it first appeared, *The Dark Knight Returns* is *not* set in the "near future" but in the present day. Miller didn't create his main character by aging the perpetually thirty-year-old Bruce Wayne of the comics by twenty years. Instead, he simply imagined what the Bruce Wayne of the 1966 television show would look like twenty years older—in 1986.

Comics Alliance writer Chris Sims explains:

> Just look at the first things he does when he comes [out of retirement]: He throws batarangs that stab into his enemies' arms instead of conking them upside the head, and kicks a dude in the spine so hard that he'll only "probably" walk again. It's brutal stuff, and it's exciting—and the reason that it's exciting is that it's different, especially if the image of Batman that you have in your head is the bright, cheery, non-spine-injuring Batman of the '66 show. That shock, that contrast, is what sets the tone for the story, that we're seeing a Batman and a Gotham City that have changed.
>
> There's a reason that when Bruce Wayne finally puts on his costume and comes out of retirement, it's ... the bright, blue-and-grey suit with the bulky utility belt that'd be right at home around Adam West's waist.

The story of *The Dark Knight Returns* is the story of Bruce Wayne learning that his old methods are no longer suited to the modern world. On one level, it's Miller's cheeky comment on the state of superhero comics, a genre that he felt needed to adapt or die. But it's also a sly testament to the mutability of Batman as a character, as Miller edges him closer and closer to his roots with each issue: once his familiar blue and gray costume gets destroyed, he dons the suit he wore in his earliest adventures. The final glimpse we get of him is in his civilian identity, bookending how he looked when we first saw him, back in 1939, as Commissioner Gordon's bored socialite friend.

As O'Neil did before him, Miller looked to the original Bill Finger and Gardner Fox stories of Batman's first year for inspiration. But he found something O'Neil hadn't, something he considered essential to who his Batman would be. In a panel from *Detective Comics* #27,

Commissioner Gordon pulls up to a house, spies the Bat-Man on its roof, and orders an officer to shoot him.

For most of his existence, writers had paid merely dutiful lip service to Batman's status as a vigilante. But Miller knew that the image of Batman that hovered in the collective consciousness was one of Adam West's duly deputized do-gooder. His Batman, then, would be a figure of violent opposition, a man isolated and alone, at odds with criminals, the police, and—ultimately—society itself. The world Miller created was a place where those in authority were just as venal and morally bankrupt as the criminals. Wayne ultimately decides to fake his death and abandon the Batman identity when he realizes his role as an enforcer of the status quo renders him inadequate to the enormity of the task at hand. By turning Batman into an antiestablishment figure, Miller, like O'Neil before him, upends the character's 1939 formulation as a lackey who protected Gotham's wealthiest from assaults by working-class criminal scum.

Miller also took up Batman's driving obsession and further amplified it to blend into his more extreme, Schwarzeneggerized fictive universe. In Miller's hands, obsession became full-blown schizophrenia. We learn that Batman's persona lives in Bruce Wayne's mind as a huge, demonic bat that torments him; Batman says, "In my gut the creature writhes and snarls and tells me what I need . . ." In Batman's 1939 origin, a bat had accidentally flown into Bruce Wayne's study through an open window, but Miller gives even that prosaic detail a booster shot of adrenaline, by having Bruce Wayne's imaginary bat-monster crash though a thick glass window to claim him as its victim.

Miller also struck on a simple way to obviate the gay panic that so often hangs over depictions of Batman and Robin in the wake of Wertham: he made Robin a girl. Inspired by Batman's return to action, plucky teen Carrie Kelley dons a makeshift Robin costume and pitches in. "Until Robin is part of Batman in *Dark Knight*, he feels incomplete," Miller said. "I think that's a necessary part of the chemistry for the character, and Robin works better with Batman being an older man . . . I made Robin younger and Batman older." Over the course of the tale, she proves herself brave, resourceful, and, thanks to her affinity for technology, invaluable to the Caped Crusader's mission.

Miller works hard to avoid sexualizing young Carrie and instead shunts all of the story's sexual tension onto his Joker, a screaming, lipstick-wearing poof straight out of a seventies sitcom. Miller says he deliberately turned the Joker into "a homophobic nightmare" to make him a foil for his frigid Batman. "Batman's sexual urges are so drastically sublimated into crime-fighting that there's no room for any other emotional activity. Notice how insipid are the stories where Batman has a girlfriend . . . it's not because he's gay, but because he's borderline pathological, he's obsessive. He'd be MUCH healthier if he was gay."

The mincing depiction of the Joker, along with Miller's hypertrophic embrace of the "power = right" ideation lurking at the heart of the superhero concept, earned him criticism from some on the political left. When the series was collected and issued as a trade paperback, the *New York Times'* review consisted of an airy dismissal comparing Miller's Batman to Rambo, while the *Village Voice* dissected the book's politics in an article titled "Is Batman a Fascist?"*

The critics weren't alone: many readers conflated Miller's knowingly over-the-top and nakedly manipulative emotionalism with the cynical bloat of a Hollywood action movie. But in *The Dark Knight Returns,* Miller's treatment of fascistic imagery and ideas is so self-consciously baroque it becomes ironic; there's more Robocop than Rambo to Miller's Batman. "I don't want Batman as president," Miller said when asked about *Dark Knight's* reactionary themes, "and I don't think the books say that. There's a tendency to see everything as a polemic, as a screed, when after all these are adventure stories. . . . Batman works best in a society that's gone to hell. That's the only way he's ever worked."

---

* The author's unequivocal answer: yep.

Rolling Stone agreed, saying, "Batman is bigger than a comics icon; he is a violent symbol for American dissolution and American idealism."

This is Batman-as-inkblot, an endlessly interpretable figure who accepts the meanings projected onto him by authors and audience alike. He can uphold the status quo and violently overthrow it. He can represent fascism and liberal democracy at once. He employs the iconography of darkness to become a beacon of light. He's a laconic soldier and a wounded orphan. He's whatever the reader brings to him.

The collected series made the *New York Times* bestseller list, something no superhero comic had done before (or technically could have, as it was only *The Dark Knight Returns*'s trade paperback status that made it eligible). It remained on the list for thirty-eight weeks, buoyed by sales to normals who stumbled across it in chain bookstores. Historian Mila Bongco said, "Miller succeeded where comics publishers and other comics artists have not—he broke through the limits of the comics ghetto and managed to get people to buy a comic book—people who were unaware of this medium or who have not touched a comic book since their childhood. *The Dark Knight Returns* became a media event."

To the normals who picked it up, *The Dark Knight Returns* took the idea of Batman that had been unleashed on the culture in 1966 and matched it to the times, replacing the ebullient Pop Art sensibility of old with a steroidal and militarized action-flick mise-en-scène. Miller's ideas were bold, broad, and unsubtle enough to blast through the accretion of niggling details and Byzantine continuity that the fans loved— and render them superfluous.

That continuity no longer mattered, because DC had granted Miller the freedom to provide Batman an ending—something the medium explicitly denied perpetually licensed properties like superheroes. This was the secret of its appeal to non-fans, who had no interest in, and still less patience for, the eternal iteration and dense history that are endemic to the superhero genre. The nerds wanted adventures, but the normals wanted *stories*.

And a story is what Miller provided them, with an ending that transformed Batman's long decades of endless adventuring into one finite tale with a discernible shape. But as the publisher was quick to point out to fans, it was only *an* ending, not *the* ending: one possible fate out of thousands, not a prophecy. Not, perish the thought, canon.

Which is one reason that, once the initial ardor cooled, the Batman fan base began to reevaluate the series. Recently, for example, the website Comics Bulletin listed *Dark Knight* as one of the most overrated comics in history. "Gone are the traits that define Batman. . . . Batman went from a figure of the night who never kills to a hulking brute . . . *The Dark Knight Returns* falls flat due to its misuse of the central character."

It's not my Batman.

LET'S START AT THE VERY BEGINNING

Miller wasn't done with Batman; his contract with Dick Giordano called for him to tackle the Caped Crusader's origin as well. But this would be a far trickier task.

It meant Miller now had to enmesh himself in the thorny continuity he'd managed to sidestep in *The Dark Knight Returns.* Over the decades, many writers had fussed with the origin's triggering incident: In 1948, Bill Finger had given the mugger who killed Bruce Wayne's parents a name, and eight years later revealed that the act had been no accident but a mob hit. This same story suggested that Bruce's true, subconscious inspiration for the Batman identity came from the time he saw his father dressed for a masquerade party in a bat costume. In 1969, writer E. Nelson Bridwell twisted this narrative feedback loop into farce by revealing that the woman who'd looked after Bruce in his childhood was secretly the mother of the man who'd killed his parents. And several writers had offered glimpses of young Bruce Wayne traveling the world to acquire the skills he'd need as Batman.

Editor Denny O'Neil assured Miller he was being given the keys to Batman as he would exist in the new, fresh-slate DC Universe, which would be completely remade by the events of *Crisis on Infinite Earths*. The only continuity he'd need to worry about was the one he was about to create for himself.

There was one caveat: to underscore the fact that Miller's Batman was to be the one and only Batman of the new DC Universe—and to give the comics a much-needed sales boost—O'Neil insisted that the story be told over the course of four issues of the existing Batman monthly title. That meant Miller would have to dial back on the technical pyrotechnics: newsprint paper was too thirsty to reproduce the dazzling ink and colors on display in *The Dark Knight Returns*. And Miller would have to alter his pacing to account for the pages that would be turned over to advertising.

But he'd done that before. O'Neil tapped artist Dave Mazzucchelli, with whom Miller had just worked on a critically acclaimed run of Marvel's *Daredevil* comic, to help him with a dark, grounded take on Batman's origin. When O'Neil offered to restart Batman from scratch, with a brand-new issue #1, as DC had decided to do with Superman and Wonder Woman, Miller objected. "I don't need to slash through continuity with as sharp a blade as I thought," he said. "Doing the *Dark Knight* has shown me that there's been enough good material . . . that I wouldn't want to throw the baby out with the bath water. . . . I didn't feel that fleshing out an unknown part of Batman's history justified wiping out 50 years of [adventures]."

In this, Miller stood apart from the very fans who would soon come to prize his highly stylized, grim-and-gritty take on the character. The bathwater Miller decided to retain, after all, contained some of the most whimsical excesses of midcentury Batman—perhaps even the Batusi.

Miller began by looking for aspects of Batman's origin that hadn't yet been explored. He left the murder of Bruce Wayne's parents more or less alone, reducing it, as he had in *The Dark Knight Returns*, to stark flashes of imagery to evoke how vividly it lived in Bruce Wayne's memory. Neither was Miller interested in globe-trotting adventure or endless training montages. Instead, he chose to indulge his love of hard-boiled crime fiction with a tale about young Bruce Wayne's return to Gotham and his first, inexpert forays into crime fighting.

Batman: Year One is told from the perspective of its two main characters: a twenty-five-year-old Bruce Wayne, just back from twelve years abroad, and police lieutenant James Gordon, an incorruptible cop newly arrived in a crooked city. Both men stumble as they set out to clean up Gotham, make powerful enemies among the city's elite, and ultimately arrive at the mutual trust that will see them through their respective crime-fighting careers.

Everything about *Year One* is darker, smaller, and more sober-minded than *The Dark Knight Returns*. Miller eschews the symbolist riot he indulged in to craft his latter-day Caped Crusader for the straight-ahead plotting of a police procedural. Gone is the broad political satire, the cynical irony, the deification of eighties action-movie machismo: where Miller had rendered *Dark Knight's* Batman as a larger-than-life mountain of muscle, Mazzucchelli's *Year One* Batman is a human man of average build wearing a cloth costume that wrinkles at the knees and elbows.

More importantly, and utterly unlike the swaggering alpha male of *The Dark Knight Returns*, *Year One* Batman screws up. Kind of a lot: his first outing goes south when he underestimates his opponents, nearly kills a petty thief by accidentally knocking him off a fire escape, gets shot by police, and ends up trapped in a burning building.

The tone is dour; the violence is kept strictly street-level and studiously leached of any superheroic glamour. Miller also tones down the melodramatic excess that gave his *The Dark Knight Returns* narration its bathetic poetry, favoring staccato bursts of noir-inflected internal monologue: "It kicks. Gunpowder burns my eyes and fills my nostrils. A wad of lead flies . . ."

But amid all the setbacks and spare *Dead Men Don't Wear Plaid* dialogue, Miller gives his Batman a fleeting yet memorable moment of triumph that embraces the soaring theatricality on which the character was built.

In a scene that has come to define *Batman: Year One*, the Caped Crusader steals up to the corrupt mayor's mansion on the night of an elegant dinner party. We see a smoke bomb crash through the window and land on the sumptuously appointed dinner table near a flaming cherries jubilee. The lights go out. A huge explosion tears a hole in the mansion's wall. Before the terrified partiers can run, the harsh beam of a floodlight fills the smoking gap in the wall. An imposing cloaked figure steps into it.

"Ladies. Gentlemen," the silhouette declares, entering. "You have eaten well. You've eaten Gotham's wealth. Its spirit. Your feast is nearly over. From this moment on"—here the figure of Batman reaches over and snuffs the flaming dessert at the very same second the floodlight cuts out, sinking the room into utter darkness—"NONE of you are safe."

That this scene attains the simple, iconic power it does is not merely a function of Mazzucchelli's skills. It works because, as he did in *The Dark Knight Returns*, Miller places Batman in stark opposition to the existing power structure: he takes a break from beating up street thugs to lash out at the wealthy who have corrupted the system.

And Mazzucchelli's Gotham City exhales corruption; it's a dirty and crumbling burg drowning in Richmond Lewis's washes of muted browns and deep blacks. Where other artists make Gotham a baroque urban hellscape, Mazzucchelli's is a prosaic and palpably real place devoid of anything so abstract and ineffable as hope. We take one look at its grubby, ominous alleys and we know: it *needs* a Batman.

Tellingly, neither *Dark Knight* nor *Year One* finds the Caped Crusader at the height of his powers. Miller knew that a hero is least interesting when he is most effective—which is how he appeared each month in the anodyne adventures collected and combed over by hardcore fans. By focusing instead on the Batman that exists at either end of his career's bell curve—hampered by inexperience on one side and age on the other—Miller made the obstacles that much tougher for his main character to clear, and the stakes that much higher.

As Denny O'Neil had hoped, phenomenal sales of the four *Year*

One issues of the *Batman* comic (#404–407, February–May 1987) drove the title back up the charts. From the all-time low of 75,000 copies per month just two years before, the book now averaged 193,000 per month—numbers not seen since the early 1970s, but still not enough to dislodge Marvel's *Uncanny X-Men* from the top position.

While the darker, more muted tone of *Year One* made it a tougher sell to normals—bookstore sales of the collected series' trade paperback, while impressive, never matched the phenomenon that was *The Dark Knight Returns*—Miller's less hyperbolic treatment of their hero delighted hard-core Bat-fans. Miller and Mazzucchelli's story served as a persuasive argument for the character by highlighting exactly those qualities that set him apart: he was vulnerable, he was fallible, he was resourceful, and *damn* could he make an entrance.

In the wake of *Crisis on Infinite Earths*, *Batman: Year One* became the canonical text of Batman's genesis; new characters and backstories Miller had introduced filtered into the new DC Universe, including a Selina "Catwoman" Kyle whom, in an on-the-nose bid to evoke the lurid noir sensibility he adored, Miller had turned into a dominatrix.

"ONE BAD DAY"

Miller had nothing to do, however, with the comic that would come to epitomize the grimmest and grittiest of the eighties Batmen. Years before Alan Moore and Dave Gibbons's 1987 *Watchmen* began to hit store shelves, Moore had written a script for a one-off Batman comic. His artist, Brian Bolland, worked slowly—so slowly that the book, called *The Killing Joke*, wouldn't see publication until March 1988.

The twelve-issue series *Watchmen* had been Moore's epic and epically mordant meditation on the superhero idea. He dissected the motivations of his heroic main characters to reveal a noxious stew of sexual dysfunction, fascist ideology, and sociopathic delight. Like *The Dark Knight Returns*, *Watchmen*'s decidedly adult approach to the whimsical notion of costumed crime fighters and its status as a self-contained story with a beginning, middle, and end helped it reach beyond loyal comics fans and find an eager audience in the wider culture.

The Killing Joke shared some of Watchmen's distrust of costumed heroes but couched it differently. Moore picked up on a theme Denny O'Neil had introduced in 1973, when he'd turned the Joker back into a homicidal maniac: that Batman and the Joker were reflections of one another.

Unlike Miller, who'd staked out the narrative real estate of Batman's beginning and his end, Moore chose to tell a tale of Batman at midlife— one that looked on the surface very like the tales served up monthly on comics shelves: the Joker escapes Arkham and wreaks some havoc, Batman finds him, they fight, the Joker is defeated, the Joker is shipped back to Arkham. Adventure, ad infinitum. Lather, rinse, repeat.

But where Miller had liberated Batman from the Sisyphean cycle of the monthly comics by appending an ending and a beginning to his existence, Moore gave Batman something else those rote monthly adventures had always lacked: consequences.

He did so by upping the violence with a grisly sequence in which the Joker shoots Barbara Gordon, the then-retired Batgirl, through the spine. He then removes her clothes and photographs her as she writhes, helpless and bleeding, on her apartment floor. He kidnaps Barbara's father, Jim Gordon; strips him naked; and proceeds to torment him with images of his daughter, who we learn has been paralyzed from the waist down. His goal: to drive Gordon insane. "All it takes is one bad day to reduce the sanest man alive to lunacy. That's how far the world is from where I am. One bad day."

The Joker fails to achieve that goal—Gordon's will does not break— but Barbara Gordon's paralysis will become a fixture of Batman's world for decades to come.

More importantly, The Killing Joke's grim tone and fascination with life-altering violence would come to be seen as of a piece with the steroidal brutality of Miller's The Dark Knight Returns, the unrelieved grittiness of Batman: Year One, and the fatalistic dread of Watchmen. Together, these books would inspire a wave of imitators who ushered the superhero genre into a cheerless era of "grim and gritty" tales that substitute extreme, nihilistic violence and dourness of mood for storytelling. The last lingering traces of whimsy were leached from the genre, replaced by anything that could deliver a shocking emotional impact. In 1988, for example, DC attempted to ape the success of *The Dark Knight Returns* with a similarly packaged story called *Batman: The Cult*, by Jim Starlin and Berni Wrightson. The numbingly violent four-issue miniseries sees Batman kidnapped, tortured, and brainwashed by an underground cult, and features a cringeworthy, unintentionally hilarious scene in which Robin finds a broken Batman seated atop a towering pile of naked, decaying corpses, murmuring, "Welcome to Hell. Welcome to Hell. Welcome to Hell."

For years after, comic book writers would profess to "deconstruct" the superhero simply by increasing the body count, adding internal monologue that imitated Miller's imitation of Spillane, or soaking every panel in murky film-noir shadows.

This was exactly what the hard-core fans wanted, more's the pity. To them, a book like *The Killing Joke* showed that Batman had to be taken *seriously*. Sure, Batman may have been created for children, but Frank Miller and Alan Moore had brought him into the *real* world, a place of bloody violence and stark sexuality, and now, finally, everybody would see him for the badass the fans had always known him to be.

What these fans saw when they looked at Batman was the object of their childhood love finally legitimized. It was as if Winnie the Pooh had escaped the Hundred-Acre Wood and run amok on the mean streets of New York. Where he brutally mauled Piglet. And ate Christopher Robin's face off.

Because that would be *real*. That would be *badass*.

THE KNIGHT DARKENS

Denny O'Neil was installed as editor of the monthly Batman titles in the new, post-*Crisis* DC Universe and set about imbuing them with the grimmest, grittiest tones of Miller's dark vision. But first, he embarked upon a little narrative housekeeping: O'Neil felt that Jason Todd's or-phaned-son-of-murdered-trapeze-artists origin story was too nakedly imitative of Dick Grayson's and needed a rethink. *Crisis on Infinite Earths* gave him the opportunity to do so. Thus, in the issue of *Batman* that immediately followed the conclusion of Batman's *Year One* story (*Batman* #408, June 1987) the tale of Jason Todd's first meeting with Batman was revised by writer Max Allan Collins.

On one of his canonical annual visits to Crime Alley, Batman in-terrupts a tough street kid who's attempting to boost the Batmobile's tires. He recruits the enterprising orphan to help him bust a crime ring operating out of a nearby school and takes the boy under his wing. After the requisite training montages, the boy becomes the second Robin.

Jason Todd's new, rough-and-tumble backstory provided an op-portunity to rework his characterization so he'd seem less like a carbon copy of Dick Grayson. To suit the grim 'n' gritty tenor of the times, Robin the Boy Wonder became Robin the Teen Sulker, careening be-tween resentful silences and angry outbursts, and perpetually chafing against Batman's authority. It was an attempt to appease the nerd fan base by taking the sole remaining touch of whimsy left to Batman— the smiling, spunky sidekick—and badassifying it. The result changed the dynamic of the Dynamic Duo in a fundamental way: while Batman brooded, Robin seethed.

But Robin exists to provide an emotional contrast to Batman's dark-ness, and in an era when that darkness became absolute, an angry, un-stable Boy Wonder didn't work. O'Neil and his writers struggled with the character. And the fans noticed.

"They *did* hate him," O'Neil said later. "I don't know if it was fan cra-ziness—maybe they saw him as usurping Dick Grayson's position . . . I think that once writers became aware the fans didn't like Jason Todd, they began to make him bratty. I toned some of it down. If I had to do it again I would tone it down more."

At an editorial retreat, O'Neil mentioned a stunt pulled by *Saturday*

Night Live in 1982: at the top of the show, Eddie Murphy had introduced viewers to a live lobster and asked them to call one of two telephone numbers to determine whether it would be boiled on live television or spared. Nearly five hundred thousand called in; more importantly, millions more talked about the stunt.*

Publisher Jenette Kahn liked the idea. "We didn't want to waste it on anything minor," O'Neil recalled. "Whether Firestorm's boots should be red or yellow . . . This had to be important. Life or death stuff."

For months, O'Neil and writer Jim Starlin had discussed sidelining Jason Todd in some way: having him adopt a new identity or find some measure of peace that would allow him to retire as Robin. It was decided: they'd leave it up to the fans. Jason Todd would be their Larry the Lobster.

Thus at the conclusion of *Batman* #427 (November 1988) Robin was caught in an explosion set by the Joker. An ad in the back of the issue informed readers, "ROBIN WILL DIE BECAUSE THE JOKER WANTS REVENGE, BUT YOU CAN PREVENT IT WITH A TELE-PHONE CALL."

Two numbers were given, which would be open for only thirty-six hours—eight a.m. Eastern Time on Friday, September 16, to eight p.m. Eastern Time on Saturday, September 17.

Two versions of *Batman* #428 had been prepared, but when the 10,614 calls were tallied, the readers had voted to kill Robin. The margin was narrow—just 72 votes separated the Kill Robin faction from the Save Robin faction. Denny O'Neil, who felt Batman needed a Robin and who dreaded the sundry logistical headaches killing a Boy Wonder would provoke, was one of the Save Robin votes.† But the deed was

---

* Larry the Lobster lived, by a margin of over twelve thousand votes. Until the following week, when Murphy ate him.

† The author of this book, on the other hand, was one of the 5,343 who voted to off the insolent punk.

done, and in the version of *Batman* #428 that went to print, Jason Todd died.

Which could have been the end of it. After all, comics characters had been killed off before. In their hugely popular *X-Men* title, Marvel had killed off the Phoenix, and it was Frank Miller himself who killed off Elektra, a character he'd created, in *Daredevil*. O'Neil had been an editor at Marvel for both of those events and remembered the angry reader reaction. He'd steeled himself for that.

But this was different.

Phoenix and Elektra came to prominence during comics' Great Inward Turn; their passing left no ripples outside of the comics shops. But Batman and Robin? *Everyone* knew Batman and Robin! Pow! Zap! Remember?

The mainstream press's coverage of *The Dark Knight Returns*—and, to a lesser extent, *Batman: Year One* and *The Killing Joke*—had raised Batman's profile among normals. As soon as *Batman* #428 hit the stands, many of the reporters who'd covered *The Dark Knight Returns* began calling the DC offices for a comment.

This had never happened before. Denny O'Neil recalled: "For three long working days and part of a fourth, until [the DC publicity department] declared a moratorium, I talked. To newspapermen. To disc jockeys. To radio and television reporters. Here and abroad."

At first the coverage was bemused: "The Boy Wonder is dead, and the readers of DC Comics' Batman want it that way," said *USA Today*, while Reuters snarked, "A group of comic book artists and writers has succeeded in doing what the most fiendish minds of the century . . . [have] failed to accomplish."

The breathless media reports surrounding the Death of Robin story line—many of which neglected to mention that the Robin in question wasn't the original—rocked O'Neil and other DC staffers back on their heels; they weren't prepared for the amount or the depth of public feeling it engendered. But within a few years, they would apply the lessons they'd learned during that time to reach out, past the hard-core fans and collectors, to generate similar media frenzies with bigger, more calculated, and more disingenuous stunts.

At the time, Frank Miller said the Robin stunt "should be singled out as the most cynical thing [DC] has ever done. An actual toll-free number where fans can call in to put the axe to a little boy's head."*

It should be noted that Miller is at least partially culpable for the fact of Jason Todd's death, if not the manner of it. He had, after all, introduced the notion of Jason's demise in *The Dark Knight Returns*. Despite DC's insistence that the story represented an alternate future, fans longed for even the faintest echo of Miller's thrillingly dystopic Gotham to turn up in the monthly books. And when the publisher handed those readers an opportunity to create the first in-canon bridge from their prosaic everyday Batman to the steroid-soaked badass of *The Dark Knight Returns*, many—or at least 5,343—of them leapt at the chance, and paid for the privilege.

Which is how it came to pass that both Batman the Comics Character and Batman the Cultural Idea entered 1989 in exactly the same way: darker than ever, and once again alone.

As they'd done before and would do many times after, DC managed to sweep the brat in pixie boots under the rug—six feet under it, this time. He'd be back, of course. Robin always comes back. But Batman was about to step out onto the world stage in a way he hadn't since the 1960s. That stage, and indeed the world, had grown darker and more ominous in the intervening decades, just as he had.

So it was just as well; the kid would only cramp his style.

---

* In point of fact, each call had cost voters fifty cents—also the Joker had used a crowbar.

6

The Goth of Gotham (1989–1996)

Michael Keaton is not a serious actor. I fear the comic talent behind
Mr. Mom, Gung Ho and Night Shift *will desecrate the Batman*
legend beyond repair.

Why would anyone choose a short, balding, wimpy comedian
to portray the Dark Knight?

—LETTERS TO *COMICS SCENE* MAGAZINE, 1988

The Batman movie will not be a good thing for the comics industry
no matter how you slice it. The best thing the industry can hope for
is to see a bomb the size of Supergirl.

—SCOTT MITCHELL ROSENBERG, PUBLISHER, INFINITY COMICS, 1988

I mean, these were very aggressive people.

—JON PETERS, PRODUCER OF *BATMAN* (1989)

When faced with a character like Batman, who carries with him more
than seventy-five years of continuous and confusing history, nerds and
normals come at him differently.

Nerds splash happily about in a huge, dark lake. The water is turbid
with silt and there's no guessing its depth. All around them the water
teems with life, some of it quite unpleasant. Nerds know this, but they
don't care. They love the lake; they are avid students of its every secret.
They could tread its murk all day.

Normals, on the other hand, swim laps in a hotel pool. The water is freshly chlorinated and clear as cocktail ice. They can see the bottom, always. If they find a good pace, they can blast through their workout in under half an hour and get out before their fingers prune, and then go about their day.

That's the difference: nerds revel in the thought that the comic they're reading is part of an ongoing narrative that began in 1939 and will go on in some form long after they're dead. All of the contradictions and complications and alternate realities and reboots and retcons* that accrete to a character like Batman over the long years are, to nerds, just so many puzzles, waiting patiently to be solved.

To normals, however, all of that baroque and mystifying detail feels like homework. "Gimme the bullet points," they say. "Walk me through it."

And that is why taking a comic book character into another, broader medium poses the prohibitive challenges it does. Of course the "bullet points," in Batman's case, are easy enough to tick off: Orphaned by a mugger. Swears an oath. Trains himself. By day, an idle millionaire. By night, a shadowy figure who punches folk a lot.

But that's at best a character sketch, not a story. To take the endlessly iterative Batman out of the recursive comics medium he was created for and insert him into a different medium with its requisite three-act structure, love interest, and action set pieces risks turning Batman into something else. It shouldn't work.

Which is why it's so astonishing that, once, it did work. Simply. Flawlessly. Wondrously. And when it did, it changed everything.

Because it represented something that had never existed before: a perfect nerd-normal nexus. It bound Batman in a tidy package that

---

* The "retcon" is a common trope of superhero storytelling in which a new story retells events that have taken place in the past and alters them to fit the new story's narrative needs.

normals could easily digest, and it did so in a way that let them see the precise combination of tone, style, characterization, and thrilling adventure that so endeared the character to nerds for years.

Also, crucially: kids loved it. Young children, whom books like *The Dark Knight Returns* and *The Killing Joke* were specifically designed to exclude, once again had a version of Batman they could, and did, love.

But before *Batman: The Animated Series* could come along and do all that, Tim Burton made a couple *Batman* movies.

BATMAN BEGINS

Michael Uslan, who would grow up to be a comic book writer and film producer, shared the nerdish distaste for the Adam West television series. As the orphaned Bruce Wayne forged his idealistic oath in the fires of his grief, so too did the young Uslan channel his outrage into a steely resolve and a long-range plan.

"My goal in life," he recalls, "which kind of crystallized in [the year of *Batman*'s debut], was to try to wipe the words *Pow*, *Zap* and *Wham* out of the collective consciousness of the world.

"I wanted to make the definitive, dark, serious version of Batman," he says, "the way Bob Kane and Bill Finger had envisioned him in 1939. A creature of the night, stalking criminals in the shadows."

That passion never left him, and in 1979, at the age of twenty-seven, he and a partner wrote a screenplay about a dour, middle-aged Batman coming out of retirement to clean up Gotham City. He hoped to use the treatment to convince studio executives that Uslan's vision of a grim, lone-avenger Batman was viable.

But the Great Inward Turn comics had taken since the sixties television series went off the air meant that no one but hard-core comics fans had even glimpsed the gothic Dark Knight of Denny O'Neil, Neal Adams, and others. According to Uslan's autobiography *The Boy Who Loved Batman*, once he'd secured the rights to Batman from Warner Bros., one studio executive wished him luck finding a producer, warning him that "the only Batman people will remember is the pot-bellied funny guy." They were right. Uslan took his script to Columbia and United Artists, but even after Uslan's explanations, executives assumed his Batman treatment must have been based on the TV series and refused to bite.

Finally, Uslan approached young producer Peter Guber. Smelling franchise possibilities, Guber jumped at it, and soon after started a production company with the notoriously headstrong and bellicose producer Jon Peters, who considered himself a fan of Batman. Peters had been twenty-one years old when the Adam West *Batman* series premiered; the self-styled "tough kid from the streets" (his family owned a hair salon on Rodeo Drive) detested everything about the television show, which he deemed "fruity." He loved the notion of a blockbuster action movie with Batman at its center. "I thought, what a great chance to get a Batman who kicks some ass," he told an interviewer.

After two years of failed attempts to interest studios, in 1981 the Guber-Peters Company convinced Warner Bros. Pictures to proceed with a Batman film. Soon after, despite all his efforts, Uslan was effectively sidelined by Guber and Peters.

Uslan's script was given to screenwriter Tom Mankiewicz, who'd written several Bond films as well as the screenplays for *Superman* and *Superman II*.

In 1983, Mankiewicz turned in his draft, which bore no resemblance to Uslan's screenplay about a middle-aged Batman. As Lorenzo Semple Jr. had done when working on the 1966 *Batman* television series, Mankiewicz looked to the comics for inspiration. Specifically, to the 1977–78 run of *Detective Comics* issues by Steve Englehart and Marshall Rogers, considered by nerds a definitive take on *their* Batman.

His first draft was stuffed with events and familiar characters from the stories in question—the Joker, the Penguin, crooked city councilman Rupert Thorne, Dick Grayson/Robin, and love interest Silver St. Cloud. As Englehart had done, Mankiewicz paid tribute to the "big props" era of forties and fifties Batman comics by setting the film's climax at an exhibition featuring a giant typewriter, inkwell, eraser, and pencil sharpener.

Mankiewicz's screenplay, unsurprisingly, hewed closely to the chronological model of his first, hugely successful *Superman* film: we see our hero's traumatic origin, we watch him train for his great task, we follow him as he performs a montage of heroic deeds in a single night. Only after all of that scene-setting has been accomplished, which takes up the script's entire first half, does Mankiewicz's plot kick in.

Originally slotted for release in 1985, *Batman* was beset by delays when Warner Bros. executives, who had expected Mankiewicz to infuse his script with the witty dialogue and sardonic humor he'd brought to *Superman*, expressed worry at his screenplay's dark tone. Mankiewicz patiently explained that while his *Superman* script had intentionally embraced elements of screwball comedy, that approach couldn't work for Batman's world, where the rules were fundamentally different.

Producers were also having difficulty lining up a director: Ivan Reitman, Joe Dante, and Robert Zemeckis, who'd come under consideration for their bracing humor, begged off. Richard Donner was flattered to be asked but was busy on *Ladyhawke*—and summarily poached his old friend Mankiewicz to come help him with the script.

Now Guber and Peters had no director and an abandoned screenplay about a costumed superhero who, it seemed to them, could stand to lighten up a little. They approached young filmmaker Tim Burton, whose first feature, *Pee-wee's Big Adventure*, had just been an unexpected hit for Warners, to fix both problems.

Burton doesn't seem a surprising choice today, in the light of three decades' worth of output that evinces his penchant for pale, freakish outsiders; emo humor; and goth-inflected grotesqueries. But when Guber and Peters reached out to him, *Beetlejuice*, *Edward Scissorhands*, *Sleepy Hollow*, *Dark Shadows*, and all the rest lay still ahead of him; the world had seen only his Technicolor, quirkily picaresque tale of a fey, bicycle-obsessed man-child. Perhaps Guber and Peters were hedging their bets, then, when instead of officially signing Burton to direct, they brought him in to help develop the script.

The idiosyncratic Burton felt Mankiewicz's screenplay too closely aped the structure of his *Superman*. Far worse was how thoroughly it neglected the very thing that had attracted Burton to the character in the first place, the thing he'd keyed into: Batman's dark, twisted, outsider psychology.

He and then-girlfriend Julie Hickson filleted Mankiewicz's screenplay and produced a new treatment in October 1985. The homage to the big-prop era made no sense to them. Instead they introduced a new finale: a Christmas parade featuring giant balloons filled with the Joker's deadly Grimacing Gas. To an already overstuffed cast list, they added cameos by the Riddler, the Penguin, and Catwoman, who band together with the Joker to murder Dick Grayson's parents and set the boy down the path to Robin-hood.

But Burton and Hickson's main contribution was to impose the three-act structure of a revenge movie—"Act 1: Loss; Act 2: Preparation–Transformation; Act 3: Retribution"—effectively funneling the character's roiling psychological underpinnings into a familiar and overtly schematic Hollywood trope.

Thus, in the new treatment, Bruce Wayne's parents are mowed down by a gunman in a Mister Softee truck; young Bruce looks up in time to see the culprit—a white-skinned, red-lipped, green-haired young man.

Stakeholders—including DC Comics—grew concerned about the protracted development process and quibbled with the script. Ultimately the project found its official screenwriter in a confessed Batman nerd named Sam Hamm. Over the summer months he and Burton enjoyed a spirited collaboration and in October 1986, Hamm delivered his first draft.

Hamm felt strongly that earlier attempts to focus on Batman's origin would result in a film that took too long to get started. He decided they could begin in media res, with the Batman already established in

Gotham City, and deal with the origin in flashback. Taking a cue from *The Dark Knight Returns*, he kept paring away the origin until he'd reduced it to an expressionistic montage.

As any fan of the character would, he studiously ignored Burton's notion that it had been the Joker who'd killed Bruce Wayne's parents. He also swapped out Englehart's characters with new ones: city councilman Rupert Thorne out, mob boss Carl Grissom in. Silver St. Cloud out, and in with Vicki Vale—a character with a much longer comic book history.

On Burton's urging, Hamm followed Frank Miller's example and doubled down on the idea that Batman existed as a physical manifestation of Bruce Wayne's psychopathology. His Wayne is a true split personality, psychologically addicted to donning the Batsuit. In one scene cut from subsequent drafts, that addiction stands revealed as true dependence: Bruce Wayne witnesses the Joker's men assassinate a rival mob boss in a city plaza, but because it is midday, he is unable to change into Batman. The inner conflict paralyzes him; he enters a panicked, sweaty, near-catatonic state until Vicki rouses him. Where the plausibility-obsessed *Dark Knight* trilogy of Christopher Nolan would spend long minutes expositing that Bruce dons the Batman identity to become "an idea, a symbol," Hamm and Burton don't bother with any such semiotic chin-scratching. To them, he dresses up like a bat because he's psychotic.

Burton was ready to go ahead with Hamm's screenplay, but studio executives remained wary of putting a project of such scale and budget in Burton's hands, at least until they saw how his more modest Warners film, *Beetlejuice*, performed. So Burton went off to make his quirky comedy-horror tale, and Hamm continued to plug away at the Batman screenplay, taking it through five revisions over the next two years.

In April 1988, *Beetlejuice* landed in theaters and promptly made Warners more than five times its modest $15 million investment. Warners was satisfied, and nearly a decade after Michael Uslan had first

pitched his "dark, serious" idea, a major Hollywood blockbuster starring Batman was finally green-lit.

BACKLASH BEGINS

Casting began in earnest. Willem Dafoe, James Woods, David Bowie,
Crispin Glover—if you were an actor who was well-known, eccentric,
and skinny in the spring of 1988, your name got attached to the role
of the Joker in Warners' upcoming *Batman* film. Robin Williams campaigned hard for the part, but Guber and Peters had only ever wanted
the fifty-one-year-old Jack Nicholson. He agreed to the then-record-
breaking sum of $6 million plus a percentage of the gross and a cut of
the film's merchandising. It would turn out to be one of the savviest, and
perhaps the most lucrative, handshakes in Hollywood history.

As for the title role, Burton and his producers at first convinced
themselves that they wanted to go the *Superman: The Movie* route and
find an unknown. But given the anarchic nature of Nicholson's character, they resolved they needed an actor who wouldn't "get wiped off the
screen."

Many dark-haired, square-jawed actors were considered: Mel Gibson, Tom Cruise, Daniel Day-Lewis, Alec Baldwin, Pierce Brosnan,
Charlie Sheen, and even, briefly, and only half-kiddingly, Bill Murray.
Consultant Michael Uslan, delighted that his first choice for the Joker
role had accepted the gig, argued for Harrison Ford or Kevin Costner.

In the end, Burton chose Michael Keaton.

"I was apoplectic," recalls Uslan. "I had now spent seven years of my
life to bring a dark, serious Batman to the screen, and it was like all my
hopes and dreams were going up in smoke."

Burton attempted to mollify Uslan by pointing out that Batman was
more than a lantern jaw. In fact, by the director's reasoning, the part
cried out for something closer to a character actor. It didn't make sense
to Burton for Bruce Wayne to be a blandly handsome, predictably muscular cipher. By casting the less-than-imposing—and indeed vaguely

squirrelly—Keaton, the film could drive home the character's deeply fractured self. "I always had trouble with the Bruce Wayne in the comic book," Burton said. "I mean, if this guy is so handsome, so rich, and so strong, why the fuck is he putting on a Batsuit?"

But to hard-core fans, a handsome, debonair Bruce Wayne was a core principle. The preceding decade of comics had underscored this belief by deliberately playing up the James Bond notes in Wayne's character. Where the Batman persona spoke to fans' wish-fulfillment fantasies of kicking butt, Wayne addressed their more esoteric but equally powerful longing to look great in a tux.

Which is one reason why, when news of the Keaton casting broke, Uslan's reaction would serve as but a tiny amuse-bouche to the all-you-can-eat buffet bar of fulminating nerd-rage that followed.

In reporting on the casting news, the comics news magazine *Comics Buyer's Guide* neatly encapsulated the fans' sense of betrayal with a single phrase: "Holy Adam West!"

Fans worried that all of the progress that had been made over the past two decades, all of the work that had been done to get the character out from under Adam West's shadow, might have been for naught. Hiring Mr. Mom to portray the Dark Knight was seen as proof that what Hollywood wanted was to take the character not, as it had promised, back to his 1939 roots, but back to his 1966 leaf rot.

Comics Buyer's Guide reported that they were receiving several calls a day from Batman fans begging to be told that reports of Keaton's casting were in error. One writer noted that his non-comic-book-reading friends were now excited about the movie, assuming it would be a broad parody. "They thought Martin Short would make a good Robin," he wrote plaintively.

Later, when the magazine reported hearing that the film was being revised to "make it more like the TV show people were familiar with," nerd unrest bubbled over into nerd protest.

Up to this point in the production process, Burton had been imprecise in publicity interviews and to fans his attitude seemed to bode decidedly ill. In one interview he'd abstractedly mentioned that his *Batman* film would borrow from "all eras" of the character's life, including the television show's humor. Elsewhere, he'd noted that he found the idea of someone dressing up in a Bat costume "ridiculous."

During the film's production, Warners received over fifty thousand petitions and letters of complaint. Among them was a petition started by the owner of a Toronto comics shop, signed by twelve hundred of his customers as well as several writers, artists, and editors of Batman comics, whose signatures he'd secured at the Chicago Comic Con in July.

When Bob Kane publicly criticized the choice of Keaton, the producers kicked into crisis mode. For the first time in Hollywood history, a studio launched a campaign targeted to the hard-core fan base of an existing property with the express purpose of mollifying their fears. In the summer and fall of 1988, Warners sent a publicist on the comics convention circuit who was specifically tasked with assuaging fans by promising them a dark, brooding Batman film. But the first step was to get Bob Kane onto the reservation by paying him as an official consultant on the film.

In early August, at a San Diego Comic-Con panel, the Warners flack proudly introduced Bob Kane, who proceeded to plead with the audience to give Keaton a chance.

Comics Buyer's Guide coeditor Don Thompson was, to put it mildly, skeptical: "Most people are dismissing Bob Kane, saying Warner is paying him to say nice things about the movie," he said. "No one seems to be taking him seriously."

Outraged fans wrote in to *Comics Buyer's Guide, Comics Scene, Amazing Heroes,* and even movie magazines like *Premiere*: "Michael Keaton is IN NO WAY suited to play the role of the Dark Knight," read a typical example. "His personality, screen image and physical makeup are the AB-SOLUTE OPPOSITE of the time-honored character of Bruce Wayne, regardless of what cartoonist Bob Kane may think. Holy Sellout!"

In September, the Warners publicist presenting a *Batman* panel at the World Science Fiction Convention in New Orleans was booed and hissed. But although the fans were in full riot, word of their dissatisfaction hadn't yet escaped the confines of the furiously fractious nerd ghetto. That changed on September 11, 1988, when the *Los Angeles Times* ran an article highlighting the controversy.

The *Times* article turned under-the-Hollywood-radar fan grumbling into a corporate headache. "One of the most powerful men in Hollywood called the Warner chairman to say *Batman* would ruin Warners," Jon Peters said. "That it would be another *Heaven's Gate*."

ONSET OF ON-SET TENSIONS

Filming began in October on a huge ninety-five-acre lot at Pinewood Studios, near London. A harried Jon Peters became a familiar presence on the set, having insisted that Hamm's script needed further rewrites. Hamm, who had already taken the script through five revisions, begged off, citing a Writers Guild strike. Peters brought in Warren Skaaren to up the film's emotional punch.

Skaaren began by excising Robin. Burton agreed with the decision not to introduce yet another origin to the mix. "It was too much psychology to throw in one movie," he said later.

Hamm's script had ended with the death of Vicki Vale, but Skaaren let her live. In fact, he felt the film needed to honor the Bruce-Vicki relationship more deeply, as well as establish Alfred's fatherly concern for Bruce's well-being. He addressed both issues by adding one of the most reviled scenes in Batman's cinematic history, in which Alfred, worried that Bruce is shutting out his one chance at romance, ushers Vicki into the Batcave, exposing Batman's secret identity.

Years later, Burton would castigate himself for acceding to that particular change, though he knew it would upset hard-core fans. "That was the one thing I got killed for," he said, referring to the nerd outcry over the scene. "It was rough. I said to myself, Fuck this bullshit! This is comic book material. I thought, you know, who really cares? But it was a mistake. It went too far."

But the decision that would earn the film its harshest and most en-during criticism from the nerd community came next. Skaaren, who spent a significant amount of time on set with Jack Nicholson looking for ways to expand the role, reintroduced Burton's previous idea that it was the Joker who'd murdered Bruce Wayne's parents.

When Hamm learned of the change, he called it grotesque and vul-gar. It might simplify the storytelling, he argued, but it would compli-cate the ending, as it would introduce a new question: once the Joker is dealt with, why doesn't Batman hang up his cape?

As far as Burton was concerned, the script answered that question: because he's nuts.

While filming the movie's climax, set in a cathedral's bell tower, an annoyed Nicholson confronted Burton, demanding to know why the Joker would climb to the top of the bell tower in the first place. Burton, physically and mentally exhausted by the grueling schedule, had no an-swer and acquiesced to changes. Tensions on the set increased as Peters halted production and brought in screenwriter Charles McKeown to tinker with the film's final scene.

McKeown also spent a day brainstorming with the actors and Bur-ton to completely rewrite a scene in which the Joker confronts Bruce Wayne in Vicki Vale's apartment. The result, which stops the film dead as Keaton's Bruce struggles to explain himself to Basinger's Vicki, stands out as the film's oddest scene, as it radiates the elliptical and tortuous feel of the acting class exercise it essentially was.

Just as the end of the twelve-week shoot was finally in sight, as tem-pers flared, delays stretched on, and the budget ballooned, a front-page article in the *Wall Street Journal* rocked the entire production back on its heels.

"Batman Fans Fear the Joke's on Them in Hollywood Epic" blared the headline. Like the earlier *Los Angeles Times* profile, the piece listed the usual fan complaints, but it added a business angle by including ner-vous quotes from licensors and distributors.

Although it concluded with reassurances from Warners that Burton was listening to fans and the film would indeed be dark and serious, the damage was done, and it was extensive. The mood on the set turned somber. "Everyone I knew sent that article to me," said Guber, "it deflated *everybody.*"

But Peters had already moved to stanch the bleeding. Earlier in the month he'd ordered editors to stitch together a brief promotional trailer. The result was little more than a montage, but it was enough to establish the film's tone and to show off production designer Anton Furst's deco-gothic-nightmare Gotham City. At a convention in New York City over Thanksgiving weekend, a select group of fans was shown the teaser trailer, and an excited buzz began.

The film's unprecedented publicity blitz commenced when Peters tasked Furst with designing a logo for the poster. Furst took the classic Bat-emblem of the comics (tellingly, not the one featured on the film's Batsuit) and rendered it as a metallic badge against a black background. It was simple, essential, iconic, and—once the poster began to appear in bus stations—frequently stolen. In January, a longer version of the teaser trailer appeared in theaters and was broadcast on *Entertainment Tonight.* Newspapers reported that some cinema patrons were buying tickets to see the trailer and leaving before the movie started. A puff piece in the *New York Times* offered a flattering portrait of Burton as a director and a person; the reporter dubbed the footage he'd seen in the production's editing suite "dazzling."

As the premiere date neared, over three hundred tie-in products bearing the Bat-logo appeared. Taco Bell offered a series of *Batman* plastic cups. MTV gave away a Batmobile. Topps offered trading cards. *Batman* games, puzzles, coloring books, and ToyBiz action figures flooded the shelves of toy stores. The 1,100 JC Penney department stores across the country set up *Batman* shops stocked with all manner of prominently emblemed gewgaws and—especially— *Batman* T-shirts.

In the summer of 1989, those shirts—black, yellow, and tie-dyed— were everywhere; the Bat-symbol became a fashion statement that graced hats, jean jackets, sneakers, and necklaces. Unlike the Batmania of 1966, which had sprouted more or less organically, this one had the backing of a media conglomerate with a $10 million marketing budget. Over $1.5 billion of officially licensed Bat-products were sold in stores—and hundreds of thousands more at the kiosks that hawked bootleg Bat-merch in places like Greenwich Village.

The only hiccup in Warner Bros.' massive marketing and promotion effort had to do with the film's soundtrack album. Or technically, albums. Peters wanted Prince to write the score, while Burton tapped Danny Elfman. When Peters asked Prince for two songs to include in the film, the purple paisleyed pop star produced a full album's worth, and that album, bearing Furst's Bat-logo and named simply *Batman*, appeared in stores three days before the film debuted. Its first single, the exultantly and unapologetically cheesy "Batdance," saturated the airwaves throughout the summer of 1989; the album sold six million copies in the US alone. Elfman's orchestral score would get its own album as well, but production glitches delayed its release until August.

The advance hype kept building. The *New York Observer* tartly observed that the film was "less a movie than a corporate behemoth." A segment on the ABC newsmagazine *20/20* featured Barbara Walters asking viewers, "Is America dying to see another comic book character brought to the silver screen? *Superman* soared. But *Popeye* got sand in his face. So will *Batman* go 'Zonk!' or 'Zowie!'?"

When the film finally debuted on June 23, 1989, its opening weekend didn't simply break the existing box-office record,* it doubled it. It would go on to be the first film to pass the $100 million mark in ten days and would ultimately take in over $411 million to become the highest-grossing film of 1989.

Critics universally praised the look and feel of the film, though they were decidedly split on the rest of it. Roger Ebert, in fact, called it a

---

* Set by *Indiana Jones and the Last Crusade* just weeks before.

"triumph of design over story, style over substance—a great-looking movie with a plot you can't care much about." His colleague Gene Siskel was more favorable, noting, "[It's] the first summer spectacular I've really enjoyed."

Later, Burton would express his dissatisfaction with the movie, calling it "boring," and look back on the months of filming as "the worst period of [his] life. A nightmare." He also admitted to being puzzled by the popular reaction. "The reality is *Batman* was a success because it was a cultural phenomenon," he said, "which had less to do with the movie than with something else I can't begin to put a finger on."

So let's give it a shot.

"I'M BATMAN"

The most immediate explanation for the film's record box-office take, of course, is the millions spent on promotion, which forever altered the formula of movie marketing. The Bat-logo hadn't simply increased public awareness on the back of its tie-ins and licensing deals, it had achieved true, inescapable market saturation and expanded the potential audience.

If *Batman* had been the first major blockbuster to hit theaters in the summer of 1989, at least some of its success might have come from people who'd waited through the long winter to experience the thrill ride of a major Hollywood action movie again. But *Indiana Jones and the Last Crusade* had occupied that role by beating Burton's film to movie houses by more than a month.

It would be tidy to chalk the success of Burton's *Batman* film, as several reviewers did, up to its affinity with an increasingly pessimistic national mood. After all, the decade had begun brightly enough, with a blockbuster *Superman* film in theaters and uplifting "It's morning again in America" political rhetoric. And by any measure, 1989 was a pretty lousy way to close out a decade. In the months leading up to the film's release, the news had been led by the Exxon *Valdez* oil spill and the Tiananmen Square massacre; consumer confidence was down and a recession loomed.

The problem with the notion that the darkness of Burton's *Batman* resonated with the darkness of the times, however, is that Burton's *Batman* isn't dark.

It's *literally* dark—the cinematography is steeped in impenetrable shadows—but it's far too formulaic and anodyne to evoke any real sense of foreboding. And any film that contains a scene like the one in which a bereted Joker defaces an art gallery while shaking his fifty-one-year-old moneymaker to Prince's contractually required "Partyman" can only make the 1966 television series look like *Requiem for a Dream*.

No: what Burton produced was a perfectly workable eighties action-comedy—not a Batman movie.

While it's true that Batman is an elastic concept, and while many versions of Batman can coexist peacefully, Burton's film doesn't so much create a new and unique version of the character as slap a pair of bat-ears on Charles Bronson.

It could have been a Batman movie. For a while, it was on track to become one. But all of those last-minute deviations Peters ordered to Sam Hamm's screenplay exemplify the conflicting worldviews of nerds and normals. Hamm roped off a small area of Batman's dark, vast lake, but Peters insisted on building an inground pool.

Action-movie heroes get revenge on those who have wronged them by the end of the third act, but Batman's war on all criminals never ends. Action-movie heroes liberally avail themselves of lethal force, but Batman never kills. Action-movie heroes rescue, and ultimately end up with, the girl. Batman doesn't do girls.

There's certainly an attractive, steel-trap logic to having, say, the Joker kill Bruce's parents, but it's the logic of the Hollywood screenplay, in which everything set up in the first reel comes back in the last. This construction is tight, even hermetic, and it pervades film, television, genre fiction, and even theater, in the form of Chekhov's gun. Its universality makes it familiar, and that familiarity makes it satisfying. Stories whose endings recall their beginnings in this way feel more complete to us, more whole than others.

Batman's status as a creature born of ongoing serialized narrative makes him essentially a bold, open-ended, simple idea: a guy who wants to prevent what happened to him from happening to anyone else. For Batman to work, his mission must be larger than the act, and the criminal, who set him on it.

It's a caped crusade, not a caped vendetta.

That idea is too feathery and abstract to sell Taco Bell collectible cups, however, so Burton's film attempts to explain Batman's motivation by making Bruce Wayne crazy. The film's climactic dialogue between Batman and the Joker is not merely too puerile to carry much weight, it also renders the underlying resonance between the two characters completely banal.

JOKER: YOU MADE ME!
BATMAN: I made YOU? You made me first!

It reduces a pair of elemental figures to a closed feedback loop of cause and effect.

Burton depicts the Batmobile firing its mounted machine guns into a crowd of goons and blowing up a factory filled with people. In another scene, Batman lassos a criminal around the neck and pulls him over a railing. These scenes were engineered to trigger our reflexive action-movie response: we cheer the hero's latest bit of lethal badassery.

But Batman is a superhero, not an action-movie hero. His refusal to kill his enemies isn't simply a vestigial remnant of his roots as a children's character. It's a deliberate storytelling choice: it would be *easy* to mow down a roomful of bad guys with an Uzi. But by taking that option off the table, the story's tension increases, the challenge our hero faces becomes far more difficult, and his chosen solution must become more ingenious: *Batman* isn't *Commando*.

Ending the film with the death of the Joker satisfies the normal's need for a complete, self-contained story, but it dispenses with the superhero genre's core tenet of eternal return: the bad guy always comes back.

While the changes made by Peters and Burton paid off at the box office, at cons, in comics shops, and on letters pages, fans dutifully groused: the muscled body armor was cheating; Batman would *never* sit passively by as a family is mugged; in many screenings, the Alfred-shows-Vicki-into-the-Batcave reveal elicited anguished and primal shouts of nerd-rage.

But as Warner Bros. knew they would, they bought tickets. Of course they did: Warners had spent millions on a targeted campaign to assuage their fears. And although the hard-core fan's satisfaction with the final product was less than total, it was still a multimillion-dollar *Batman* film. The mere stunning fact of the thing was enough to send them back to see it a second and even a third time. When the movie was released on VHS in November* they were among the horde who bought up over $150 million worth.

BAT-BUMP, OR BAT-BUBBLE?

The success of the *Batman* film did precisely what DC Comics desperately hoped it would: it drove new buyers—normals and lapsed nerds alike—into comics shops. There they found stand-alone, new-reader-friendly Bat-books like *The Dark Knight Returns*, *The Killing Joke*, and *Year One*.

In September, any normals who wandered into a comics shop found a brand-new monthly Batman comic waiting on the shelves—one aimed squarely at them. *Batman: Legends of the Dark Knight*

---

* *Batman* was priced much lower than most other VHS tapes at the time, as Warners had decided, for the first time, to target the home buyer, not the video rental store manager.

presented new tales that focused on a Caped Crusader just beginning his crime-fighting career.

The other monthly Bat-books churned blithely on through the murky waters of their nerd-focused backstories: in a tale that stretched over half a year's worth of *Detective Comics*, a savvy thirteen-year-old boy named Tim Drake (who had figured out Batman's secret identity at age nine) noticed that his hero's behavior was growing more erratic in the absence of Robin. He sought out Dick Grayson to entreat him to give up his identity as Nightwing, become Robin once again, and rejoin his mentor. When Grayson refused, Tim Drake became the third Robin himself.

The pages of *Legends of the Dark Knight*, on the other hand, contained lean and muscular stories that could be picked up and understood without AP-level Bat-knowledge.

This was intentional—strategic, even. Earlier in the year, Warner Communications (which owned DC Comics) had merged with Time Inc. to form Time-Warner. This meant that DC was now a part—albeit a small one—of what was suddenly the largest media conglomerate in the world. The company now had access to more resources than ever to promote, market, and merchandise its characters, and—almost as an afterthought—the comics in which they appeared.

The appearance of *Legends of the Dark Knight* in comics shops changed the comics landscape. Over and above its appeal to curious new readers, its status as the first solo Batman title introduced since 1940 (a fact prominently spelled out on the special "collectors edition" cover) made it attractive to speculators—collectors who bought multiple issues and squirreled them away to await the day they would markedly increase in value. The fact that DC released the first issue of *Legends of the Dark Knight* with different covers in a range of special-edition colors ensured that the title would have sold well to collectors even if Batman hadn't just starred in a major Hollywood blockbuster. *Legends of the Dark Knight* became the top-selling comic of the year. Astonishingly, its surging sales, combined with those of the other Bat-titles, effectively doubled the size of the American comics industry in the span of a few short months.

It was during this period that an odd, and oddly gorgeous, tone poem of a Batman story appeared in comics shops. *Arkham Asylum: A Serious House on Serious Earth* was a "prestige hardcover edition" written by a young Grant Morrison with art by Dave McKean that looked and felt like nothing DC Comics had published before.

By this time, "grim and gritty" had become the default narrative mode of comics. Marvel's Punisher, a machine-gun-toting, mass-murdering vigilante, introduced in the previous decade as a villain, was now starring in two bestselling titles of his own, sharing the top of the charts with Wolverine, a hero whose power was the disemboweling of others.

But although *Arkham Asylum* offered a dutifully grim take on Batman's world, it was anything but gritty. In *Supergods*, his 2011 treatise on the superhero, Morrison describes how he set out to make the book "deliberately elliptical, European and provocative" as well as "dense, symbolic, interior."

He succeeded. Ostensibly the story of Batman intervening in a hostage situation at Gotham's house for the criminally insane, *Arkham Asylum* walks the reader through a harrowing series of encounters with the Dark Knight's deadliest foes. In McKean's surreal and discomfiting painted panels, figures are reduced to impressionistic streaks and splotches of color and shadow. Morrison ransacked his dream diaries for nightmare imagery and worked on the script in a sleep-deprived state that makes the finished product read like a willful rejection of groundedness and realism. *Arkham Asylum* is as unapologetically flamboyant and outré as its Joker, who sports long, jungle-red fingernails as he capers through the story in hurt-me pumps, and it gave readers who'd loved Burton's film a sense of what a *truly* dark take on Batman looked like.

As the 1990s dawned, a corner was irrevocably turned. Whatever the metric—comics sales, licenses, press mentions, fan letters, overall cultural impact—the Dark Knight had finally and permanently displaced the Last Son of Krypton as DC's flagship character.

But it soon became apparent that the "Bat-bump" in sales predicated by the Burton film was just that: sales of DC's Batman books were surging, but the effect did not extend to other comics in the publisher's line. So DC fed demand by introducing yet another new monthly Batman comic tied closely into the existing continuity called *Batman: Shadow of the Bat*.

They also seeded their new premier character in more and more titles, including a series of disparate graphic novels that read as extended thought experiments. The first of these, called *Gotham by Gaslight*, imagined an alternate-history version of Batman in Victorian London, stalking Jack the Ripper. Over the next few years it would be joined by a host of graphic novels that would come to be labeled "Elseworlds," which iterated Batman in a host of alternate-reality settings: a digital future, a steampunk past, Arthurian Britain, World War II, the Civil War, the French Revolution, and many more.

Although Batman's fellow DC heroes weren't feeling the same level of love as Batman, it was a boom time for the comics industry. In 1990, over six thousand comics shops had sprung up across the country—up from four thousand just four years before. By 1993, that number would rise to ten thousand. Nerds in even the most rural areas could now find a place within a few hours' drive where they could commune with their people and buy up the vast swath of Batman comics now extant. While there, they could also peruse titles featuring a new batch of gun-toting, überviolent antiheroes in the Punisher mold, who shared an odd sartorial preference for strapping packets of ammo to their mesomorphic thighs, arms, chests, and torsos. These characters, born of writers and artists who'd taken the testosterone-soaked satire of *The Dark Knight Returns* gravely seriously, bore names like Shadowstryke, Knightsabre, and Shrapnel. Their stories were witless, nihilistic paeans to unleashing military ordnance while grimacing. And they sold like hypertrophically muscular hotcakes.

Their success hinged on how generously they fed the hard-core fanboy's love of action-movie, death-dealing badassery, reading as they did like the adventures of Rambo in spandex.

This trend was compounded by another: the spectacular sales of *Legends of the Dark Knight*'s variant covers had ushered in an era when comics publishers began pandering to the speculator mind-set. Ever since the mideighties, when Marvel's *Secret Wars* and DC's *Crisis on Infinite Earths* boosted sales by telling a single, sprawling tale across multiple titles, publishers had taken to busting out a new crossover "event" every summer, with names like *Legends, Millennium, Invasion!, Inferno,* and *The Infinity Gauntlet*. They also began to publish more miniseries, which meant that at any given time, several comics on the stands bore the designation "Issue #1!" so prized by speculators.

The variant cover took its place alongside the event and the miniseries in the industry's arsenal of go-to gimmicks that inflated sales. The number of titles in each publisher's line swelled larger than ever before, and most came in an assortment of die-cut covers, hologram covers, embossed covers, foil-stamped covers, gatefold covers, or glow-in-the-dark covers, and comics encased in airtight polybags. Fans ravenously bought up multiple copies of each.

What could possibly go wrong?

BURTON RETURNS

Given the huge grosses of Burton's *Batman* film, Warners executives knew they wanted a sequel as soon as possible, and they set Sam Hamm to work on a script. They were equally sure that they wanted Burton back at the helm.

Burton, for his part, was a good deal less certain.

Shooting *Batman* had been a profoundly unpleasant experience that left him emotionally and physically drained. He resented the interference from producers, and he was not at all inclined to follow up the years he'd spent shackled to a corporate-owned nugget of intellectual property with yet more. The story he wanted to tell now, about a frail orphaned outcast with scissors for hands, was smaller and more personal, and he went off to 20th Century Fox to tell it.

Meanwhile, Hamm hammered out multiple drafts of *Batman II*, which picked up where the first film ended, with more details coming to light about the Joker/Jack Napier's murder of Bruce Wayne's parents, while Bruce's relationship with Vicki Vale deepened.

Warners executives believed the Penguin to be Batman's number two villain and demanded he be featured in the sequel. Hamm felt Catwoman represented a more intriguing foe. He added both, believing the presence of two villains sent the signal that this film upped the ante on the first. Hamm's initial plot had the two villains stealing priceless artifacts from the "Five Families" of Gotham City, which led them to a secret treasure buried in the Batcave. Robin, meanwhile, was finally introduced to the cinematic universe as a feral street urchin.

As Burton finished work on his twee goth fairy tale *Edward Scissorhands* at Fox, Warners approached him with the assurance that if he were to take on *Batman II*, Guber and Peters would be out of the picture, and he would be given full creative control as a producer. He could make the *Batman* film he'd wanted to make in the first place, true to his singular vision: a Tim Burton film in more than name alone.

Burton agreed; in August 1991 the official announcement was made. And now that he'd been handed the power to approve the film's screenplay, Burton's first step was to reject the one Hamm had been working on.

He reached out to screenwriter Daniel Waters on the strength of his pitch-black, mordantly funny script for the high school suicide comedy *Heathers*. Waters, who was spending his days cranking out last-minute rewrites on the set of *Hudson Hawk*, eagerly bolted from that production and rose to Burton's challenge: write the still-reluctant director a script he'd actually be interested in directing. Waters ditched Hamm's Five Families idea, turned Robin into the leader of a street gang, and at the director's urging, intensified Hamm's freakish take on the Penguin into a familiar Burton trope: a pale, deformed, and grievously wronged outcast—in essence, Edward Flipperhands.

Burton took to heart Warners' offer to make the *Batman* film he'd originally wanted, and he decided that everything about *Batman Returns* should feel like not a sequel but a wholly distinct new story. That meant cutting all narrative and thematic ties to the first film (out went the Jack Napier subplot and Vicki Vale) and hiring an all-new production and post-production crew (with the notable exceptions of the first film's costume designer and composer). Though this team was new to Batman, they weren't new to Burton: he simply hired the crew who'd worked on *Edward Scissorhands,* to better bring that film's wounded, emo sensibility to bear on the subject at hand.

From that moment on, *Batman Returns* was destined to become what it ultimately turned out to be: *un film de* Tim Burton . . . with Batman in it.

The first film had shown how difficult it was to preserve Batman's core elements amid the overpowering commercial demands of blockbuster moviemaking. With *Batman Returns,* that same challenge now had to be navigated while Burton sought to impose his highly specific vision on the Dark Knight and his world. That vision worked ceaselessly to pull the character away from his pulpy, two-fisted comic book roots and into the realm of the grotesque, where Burton's pale-skinned, black-lipped, sulky goth aesthetic held sway.

Some degree of idiomatic affinity existed: the Batman of 1939 was a creature of German Expressionist shadows and theatricality, and certainly Burton's visual and emotional sensibility ran in that direction. This was borne out when a script revision replaced Harvey Dent with a new antagonist, a wealthy Gotham businessman originally conceived as the Penguin's long-lost brother. His name: Max Shreck, an homage to the actor who'd portrayed the vampire in F. W. Murnau's 1922 silent film *Nosferatu.*

Waters turned in more drafts: Robin became a tough-talkin' African-American mechanic, referred to only as "the kid."

After Waters turned in his final draft, Hollywood gossip began floating many names for the Penguin role: Bob Hoskins, John Candy, Christopher Lloyd—even Marlon Brando. But as had been the case with Jack

Nicholson's Joker, only one actor had ever been seriously considered: Danny DeVito.

No such consensus existed on Catwoman, and for months the rumor mill cycled through names that today seem perfectly solid (Lena Olin, Bridget Fonda, Jennifer Jason Leigh), weirdly intriguing (Jodie Foster, Geena Davis, Debra Winger), flat-out mystifying (Cher, Madonna), and you've-got-to-be-kidding-me (Meryl Streep). Sean Young, who'd originally been hired to play Vicki Vale in the first film but had to bow out when she broke her arm while rehearsing a horse-riding scene, felt she was owed the role. When the production refused to return her calls, she donned a makeshift Catwoman costume and slinked onto the Warners lot, demanding a meeting with Burton. She was turned away. Later, she appeared on the Joan Rivers daytime talk show in Cat-drag, daring Burton to meet with her as she cracked a cat-o'-nine-tails.

Burton swiftly hired Annette Bening. When Bening became pregnant, however, the role went instead to Michelle Pfeiffer.

Christopher Walken was hired as Shreck, and Marlon Wayans was tapped for the role of Robin the streetwise mechanic. Warners bought Wayans's option for two Batman films and fitted him for his wardrobe.

But with principal photography just weeks away, Burton asked screenwriter Wesley Strick to take another pass at the script. As was fast becoming Batman-movie tradition, he cut Robin out of a screenplay overstuffed with characters. He also rewrote the Penguin's master plan—instead of resolving to freeze Gotham City, he would seek serious Old Testament vengeance by murdering the firstborn son in every household.

Filming began in September 1991 as scheduled, but the shoot ran behind schedule, ballooning the $55 million budget to $80 million. When test audiences expressed dissatisfaction with the ambiguous resolution of Catwoman's story, a new sequence showing her alive and well, gazing up at the Bat-Signal, was shot at the last minute, at a cost of $250,000, using a body double for Pfeiffer.

Compared to the shock-and-awe promotional approach of the first

Batman film, the marketing push behind *Batman Returns* was relatively restrained—if securing only 130 officially licensed partners, including Coca-Cola, McDonald's, and Six Flags, can be considered restrained.

In the run-up to the film's release, hard-core fans—even those who maintained their antipathy toward Michael Keaton's casting—studiously kept their powder dry. A promotional interview with Tim Burton on *Entertainment Tonight*, in which the director enthusiastically described DeVito's character by saying, "In the comics, he's just a funny guy in a tuxedo. But we're really going to make him the Penguin," ignited a round of kvetching. Nerds heard in Burton's tone an airy dismissal of the comics that felt disquietingly familiar.

When *Batman Returns* opened on June 19, 1992, its opening weekend take of over $45 million broke box-office records, just as its predecessor had done. However, its domestic take of $163 million was $90 million short of *Batman*'s. It ended up only the third-highest-grossing film of 1992, behind *Aladdin* and *Home Alone 2*.

The reviews were likely blameless in this regard, as most were quite positive. *Time, Variety*, and the *New York Times* agreed it was superior to the first film, and the *Washington Post* preemptively dismissed any nerd quibbles by noting that "comic book purists will probably never be happy with a *Batman* movie. But *Returns* comes closer than ever to Bob Kane's dark, original strip." Roger Ebert, however, wasn't a fan of the film's muddled storytelling, stating his belief that any attempt to graft superheroes onto film noir was doomed to fail.

Pfeiffer's Catwoman performance—and fetish gear—while praised by critics, came under fire from parents' groups, who launched letter-writing campaigns and protests against the film's frank, kitten-with-a-whip sexual content and violence. Warners pointed to the film's dark tone and PG-13 rating in an attempt to refute accusations that it was being marketed to young children—a position that proved difficult to maintain in the face of McDonald's *Batman Returns* Happy Meals promotion. The fast-food chain eventually bowed to pressure and withdrew the campaign.

On the op-ed page of the *New York Times*, the film drew criticism from Jewish writers who had somehow managed to discern in its depiction of the Penguin—a beak-nosed outsider who begins the film by floating down the river in a basket and ends it by visiting on Gotham the tenth plague of Egypt—a note of anti-Semitism.

Go figure.

Despite the record-breaking box office, the $267 million it earned worldwide, and the extra $100 million the film went on to make in video sales and rentals, Warners executives felt certain this two-pronged backlash, and the film's fixedly emo atmosphere, had hurt ticket sales. They resolved that the franchise must and should continue, but in order to do so, it needed to move in a new, brighter, more family-friendly direction.

THE BAT, THE CAT, AND THE BIRD

You can kind of see their point: *Batman Returns* is a weirdly nasty piece of work.

That's not a function of the film's body count per se, though Batman does gloat as he kills one criminal and burns three others alive. The script's humor, like its nonsensical story, can't seem to decide what it wants to be, cycling endlessly through on-the-nose puns that would shame Cesar Romero, stone-faced camp, and whatever the hell *this* is supposed to be: "The sexes are all equal when their erogenous zones are blown sky high!"

Throw in the Penguin's out-of-precisely-nowhere mayoral bid (a plotline lifted intact from the 1966 television series) and his abstruse and ever-shifting evil scheme(s), and the result is a weirdly nasty yet *aggressively* silly movie.

Critics who labeled this broad, goofy film "dark" must have been distracted by its wintry color palette and by the disquieting degree to which Burton allows the threat of sexual violence to hang over Pfeiffer's Selina Kyle. Her Catwoman is a distinctive and memorable screen villain, and her status as a victim of crime is intended to thematically pair her with Bruce Wayne. But where Wayne's childhood trauma inspired him to train his mind and body for his great mission over the course of a decade, the film's Catwoman is born when Selina Kyle is thrown out a window and is somehow brought back to life . . . by alley cats. The agency she finds is both magical and external. Thus the film seems to posit that what empowers her transformation into Catwoman is not any choice Selina Kyle makes, but the abuse itself.

That's messed up.

All of Burton's films, to some significant degree, revel in the self-consciously transgressive frisson bestowed by macabre humor. But elsewhere, at least, the mordant and gruesome gags are leavened by a wistful fabulism, a longing for a very specific, and very stylized, lost innocence.

Batman, given the surfeit of cooks in its cinematic kitchen, had felt more like a Hollywood behemoth than a Tim Burton film. *Batman Returns*, however, exudes every stylized, quintessentially Burtonesque artisanal quirk in his toolbox—except that sense of melancholy. Without it, the film powers through the confusing switchbacks of its plot, cynically risking nothing, and about nothing except itself.

The hard-core fans were split on the film. To some, the violence and sexuality that had alarmed parents served as a sort of validation: here, then, was a serious, badass Batman for grown-ups; also Catwoman was hot. In others, the film inspired a strange cognitive dissonance: *Batman Returns*'s weirdest and, among normals at least, most buzzed-about elements were the Penguin's tragic origin and his freakish deformity, Catwoman's Ike-and-Tina backstory, and the black latex gimp suit into which Pfeiffer was vacuum-sealed before each shot. These aspects bore no comics provenance whatsoever, having been hatched from the minds of Waters and Burton specifically for the film. To nerds, this was like watching someone else tell their favorite joke at a party and mangling both the setup and the punch line—yet leaving everyone in stitches.

The comics industry duly braced itself for another inrush of new and lapsed readers in the wake of *Batman Returns*'s release. Shops pre-ordered Batman comics in higher-than-usual numbers, though with the comics boom at its peak, their usual numbers were plenty high already.

But a second Bat-bump failed to manifest, and those extra Bat-comics—which could not be returned to DC—went into overstock.

CHECKPOINT

There is Batman the character and Batman the idea.

Batman the character lurks and broods on the comics pages prized by nerds. His history is a vast black lake of narrative some seventy-five years deep, and—barring the occasional editorially mandated course correction—he exists in a state of perpetual narrative equilibrium, changing only rarely and incrementally.

Batman the idea floats in the cultural ether. He is endlessly mutable, as he is constantly shaped and reshaped by the numerous iterations that keep him alive in the collective consciousness: films, television shows, video games, and Pez dispensers.

For more than twenty years, this collective-consciousness Batman had looked like a po-faced Adam West. Now, suddenly, he looked a lot more like a body-armored, stiff-necked, pillow-lipped Michael Keaton. Until 1989, the Batman who'd adorned Pez dispensers, lunch boxes, and key chains sported a cape and cowl the color of a cloudless April sky; now they were black as neoprene. It was this same Batman who stared out from kids' backpacks at the Warner Bros. Studio Store.

It could have easily gone on like that indefinitely, with the world's imagination contentedly mistaking Tim Burton's flamboyantly stylized and idiosyncratic take on the character with the character's essence, like a moth mistaking a porch light for the moon.

But it didn't. Because at ten a.m. on Saturday, September 5, 1992, a television series premiered with the primal idiomatic power to seize the stewardship of the character's public conception from Burton's pale hands. It would do so by combining a deep, comprehensive, and *profoundly* nerdy understanding of Batman with a compact, concise, and normal-friendly narrative format.

The name of the show was *Batman: The Animated Series,* and it would go on to serve up the essence of Batman six times a week to an audience of nerds, normals, and—finally, some twenty-two years after the comics industry's Great Inward Turn had left them to fend for themselves—kids.

ANIMATING PRINCIPLES

Warner Bros. Animation was deliberating which of the studio's deep bench of characters it could leverage as television properties when the unprecedented success of Tim Burton's 1989 *Batman* (and the 1989 Time-Warner merger) made a Batman animated cartoon all but inevitable. Their first foray into TV animation, *Tiny Toon Adventures*, had yet to premiere when the Warner Bros. Animation vice president announced at a staff meeting that the company would be developing a Batman series, and any animators interested should pitch their ideas. Eric Radomski and Bruce Timm stepped forward.

Background artist Radomski used colored pencils on black paper to suggest a foreboding, impressionistic, Art Deco Gotham City. Timm's character designs riffed on both the Fleischer Studios *Superman* cartoons of the 1940s and Hanna-Barbera's stripped-down house style. But where Hanna-Barbera's design economy often looked merely crude and stiff, Timm's Batman sketches seemed elegant, clean, and—more than anything—*pure*. He'd worked for years on shows like *GI Joe*, where producers urged animators to draw "realistically," aping the photorealistic style of comic books—which as far as Timm was concerned meant loading figures down with extraneous lines that were hell to animate. His Batman would instead embrace and epitomize the very word his old bosses had tossed around as the ultimate insult: "cartoony."

Together, the two men produced a two-minute promotional reel that showed off Radomski's retro forties "Dark Deco" Gotham and Timm's sleek, fluid animation. Their styles wove together seamlessly; this new world had a weight and volume—backgrounds didn't look flat but swallowed the characters in film-noir shadows. And the characters weren't the two-dimensional cutouts that had become the Saturday-morning cartoon stock-in-trade; they were solid, rounded, whole—figures that took up space.

Alan Burnett, who'd tried unsuccessfully to pitch a dark take on a Batman cartoon to Hanna-Barbera years before, came aboard as writer-producer, and Burnett brought writer Paul Dini over from *Tiny Toon*.

The show's initial production bible laid out four ground rules for writers to adhere to, each of which intended to set the series apart from all previous television incarnations of the Dark Knight:

1. *Batman works alone.* The producers wanted to ensure that Batman remained the sole focus—a lone avenger of Gotham's night. This rule survived only the show's first season intact, after which network executives insisted that Robin be featured in every episode: "Kids," they said, "sell toys."

2. *Batman is a vigilante, not a duly deputized agent of the law.* That meant the cops wouldn't reach out to him via hotline phone or Bat-signal. Alan Burnett fought against this rule, reminding Timm and Dini that they'd overlooked something: the Bat-Signal *looked* cool. They relented, and the signal made its first appearance in the series with the twenty-fifth episode, "The Cape and Cowl Conspiracy."

3. *No Dick Grayson.* The Batman and Robin of the *Super Friends* show, for example, had offered up their familiar, flavorless two-man act for years. To allow Batman to claim the spotlight—and neatly short-circuit any concerns about their strange living arrangements—the producers decided that in the timeline of the series, Dick Grayson would be a grown man leading his own life apart from Bruce Wayne and would visit only occasionally. This rule, like rules one and two, was frequently bent and ultimately broken.

4. *Each episode would feature a big action set piece and villains who were darker, stranger, and more anarchic than anything Saturday-morning television had permitted before.*

The rules on the depiction of violence in television animation had indeed loosened—back in the seventies, for example, fear of parents' watchdog groups had turned Tom and Jerry, who'd spent decades locked in a psychopathically violent death match, into chummy milquetoasts. But now, on the back of the cultural phenomenon of Burton's *Batman* films, producers were given leeway to embrace the dark tone they set out to achieve. Though Fox's Standards and Practices department still hovered over the proceedings, forcing last-minute rewrites and work-arounds, it was understood that fistfights with gun-toting bad guys had a necessary place in Batman's world.

Voice actors were chosen carefully, as the producers wanted the series to sound as different from the other Saturday-morning cartoons as it looked. That meant extending the talent search beyond the usual stable of old cartoon pros—who tended toward bright, high-energy, highly performative interpretations—to locate actors who would instead find the naturalistic, restrained rhythms the producers sought. Dini recalled that of the over forty actors who tried out for Batman, most came at the role with a showy "Clint Eastwood rasp" that felt forced. When Kevin Conroy auditioned, however, he simply used his regular speaking voice, albeit a bit lower and more intimate, and was hired.

Tim Curry was originally tapped to voice the Joker, but while the actor nailed the villain's chillingly sinister side, producers felt the role's giddier notes eluded him. Mark Hamill auditioned, displaying a vocal range and dexterity that underscored the character's mercurial nature, and took over the part.

I AM THE NIGHT

The calm, unforced quality of the series' voice acting was no after-thought—it was a function of the producers' guiding aesthetic.

Other Saturday-morning cartoons lunged out of the television screen in a desperate bid to grab their audience's flickering, sugar-cereal-dazzled attention and sell them the tie-in merch. Characters crouched in stiff action poses and shouted thick clots of toyetic exposition against brightly colored, retina-sizzling backgrounds.

Batman: The Animated Series, on the other hand, looked and felt like nothing else on Saturday morning, and indeed, nothing else on television. Its emotional palette matched its visual palette: *cool.*

Its Gotham was a world submerged in shadow, inviting the viewer's eye and imagination to fill in the details that vanished into the murk. Characters didn't stand around and shout at one another—they had conversations that sounded like conversations, inflected with layers of nuance. Not that there were a hell of a lot of conversations: by the time an episode made it to air, story editors and producers had ruthlessly stripped away unnecessary dialogue to emphasize purely visual story-telling.

Which was where the show captured something no other interpretation had before. Its Batman moved with a swift, balletic grace, stepped in and out of the shadows like an apparition, and—when he wanted to—looked convincingly terrifying.

"Batman's fearsome look is arguably more effective in animation than in live action," said Paul Dini. "In our series, the artists are frequently able to depict him as living darkness, a grim, blank-eyed shadow."

Every other mass-media iteration of Batman imposed itself on top of the character: the forties movie serials their cheesy xenophobia; the 1966 television series its go-go-booted, brightly colored camp; the seventies television cartoons their stiff, anodyne predictability; Burton's Batman films their flamboyantly gothic commercialism. *Batman: The Animated Series*, on the other hand, felt as if it delicately peeled things away from the character—layer upon layer of useless accreted detail—and what remained, glowering out at us from the darkness, was the thing itself, revealed at last: Batman.

Each episode opened with a one-minute introduction that served as a visual mission statement: The Warner Bros. logo morphs into a police blimp, piercing the bloodred night sky with its searchlights. We pan down to the streets of Gotham, to watch two thugs stage a bank heist. The police give chase; we cut to a shot of the Batmobile's exhaust belching flame (a wink to the 1966 series) as it speeds toward Gotham. The goons run along a rooftop, stopping short as a shadowy figure leaps out of the night and rears up at them. Its eyes—two blank white slits, the only details visible on the imposing silhouette—fix themselves upon the two men.

And *narrow*.

It's a small moment, barely a beat, an almost imperceptible break in the action before he knocks the guns out of the thugs' hands with a batarang and proceeds to smack them upside their respective heads— but fans felt in that instant the thrilling shock of recognition. It was something they had imagined since childhood but had never seen—a gesture charged with years of meanings and metameanings, expressed with a purity and simplicity only animation could deliver. In that moment, they saw all of the character's grim intentionality given life, the oath that defines and drives Batman distilled to its essence: *Never again*.

If the intro's concluding voice-over went a bit too big ("I am vengeance. I am the night. I am . . . Batman"), nerds forgave. That half-second pause before he launched himself into combat, when his implacable purpose was made plain, landed on them with the weight of a promise, and it felt like a gift. An assurance that, finally, Batman was in safe hands.

The series premiered with an episode pitting Batman against Catwoman. Producers, learning from the past, wasted no time in establishing Bruce Wayne's heterosexual bona fides by emphasizing his powerful attraction to Selina Kyle/Catwoman. Though "The Cat and the Claw, Part I" had come fifteenth in the production pipeline, it was moved to the top of the schedule as a deliberate feint to capture the eyeballs of normals who remembered Pfeiffer's *Batman Returns* performance. This wasn't the only nod to the films made by the series: Warners insisted that the show's depiction of the Penguin accord with Burton's take on the character as a tragic, deformed freak. The show's producers—nerds all—grudgingly agreed.

In addition to its berth on Saturday mornings, *Batman: The Animated*

Series anchored the Fox Kids bloc of animated programs on weekday afternoons at four thirty, where it quickly became the highest-rated cartoon in America. This success inspired Fox to try the program in a friendly-to-adult-audiences Saturday-evening time slot. As the show's popularity grew, merchandising followed, and the critical and industry praise began to flood in. The episode "Robin's Reckoning," which retold the origin of the Boy Wonder with deftness and restraint, received an Emmy—the first of four the series would earn over the course of its run.

Despite pressure from Warners to feature tie-in merch, the Batman of the series rarely availed himself of the gimmicks that came packaged with his ever-burgeoning line of action figures (Rocketpack Batman! Air Assault Batman! Cyber Gear Batman!). Instead, the producers hewed closely to their original, elemental conception of the character. In this, they were aided considerably by a core team of writers with a deep, and deeply nerdy, understanding of the character.

"Our strongest scripts were those developed by our in-house writers and story editors," said Dini. "As a rule, most of the freelance submissions we received would be either clichéd cartoon plots (hero gets shrunk, hero goes back in time, hero gets split into good and bad personas, etc.) or contrived team-ups between Batman and other DC superheroes."*

When they did seek outside writers, producers availed themselves of stories and scripts by many of the men who'd shepherded Batman through the previous twenty years—Len Wein, Gerry Conway, Steve Gerber, Marv Wolfman, Elliot S. Maggin, Martin Pasko, Mike W. Barr, and Denny O'Neil.

Fans who watched the series sensed that Batman was under the

---

* Sixteen years later, the gimmicks and team-ups that got freelance scripts rejected for *Batman: The Animated Series* would make up the organizing principles for another hugely successful animated series starring the Dark Knight: *Batman: The Brave and the Bold.*

stewardship of fellow nerds who knew the character intimately. This was as much a function of what was on-screen as what was not. "Although a common theme in the movies, we did not want to ever have Batman tempted to give up his costume for a normal life," said Dini. "The costume *is* his normal life."

The show was a revelation and served as a sharp rebuke to the one-note, grim-'n'-gritty bloodfests being served up for an audience of adults on comics stands. Day after day, week after week, *Batman: The Animated Series* showed that its unique synthesis and distillation of Batman, carefully pitched to an all-ages audience, could capture the core of the character, even as the Batman on comics stands still huddled in the shadow of Frank Miller.

The real genius of the series, however, and the reason it brought nerd and normal alike to the communal table as never before, was its format. The half-hour episode is the most common, most familiar, and most easily digestible television format, and television itself is the most convenient, intimate, ubiquitous—and indeed the most normal—of entertainment mediums.

The series' episodic nature closely echoed the serialized aspect of comics and each installment ended with a reversion to the status quo: the case solved, disaster averted, justice done—a beginning, middle, and end. But a half-hour television show has the ability to engage a viewer more powerfully and permanently than even the most spectacular film, as it offers the one thing that film can only gesture toward: time, and lots of it.

Episode to episode, Batman's situation didn't change much. But as those episodes stretched into seasons, subtle, cumulative, permanent changes grew visible: characterizations deepened, friendships formed and frayed and formed again, villains revealed unguessed-at layers below their chilling surfaces. As time went on, writers introduced tonal variations to the series, allowing occasional comedic episodes to leaven the grimness of Batman's world. The sense of intimacy this steadily mounting richness of nuance imparts was something that any comics-reading nerd knew well; now, however, it was being served up to normals—and their kids—every day after school.

Among those kids, a mini-Batmania flared: Warners flooded stores with action figures, vehicles, and play sets while the sixty-five episodes of the show's first season aired over the course of two years. The second season, consisting of twenty episodes, premiered in May 1994, redubbed *The Adventures of Batman and Robin*.

Late in 1996, Warners asked for more episodes. Reruns of the show were moving from Fox to the WB network (where they would join the Timm/Dini-produced *Superman: The Animated Series*) and the network wanted to beef up the Batman content. But Warners had two stipulations: the show had to feature not only Robin, but also the character Batgirl each week, as she was set to costar in Joel Schumacher's *Batman and Robin*.

To challenge themselves, and ensure that the new season could not be mistaken for the old, producers borrowed young Tim Drake from the comics but tweaked his origin so it would accord with the rapidly expanding, and by now wholly independent, animated universe. They reintroduced Dick Grayson as Nightwing and hinted at a fractured relationship with the Caped Crusader.

For this new season, Timm went back to the drawing board and streamlined his character designs even further: as Miller's *The Dark Knight Returns* had done, Timm ditched Batman's blue cape and cowl/yellow oval costume for a simpler, old-school black and gray number. Every character went through a similar redesign/simplification, to bring the look of the series more closely in line with that of *Superman: The Animated Series*. Now that *Batman Returns* had disappeared from the cultural rearview mirror, Timm was given license to ditch that film's moodily Burtonesque interpretation of the Penguin and return him to his roots as simply a portly, effete crook.

Producers wanted to call this third, Bat-family-focused season *Batman: Gotham Knights*, but the WB insisted on the far less evocative, but more descriptive, *New Batman/Superman Adventures*.

Over the span of six years, three titles, and two networks, 110 episodes of *Batman: The Animated Series* were produced, along with a theatrical film (called *Mask of the Phantasm*) and two direct-to-video features.

The series remains a singular and remarkable achievement, and not only because it reintroduced the character of Batman to a generation of children—kids whom the comics had abandoned in their rush to embrace gritty nihilism, and whom Burton's films had only puzzled with their emo self-indulgence. If *Batman: The Animated Series'* sole legacy was that children once again saw in Batman something that resonated, something true and enduring that spoke to them of the inner strength that made his astonishing feat of self-rescue possible, that would be enough. But of course there's more to it.

For all the reasons outlined above, *Batman: The Animated Series* remains a beautiful anomaly, a perfect narrative paradox forever hovering in two simultaneous but mutually impossible states: it is at once the most fan-focused and nerdy, and the most accessible and normal, depiction of the Dark Knight that will ever exist in any medium.

It's more than a cartoon. It's Schrödinger's cat.

7

The Caped Crusade (1992–2003)

They're called comic *books, not* tragic *books.*

—JOEL SCHUMACHER

We grew up on Batman, and to see him exploited for the commercial marketing (which is just what is happening) is infuriating. And, more importantly, the first shot of the movie (after the credits), was a shot of the Bat-Ass. Second shot: Boy Wonder-Ass. I didn't need to see that!!! Nobody needed to see that. Even seeing Silverstone's ass and nips (rubber???!!!??) was purely gratuitous. And personally, rubber nipples don't turn me on.

—HOME PAGE, BRING ME THE HEAD OF JOEL SCHUMACHER WEBSITE

For most of their existence, Superman, Batman, and the rest of their ilk have been regarded, by those few outside the comics industry who bothered to regard them at all, as adolescent wish fulfillment. But that epithet, while a reasonable assessment of at least the root of their appeal, misses the mark in one small but crucial respect.

For their first forty years, superheroes served as *childhood* wish fulfillment: not simply to be strong, but to be the strongest; not simply to run fast, but to run the fastest—and in Batman's case, not simply to be smart, but to be the smartest. The comics of the forties, fifties, and sixties didn't lack for emotions, but they were the raw and primal emotions of the elementary school playground—joy, rage, sadness, jealousy—and they were triggered by plot mechanics: Robin suspects Batman wants to replace him with Batwoman. Choke! Sob!

Only after Stan Lee, Jack Kirby, and Steve Ditko dosed their new breed of 1960s Marvel heroes with a bolus of Clearasil did slightly more nuanced, adolescent emotions enter the mix—guilt (Spider-Man), shame (the Thing), and feelings of alienation (the X-Men). More importantly, these emotions didn't surface in reaction to events—they were intrinsic to the heroes' psychological makeup. Suddenly, superheroes had personalities.

With these new emotions and characterizations, superheroes began to address longings more abstract than simply to fly far and run fast and be strong: these new heroes endeavored instead to win the girl, to find acceptance, to live up to responsibility, to be considered worthy: *adolescent* wish fulfillment, at last.

And so it went, from the 1960s to the 1980s—an age in which the adolescent emotionalism of Marvel heroes overran the superhero universe, a process accelerated by the Great Inward Turn of the 1970s. By the end of the eighties Batman had transformed from boilerplate cop-in-a-cape into a taciturn, obsessed loner, or a depressive schizophrenic.

But in the early 1990s, as foil covers, embossed covers, and hologram covers jostled for space on comics shelves more crowded than the industry had ever seen, the superhero's recently acquired adolescent yearning erupted from subtext into hilariously overt text.

It was a comics culture predicated upon gleefully hormonal visual excess. The eighties emphasis on Schwarzeneggerian muscularity now metastasized into an aesthetic of swollen, distended, vascular flesh. Where heroes of the 1980s like the Punisher had toted around the odd machine gun or pistol, new heroes and teams with names like Spawn, Deadpool, Shrapnel, Cable, Bloodsport, Youngblood, and Cyberforce meted out exultantly gore-spattered justice at the ends of the blades and bazookas they kept strapped to their persons. One Batman analogue named Shadowhawk, for example, routinely maimed and paralyzed his foes.

To run one's eyes across a comics rack in 1992 was to gaze inside the testosterone-pickled brain of a thirteen-year-old heterosexual male: heroes whose grimacing faces perched atop massive deltoids like statues sunk into Easter Island, women whose medicine-ball breasts offered themselves up for inspection in poses that defied physiognomy and physics. Name your libidinal fanboy fetish: gun barrels, explosions, throwing stars, limbs that transformed into lasers, swords, or laser-swords—all of it was stripped of narrative context and splashed across full-page panels.

The vogue for "grim and gritty" stories led by Batman had soured into a mouth-breathing predilection for "extreme" visuals: page after page of pubertal pinups—comics not meant to be read but ogled.

Or, increasingly, sealed into Mylar bags and filed away. The speculator boom was at its peak, as Marvel flooded shelves with X-Men titles and variant covers. One of these, *X-Men* #1 (October 1991), sold 8.1 million copies, more than any comic book in publishing history. It was a number far too large for even the fast-growing collectors' market to soak up and sustain, so the back-issue bins began to swell with unsold comics.

Amid this die-cut, foil-embossed, gore-flecked hurly-burly, the now comparatively quaint-seeming Batman cooled his heels. The wave of X-books on the stands had already pushed his core titles out of the top one hundred in sales, and *Batman Returns* had done nothing to help matters.

Editor Denny O'Neil noticed. "We wondered if Batman might not be passé," he recalls, "because for all his dark mien he will not inflict more pain than is necessary and he will never take a life. We were looking at heroes in other comics, to say nothing of other media, in which wholesale slaughter seemed to be the primary qualification for a hero."

If Batman's moral code made him seem out of step with the prevailing comic book zeitgeist, his older brother Superman's clean-cut do-gooding made the Man of Steel seem like some kind of Mormon dinosaur. Something had to be done, and DC proceeded to do it amid no small amount of fanfare: they killed the big guy off.

Everyone inside the comic book industry recognized the publicity stunt for what it was, but news outlets like *Newsweek, People,* and *New York's Newsday* pounced upon the "story." Suddenly the death of Superman was a monologue joke on *The Tonight Show,* a sketch on *Saturday Night Live.* Comics retailers, sensing this increased public attention, placed five million advance orders for the "death issue"—which of course came in a sealed plastic bag, in black, for mourning. In addition to the usual crowd of fans and speculators, an unprecedented number of normals set foot into comics shops for the first and last time to pick up a copy, on the doomed presumption that by so doing they were helping to pay for their kids' college tuition. Ultimately, more than six million copies were sold amid a never-before-seen amount of mainstream attention.

It was a stunt, yes—but it was also a sly comment on the state of the industry. For the following year, Superman comics explored how a world without a Man of Steel would look.

O'Neil and his Batman writers, who had been planning a similar stunt for more than two years, resolved to examine the vacuum left by a hero in their own way. In a bit of narrative jujitsu, they resolved to indulge the fashionable thirst for lurid, amoral violence with a massive tale that would ultimately reaffirm Batman's stance as a moral and compassionate hero. To do this, O'Neil tightened the already rigid continuity among the Batman titles so one single story line threaded through them all. Next, he introduced his featured players.

ENTER: THE FLAMING WRIST DAGGERS OF BADASSERY

The miniseries *Sword of Azrael* debuted a character perfectly attuned to the age of throwing sops to the great fanboy Cerberus: a genetically enhanced, brainwashed assassin whose armor came tricked out with flaming wrist daggers as howlingly impractical as they were badass-looking. Batman takes Azrael under his wing and begins to retrain him, attempting to curb the young man's mercilessly murderous programming.

Meanwhile, *Batman: Vengeance of Bane* introduced the saga's chief antagonist, a *luchador*-masked mountain of muscle fueled by both rage and a powerful strength-enhancing drug. A criminal shrewd enough to deduce Batman's secret identity, Bane launches a plan to destroy Batman and rule Gotham City in his stead. To this end, he sets all of Arkham Asylum's homicidal inmates loose, an act that causes Batman to drive himself past his mental and physical breaking point in his desperate zeal to recapture them all. In *Batman* #497 (June 1993), Bane surprises an exhausted Batman in the Batcave, and the encounter ends with Bane snapping Batman over his knee, breaking his back.

The convalescent Caped Crusader taps Azrael to take over as Batman and assume what the tale, with grave pomposity, dubs "the Mantle of the Bat." Azrael agrees, but soon swaps the Bat-costume for a preternaturally goofy set of cybernetic armor complete with such I Love the Nineties accoutrements as gauntlet claws, arm rockets, a superfluous midthigh ammo belt, Spikes That Do Precisely Nothing, and, perhaps most weirdly, a laser pointer built into the torso for shining the Bat-symbol on others.

Now that the Batman titles featured Azrael in his ludicrously ultra-weaponized Bat-armor on their covers, sales were surging. The prospect delighted O'Neil and his writers—and worried the hell out of them. Azrael was always meant to serve as an object lesson, a sarcastic comment on the predominant mood, not to become the Sensational Character Find of 1993.

"We set out to create an anti-Batman," says O'Neil, "and my greatest fear was that people would love him."

As the saga continues, Azrael struggles against his conditioning and grows increasingly unhinged. He becomes paranoid and self-absorbed, experiences hallucinations, permits innocent bystanders to perish without intervening, and lets a mass murderer fall to his death. Ultimately, Batman—who's bounced back from his broken back just fine, thank you very much—challenges and defeats Azrael, and resumes his identity as Gotham's Dark Knight.

This massive story arc played out over the course of sixteen months; readers who wished to follow it were required to purchase over seventy issues of comics from eight different series. But news of Batman's broken back hadn't attracted anything like the unprecedented mainstream media attention of Superman's death, or even Robin's death. In the minds of normals unfamiliar with the mechanics of ongoing long-form narrative, death was permanent and shocking; disability, on the other hand, lacked the same charge.

Yet within the comics ghetto, it worked beautifully. All of the Bat-books surged back up the sales charts; an issue of Batman was the top-selling comic of August 1993. The fact that it was the title's five hundredth issue, a number attractive to collectors, helped a bit.

As did its variant wraparound die-cut cover.

And the fact that it came in a sealed plastic bag.

With collectible postcards.

This would prove only a fleeting success, however, when the speculator bubble finally burst, sending shockwaves throughout the industry. In April 1993, there were over eleven thousand comics shops across the country, ordering an astonishing forty-eight million comics per month. But in January of 1994 alone, some one thousand of those shops shuttered their doors. The closings continued month after month, and the number of comics distributors dwindled as well.

Meanwhile it became clear that the stunt of killing or disabling your hero offered only short-term gains: Superman's sales sagged in the wake of his inevitable return, and the Bat-titles once again plummeted from the top one hundred list, which swelled anew with angsty X-Men and antiheroes whose portable arsenals of swords and guns bristled from their bodies like so many militaristic porcupine quills. The only way Batman managed to break into the top one hundred titles at all, in fact, was by piggybacking on another property: a *Batman vs. Predator* comic cracked the list at number eighty-four, and a *Spawn/Batman* crossover with a gorgeously mind-numbing forty-eight-page fight scene became the bestselling comic of 1994.

With the industry in freefall, it didn't much matter to DC that death/ disabling stunts offered only brief sales spikes. In the years ahead, they would dutifully and desperately iterate the same strategy on all their heroes: Wonder Woman would die and be replaced, as would Green Arrow and the Flash. The Green Lantern would do them all one better by turning evil and slaughtering thousands of innocent people* before going to his great reward. None of the deaths would stick, of course— it was tough to license the likeness of a corpse—but they churned on anyway, as did summertime "event" crossovers involving every title in DC's superhero line.

It was the summer crossover of 1994, however, that would have the most profound effect on Batman. The event, called *Zero Hour: Crisis in Time*, represented DC's attempt to clean up after the previous decade's *Crisis on Infinite Earths* miniseries—which had itself been an attempt to clean up the DC Universe's various disparate threads of continuity by collapsing them all together. That process had inevitably left many contradictions and lingering questions—two things the newly energized hordes of hard-core fans could not and would not abide.

O'Neil and his writers saw the event as a chance to make some tweaks to Batman's history. The first of these was small but smart: they quietly dispensed with Catwoman's backstory as a former prostitute. In the age of comics devoted to slavishly satisfying the whims of horny fanboys, eliding such a salacious detail represented a surprising, and surprisingly progressive, move. The other changes were larger and went directly to the essence of the Batman character.

For years, Batman had known the identity of the man who shot and killed Martha and Thomas Wayne: a small-time crook named Joe Chill. The timeline-altering effects of *Zero Hour* did away with Chill completely. In the new DC universe, Bruce Wayne did not know who murdered his parents.

---

* Extreeeeeeme!

This tiny tweak served to fundamentally alter his legend. O'Neil knew what Bill Finger, and Tim Burton, did not—namely, that personifying the act of violence that birthed Batman cannot help but diminish him. His mission must be larger than the one man who unwittingly sent him on it. To function as a symbol, Batman must stand in opposition, as he'd originally sworn to do, to all criminals, and to the random violence that potentially awaits every one of us in every dark alley. He's not driven by anything so mean and petty and personal as revenge. Instead, his mission opens outward, it engages the wider world, and it's laced with a grim and knowingly Sisyphean species of hope. His goal isn't attainable vengeance, but something that will forever lie just beyond his reach: justice.

Not a vendetta, but a crusade.

The other adjustment O'Neil and his writers introduced was even more ambitious. In the new reality of the DC Universe, Batman's very existence was not public knowledge. Instead, he was now considered an urban myth, a legend of Gotham's underworld.

The move reflected Denny O'Neil's long-standing editorial mindset, taken to its logical conclusion. As both writer and editor, O'Neil had steadily if stealthily labored to isolate Batman, and Batman's world, from the rest of the DC Universe. He'd unsuccessfully resisted attempts by writers like Keith Giffen to make Batman a member of the Justice League, as well as any crossover event that would depict Batman as a high-profile public figure. O'Neil's concern was grounded in Batman's iconography. He maintained that Batman worked best in the shadows, as a figure of fear—and any story that dragged him into the light of day, much less the national news, robbed him of the very thing that made him who he was.

But the decision to turn Batman into an urban myth introduced a host of complications. If people didn't believe that Batman existed, what of Robin? Or Nightwing, who'd become the public face of the super-team known as the Teen Titans? And what about the Bat-Signal?

Just as *Crisis on Infinite Earths*' wholesale conflation/erasure of hundreds of beloved stories had inspired a wave of nerd-outrage, the notion of Batman as urban legend proved controversial. "I was at Marvel when this idea was first implemented in the Batman books," says comics writer Glenn Greenberg, "and I remember that we all laughed about it and called it completely ridiculous."

In the comics' letters pages, fans tossed around words like "preposterous," "unworkable," and "unrealistic." But O'Neil was adamant, and the change stuck, becoming DC's official editorial policy for the next ten years.

While all of this furious activity swirled through the pages of the main Batman comics and the industry proceeded with its steady implosion, an all-ages comic based on *Batman: The Animated Series* quietly debuted. This series* offered approachable, kid-friendly, done-in-one stories that captured the animated show's clean, distilled take on the character. Through the darkest years of the nineties, when comics' marketing strategy devolved into chasing the fickle collector with puerile, garishly adolescent eye candy, a comic made expressly for young children offered the truest, best-written, and most adult version of Batman on the stands.

SCHUMACHER BEGINS

The ongoing implosion of the comics industry went unnoticed by Hollywood accountants, who deemed a new Batman film inevitable. Once *Batman Returns*'s box-office and video sales were finally tallied, Warner Bros. cochairmen Robert Daly and Terry Semel reached a decision about the future of their most lucrative film franchise. "Terry and I wanted this [next] Batman to be a little more fun and brighter than the last one," said Daly. "The first Batman was wonderful. The second

---

* Written mostly by Kelley Puckett and Ty Templeton, and illustrated by Templeton, Mike Parobeck, Rick Burchett, and others.

got terrific reviews, but some people felt it was too dark, especially for young kids."

Entertainment Weekly framed it more bluntly, quoting a source saying that Tim Burton was off the picture because he was "too dark and odd" for the studio.

Too dark and odd for McDonald's as well, as the fast food chain was still smarting from having to scrap their *Batman Returns* Happy Meals promotion when parents groups protested. To stay in the good graces of the corporation whose spokesclown pimped saturated fat to children like a whimsical chalk-faced avatar of arteriosclerosis, Warners promised that McDonald's officials would be granted the ability to review the next film's script before filming began.

After feeling out John McTiernan (*Die Hard*), whose schedule was booked, and briefly considering and rejecting Sam Raimi (*Evil Dead 2, Darkman*), Warners approached Joel Schumacher, who'd made a name for himself helming a string of cheaply made hit films with distinct visual aesthetics, most notably *The Lost Boys, Flatliners*, and *Falling Down*.

"Bob or Terry," recalled Schumacher, "started the discussion by saying they wanted to offer me the corporation's largest asset."

Husband-and-wife television writers Lee and Janet Scott Batchler began work on the script for the third Batman film in July 1993. They met with Tim Burton, who'd been relegated to producer, and he encouraged them to keep exploring the notion of psychological duality in both Batman and his villains. To clearly underscore that theme, they imagined a sexy psychiatrist as Batman's love interest.

Included in their first draft was a scene set in the psychiatrist's bedroom after she and Batman have made love, which establishes that the Dark Knight doesn't remove his mask during sex—the kind of kinky throwaway joke that had Burton's fingerprints all over it.

Warners' marketing department requested that Batman don a second, shamelessly toyetic "Sonic Armor" Batsuit, the better to move action figures with. And the production department demanded that the script feature the previous film's two-villain formula. Schumacher, who'd recently worked with Tommy Lee Jones on *The Client*, was determined that the Oscar winner would play Two-Face, the Batman villain who best embodied the script's emphasis on duality and split personalities.

Once they turned in their draft, Akiva Goldsman, with whom Schumacher had also worked on *The Client*, was brought in to take another pass. Mostly, he tweaked the screenplay's tone, upping the frenetic humor and throwing in wilder jokes as he strove to capture the bright, breezy adventure of forties and fifties Batman comics. He also excised the Bat-sex completely.

Schumacher knew exactly how he hoped to achieve the studio's desired all-ages Bat-film: by throwing off Burton's grayscale somberness and embracing—nay, throttling—humor. "They're called *comic* books, not *tragic* books," he would remind his cast and crew, and he urged them to make everything about the production funnier, brighter, more colorful, more visually arresting. "A living comic book," in his words.

To this end, Schumacher, a former window dresser and costume designer, concentrated on the film's visual elements. He'd envision Batman stepping through a wall of flame, for example, and instruct his screenwriters to write whatever scenes were necessary to lead up to that moment. He'd describe to his production designer a Gotham City in which Times Square erupted at every street corner, seething with neon and fluorescent paint and lasers, and await the result in rapt delight.

Not everyone shared Schumacher's ebullient sense of how the film was shaping up. His cinematographer, Stephen Goldblatt, was nervous. "It's an extravagant opera," he said. "It borders on excess, which inevitably causes problems."

Case in point: Schumacher's pronounced visual aesthetic led him to a tiny but fateful decision. It was a run-of-the-mill costuming choice, really, the sort that happens every day during pre-production. This choice served to nudge the design of the Batsuits out of the bulky, workaday realm of Kevlar riot gear and into a slightly more body-conscious direction, toward muscle suits that deliberately evoked Hellenic statuary, as befits heroes. "They're idealized," Schumacher would say of his new Batman costumes, "almost Greek, with a little steroid in it."

Thus it came to pass that Joel Schumacher bestowed upon each of Batman's sculpted rubber pectoral muscles . . . a nipple.

He could not guess that the mere existence of said areolae would earn him the eternal seething enmity of legions of nerds and be remembered as his signal contribution to the character's legacy.

Casting the film posed a different set of challenges. Robin Williams had been eager to assay the role of the Riddler until he read the screenplay, which he felt offered an insufficiently comic take on the character. So the part went instead to Jim Carrey, ensuring that the words "insufficiently comic" could never be applied to the film.

Schumacher's desire to cast Tommy Lee Jones as Harvey Dent/Two-Face meant convincing the studio to buy out the contract of Billy Dee Williams, who'd accepted the role in Burton's 1989 film on the condition he'd be the featured villain in a sequel.

Williams wasn't the only black actor contracted for a role in the film who got nudged aside by Schumacher. Marlon Wayans's tough, streetwise mechanic version of Robin the Boy Wonder—originally slotted to debut in *Batman Returns*—didn't jibe with the new director's manic vision. Wayans's contract was bought out and Chris O'Donnell hired to play Dick Grayson/Robin.

Schumacher told O'Donnell to pack on some muscle ahead of shooting and informed the young man that in the film, his hotheaded, rebellious Dick Grayson would sport an earring.

Michael Keaton had assumed he would tackle Batman a third time but lost some measure of confidence when the studio chose Schumacher over Burton. Nonetheless, he'd hoped to be consulted during the film's development process, as he strongly felt the two-villain focus of *Batman Returns* had left his character underdeveloped. Ultimately, upon finally getting his hands on the script, he decided not to return to the role.

The search for a replacement proved a short one. Tim Burton, to the surprise of nobody, pushed for Johnny Depp. The studio favored Val Kilmer or Kurt Russell, however, and Schumacher chose Kilmer. With the casting of Nicole Kidman as improbably named Bat-shrink Chase Meridian, principal photography began.

MARKETING *FOREVER*

Warners had a nervous audience on its hands, but the studio was used to that. As they had done five years before, the Warners marketing department launched a promotional blitz to reassure and energize a very important target audience. This time, however, that target audience wasn't fans. It was licensees.

In a glitzy presentation before two hundred toy, fashion, and game executives on the studio back lot, Schumacher and the Warners marketing team eagerly promised a more "fun," "lighthearted," and "adventurous" film that would appeal to consumers of all ages. History does not record the licensees' reaction to the props Schumacher featured in this rousing presentation, which included the nipple suits and a replica of his unabashedly sex-toyetic Batmobile, though one executive would later describe the director, tellingly, as "very flamboyant."

Now that the franchise was steaming ahead under its own considerable power, the studio abandoned its previous efforts to kowtow to the character's nerd fan base. The Warners cochairs had become convinced there was no pleasing hard-core Bat-fans. Besides, Warners' research showed that they already had the nerds in their pocket—it was the dorks in costume who were always first in line, after all. This time it was the normals the studio needed to reach, and games, figures, bedsheets, T-shirts, and a whopping television ad buy was the proven strategy for doing so.

The producers did, however, once again tap the now-eighty-year-old Bob Kane as a consultant on the film, more out of tradition than deference. On set visits, Kane occasionally dropped his usual demeanor of reflexive boosterism and took Schumacher aside to actually do some consulting, voicing the very concerns that would soon be shared by multitudes.

"He didn't like the idea of Dick Grayson wearing an earring," Schumacher recalls. "He didn't understand why it was necessary. He also wasn't thrilled with the fact that the new Batsuit had nipples on it. He would come up to me every once in a while and say, 'Joel, I just don't understand.' "

Ever the company man, though, Kane dutifully talked up the new film to the fans. In an interview with *Comics Scene* magazine, he said, "Without knocking anything that Michael [Keaton] did—he did marvelously with what he had—I think Kilmer is more handsome and has an edge with his physical prowess. He is more like the Bruce Wayne that I draw."

As far as Warners was concerned, however, Schumacher was a miracle worker: for the first time, a massive Batman production came in on time and millions of dollars under budget.

The inevitable publicity campaign began in April 1995, keying off posters of the film's key players photographed by Herb Ritts, a close friend of Schumacher's. Over 130 products bearing Batman's name and likeness appeared, including a roller coaster and stunt show at Six Flags amusement parks. A McDonald's commercial clipped from the film's opening scene in which Batman tells Alfred, "I'll get drive-thru," became inescapable, and the country's Sears and Warner Bros. Studio Stores gave over huge swaths of their sales floors to *Batman Forever* merchandise.

In addition to these tried-and-true means of raising awareness and generating buzz, Warners unveiled a brand-new promotional tool, a *Batman Forever* website, the first ever to be devoted to a single film.

Batman Forever opened on June 16, 1995; it proceeded to make a record-breaking $52.7 million in its first three days and would go on to earn $184 million in the US ($20 million more than *Batman Returns*) and $337 million worldwide.

Reviews were decidedly mixed to negative, however, with the *New*

York Times lamenting the more mainstream, if frenetic, direction and slagging the hype surrounding the film, dubbing it an "empty-calorie equivalent of a Happy Meal." The *Chicago Sun-Times* seemed especially affronted by the tendency for Schumacher's camera to linger over Batman's buttocks and codpiece.

Warners, however, was deliriously happy; the franchise had never been in better financial shape. The *Wall Street Journal* predicted the film would bring Time-Warner over $1 billion in sales of licensed products alone and called *Batman Forever* a "synergistic gold mine."

"WAS THAT OVER-THE-TOP? I CAN NEVER TELL."

Batman Forever is a great big glitzy mess of a thing, albeit a fascinating one.

For all its cheeky garishness, all the neon and liquid light sticks and fluorescent paint, for all it gets howlingly wrong, *Batman Forever* does manage to get precisely one thing right.

Whenever Kilmer's Batman enters a scene by swinging into action on his Bat-rope, the moment looks about as perfect as Batman has ever or will ever look on film. Not even remotely realistic, of course—the angle of Kilmer's body is too severe, the speed and arc of his descent too controlled and even and photogenic—but Schumacher's exacting visual aesthetic ensures that as Batman's cape flutters behind him, it flutters exactly the way it would in a splash panel drawn by Neal Adams or Marshall Rogers.

For one brief, perfect moment, he gives viewers a living comic book.

That said, the screenwriters' stated intention to evoke the breezy, colorful Batman of the forties and fifties was always doomed to failure, for one very simple reason: Adam West.

He lingered still, haunting the periphery of the collective consciousness. Which is why *Batman Forever*'s deliberate tonal and narrative pastiche of Silver Age Batman comics never had any hope of registering on an audience of normals unfamiliar with its source material. Instead, what they reacted to—what critics and moviegoers alike logically assumed Schumacher was riffing on, given Jim Carrey and Tommy Lee Jones's willfully hammy performances as villains and the film's retina-sizzling color scheme—was the sixties television series, in all its groovy, go-go glory. Schumacher encouraged this interpretation with in-jokes so broadly telegraphed they were practically out-jokes—"Holey rusted metal, Batman!" Robin exclaims upon inspecting the ground surrounding the villain's lair. Like an overeager wizard's apprentice, *Batman Forever* had summoned a restless spirit from the brink of nonexistence and given it corporeal form—only this ghost rocked a blue satin cape and sported a bit of a paunch.

It happened at a time when hard-core fans, despite their quibbles with Burton's interpretation, had allowed themselves to bask in the cultural moment those films had ushered in. He was finally the badass they themselves had always longed to be, and what's more everyone knew it: in Burton's films he kicked ass; in the comics, he'd grown increasingly *extreme!*; and on the animated series he was nothing less than an elemental force.

But now this. Now Joel Schumacher had single-handedly undone three decades of painstaking work and dragged badass Batman back into the Day-Glo morass of POW! and ZAP!

That sense of loss, even betrayal, drove the ensuing nerd backlash.

Well. That and the gay stuff.

THE GAY STUFF

Look, the nipples are goofy. They're dumb. They're a joke.

But that's the thing: they are *literally* a joke.

Consider when and how they first appear: amid the "Batman suits up for action" montage that opens the movie. Burton had included similar sequences in his Batman films as a nod to the tendency of eighties action movies to pause the action and fetishize various pieces of gear as the hero loads, cocks, snaps, zips, and straps them to his person.

Schumacher, however, moves the needle from homage to parody when his camera lingers on various rubber-covered body parts: Arm! Codpiece! Butt! Nipple! He's not only lampooning *Commando* and *Rambo: First Blood Part II*, he's also taking a gentle swipe at superhero comics themselves, which idealize and objectify the physical body. The fact that the exquisitely buff male form hovers at the intersection between superhero iconography and gay porn is something Schumacher, at least, finds funny—and it's a joke he returns to often in both of his Batman films.

Just as William Dozier ensured that the sixties television show addressed itself to both kids who lapped up the derring-do and adults who keyed into the humor, *Batman Forever* also enjoyed a bifurcated appeal. Schumacher's two audiences, however, were split not by age but sensibility: 1) gay men and 2) everyone else.

In the years since the sixties television show had gone off the air, camp had come out of the closet. It called itself irony now; the era of elaborately coded messages, shibboleths, and innuendo, of embracing the tawdry and tasteless with a fervid flamboyance, of relegating oneself to the role of grotesque, sexless clown, was over. The Stonewall riots and the AIDS crisis had abraded those filigree edges away, leaving something harder, angrier, and more unambiguously and unapologetically sexual.

Thus the much-discussed "campiness" of *Batman Forever* feels fundamentally different than that of the old television show—less quaint and more defiant. Queerer.

The original *Batman Forever* casting call for Robin, for example, had specified an age range of fourteen to eighteen, which might have established Batman's bond to the Boy Wonder as strictly paternal. But Schumacher intentionally and gleefully steered into the homoerotic skid. He hired the twenty-four-year-old Chris O'Donnell as Robin and tricked him out with an earring, a tight muscle shirt, and a sneer. The result: a palpable shift in the Dynamic Duo's dynamic—from a-father-and-his-son to leather-daddy-and-his-piece-of-rough-trade.

Like the rest of the film, this change wasn't exactly subtle. It was also harmless—or at least was intended to be. Where *Batman Returns* had been kinky and brooding, Schumacher told interviewers he'd made a film that was "fun and sexy." Yes, okay, sure, maybe he'd thrown in a tradey Robin, a butt shot here or there, but it was all in fun, and it gave the gay guys and straight gals in the audience a quick, cheap laugh. Who could possibly begrudge him that?

A COMMUNITY OF COMMISERATION

Nerds could, that's who. Many had been disappointed in *Batman* and discouraged by *Batman Returns*, but *Batman Forever* was seen as a debasement.

As they had done for years, they descended on comics shops, convention panels, and letters pages to air their lists of grievances. By 1995, fanzines and the con circuit had made hard-core Bat-nerds—and comics nerds in general—members of a vast and ever-growing community of enthusiasts. They had formed fast friendships and bitter rivalries; they had sorted themselves into subniches of specialized interests: favorite characters, or artists, or writers, or story lines.

So by the time the Internet came along, they were way ahead of it.

Since the mideighties, nerd discussions had thrived in Usenet's rec.arts.comics communities, but as the personal computer found its way into more homes, the comics Internet ballooned. In the summer of 1995, as *Batman Forever* hit theaters, a Prodigy message boards user named Mike Doran began posting news items in a forum that would later grow into the comics site Newsarama. Later, Jonah Weiland created a message board to discuss the comic book miniseries *Kingdom Come* that became the website Comic Book Resources, and Harry Knowles launched Ain't It Cool News, a site devoted to rumors about upcoming films. The Web kept growing, and the comics Web kept pace. Hundreds of newsgroups and websites devoted to individual comics, characters, creators, and comics-related media sprang up, connected by vast "webrings" of affiliated content.

The advent of the Internet simply mapped an electronic, real-time infrastructure over established nerd networks. And just as the rise of comics shops had provided a safe harbor for adult nerds, a place where they could buy their *Amethyst, Princess of Gemworld* comic, far away from the sneers of grocery clerks, Internet message boards offered complete anonymity. Online personas could be created of any age, sex, gender, race, marital status, or political affiliation. It was discourse as RPG. Users for whom face-to-face social interaction proved trying or discombobulating could compose elegant, crystalline prose that elucidated their positions with cogent wit.

That combination of anonymity and mediated experience would prove both blessing and curse, but here at the beginning, as the early adopters flocked to the Bat-forums, it was mostly about cursing Joel Schumacher's name. These online commiseration-fests featured thread titles like "Batman deserves BETTER!" and "GIVE US YEAR ONE OR DON'T BOTHER" and, perhaps most pithily, "GAY!!!!!!!!!!!!" Despite the fervor of these caps-locked, superfluously exclamation-pointed exchanges, fannish discontent roiled and frothed away in this new online ghetto just as it always had in the real world, below the notice of the wider culture.

But that was all about to change.

Just weeks after *Batman Forever*'s record-breaking opening, Warners announced that it was fast-tracking a third Batman sequel scheduled to arrive in theaters in two years' time, to be helmed by Joel Schumacher.

THE ICE-PUNS COMETH

"I felt that what we were able to bring to *Batman Forever* was a lot of humor, color, and action," said Schumacher, "and if audiences liked that, we could bring them even more fun and games."

This time out, Peter Macgregor-Scott assumed the role of sole producer, officially nudging Tim Burton out of the franchise for good. Akiva Goldsman signed on as the sole screenwriter and he and Schumacher hatched the basic plot over the course of a flight to LA from the Mississippi set of *A Time to Kill.*

The studio gave Schumacher complete creative control and encouraged him to do what he'd done with *Batman Forever*, only more so. This, in fact, became the tagline for the next film: "More Heroes . . . More Villains . . . More Action." That hypertrophic impulse seeped into every aspect of production and unintentionally mirrored the steroidal bloat that had seized superhero storytelling in comics. An all-new Batcave set dwarfed those that came before, the better to house a new, larger Batmobile, a Bat-snowmobile, a Bat-fanboat, and two Bat-motorcycles.

The studio's merchandising division brought in representatives from Kenner Products to suggest new, toy-aisle-friendly hardware. Everything got bigger, including the Bat-nipples, which now poked out from the suits so pertly Batman could've hung his keys on them, and Batman and Robin's codpieces swelled to *Lysistrata*-like proportions.

This time, the production would pay no lip service to the comics. From the outset, Goldsman and Schumacher made it clear that the source material for Batman and Robin was the sixties television show. Goldsman's original draft was filled with references to the series, including a fight scene that depicted Batgirl shouting "Pow!" and "Zap!" with every punch, because as Goldsman said, "it just feels right."

Most of these jokes were later cut to make room for more ice puns, but Batgirl's very presence in the script was a nod to the television show—though her origin was tweaked by making her Alfred's niece, not Commissioner Gordon's daughter.

The original conception for Mr. Freeze was lifted from the animated series' Emmy-award-winning episode "Heart of Ice"—a brilliant scientist whose cold, emotionless affect conceals a burning desire to find a cure for his wife's terminal disease. Schumacher kept Freeze's backstory but ditched just about everything else in favor of a version that echoed the larger-than-life villains of the sixties television show. Given that Schumacher now saw Freeze as "big and strong, like he was carved out of a glacier," and that all of the actors who had assayed the role for the television series had given the character a Teutonic accent, casting Arnold Schwarzenegger proved inevitable. It came at a steep price, however. The role would be the highest-paid gig thus far in Schwarzenegger's lucrative career, earning him somewhere between $20 and $25 million, and a cut of the merchandising.

Uma Thurman was hired to bring Poison Ivy to the screen, a villainess of relatively recent vintage (having debuted in the comics in 1966) who'd come into her own on the animated series. Schumacher encouraged Thurman to forget her training and camp it up; the actress dutifully luxuriated into a role she thought of as equal parts Mae West and drag queen.

Contractual disputes over Val Kilmer's other commitments soured Schumacher on the actor, and George Clooney was signed to take over the role of Batman. Because *Batman and Robin* was shot on the same Warners lot as his television series *ER*, Clooney worked out a schedule to accommodate both: Monday through Thursday he was Dr. Doug Ross, and on Friday through Sunday he was the Dark Knight.

Well. Not the *Dark* Knight, per se. More like the Dusk Knight. "It's time for Batman to enjoy being Batman," Clooney said.

Schumacher echoed the actor's take. "This Batman is way too busy to still be tormented by the death of his parents."

As they'd done three times before, Warners trotted out Bob Kane to reassure the fans. "I feel George is the best Batman of all," he said in one interview. "He's suave, elegant, has a great profile with a strong chin, like the features of Batman in the comic books."

To normals, Kane's focus on Clooney's jawline may seem odd, but it was a coded message pitched squarely at the nerds who had railed against Michael Keaton's casting years before. Producer Michael Uslan himself had been among their number, until Burton had wearily admonished him that "a strong chin does not a Batman make."

Kane knew that the hard-core fans' oft-expressed fixation on the cinematic Batman's jawline was a marker for something deeper. Batman's costume is not Superman's, after all; in the age of muscled body armor, an actor disappears into the Batsuit completely—except for the chin. To fans, who now pore over every leaked detail from a film production with a messianic zeal, the actor's jawline represents the first indicator of the producer's commitment to the source material.

Kane was right: Clooney fit the visual bill, at least. Nerds had noticed all this talk of a lighter, more open, Marin County Batman, but for the moment—mollified, perhaps, by Clooney's chin dimple—they kept their powder dry.

Although filming began a month later than planned, Schumacher oversaw an efficient, amicable work environment and wrapped two weeks ahead of schedule. The studio had been so impressed with the machine Schumacher built that they green-lit *Batman 5* before he'd finished filming.

In February 1997, *Entertainment Tonight* aired the official *Batman and Robin* theatrical trailer for the first time, as they'd done for every other Batman film. The tried-and-true marketing strategy clicked into place immediately afterward. Warners spent $15 million on the de rigueur licensing deals (Frito-Lay, Kellogg's, Amoco, Taco Bell) and attendant marketing push. Over 250 *Batman and Robin*–affiliated products—including a rare Batgirl figure—were shipped to stores, and analysts projected Warners stood to make $1 billion on merchandise alone. "When it comes to licensing," said one analyst, "a Batman film is about the safest bet you can make."

But there was a new factor at play.

DIAL-UP DUDGEON

In his 2001 book *Batman Unmasked*, Bat-academician Will Brooker reproduces several comments posted to popular Batman message boards in the crucial months between the February release of *Batman and Robin*'s theatrical trailer and its July premiere.

On boards like Mantle of the Bat: The Bat-Board, a drumbeat of grievance and outrage was growing louder. A nostalgia for the "good old days" of Tim Burton's Batman emerged, as posters directed their increasingly monolithic antipathy at both Schumacher and the restless ghost of Adam West's Batman.

"I was floored at just how campy *Batman and Robin* is shaping up to be," said one poster. "I really prefer darker Batman as opposed to light, campy Batman."

"Will someone tell Warner Brothers that even little kids prefer Dark-night Batman compared to Caped Crusader Batman as offered in the 60s."

Booker notes that "these writers seem almost to construct themselves as marginalized unfortunates, helpless in the face of institutional decisions and the preferences of a wider, non-fan audience." This sense that their one true Batman had been ripped from their grasp could easily have been typed up on onionskin and mailed in to *Batmania* thirty years before. But in 1966, only a handful of comics fans had been sufficiently motivated to express their displeasure in fanzines and letter columns. Now there were many thousands, and the means to vent their displeasure required no patience or postage. An eager audience for their manifold opinions and outrage was always only a few keystrokes and a dial-up connection away.

Warners felt they could afford to ignore this fomenting online nerd-rage—until the day that, suddenly, they couldn't.

In the weeks leading up to the release of *Batman and Robin*, Harry Knowles's Ain't It Cool News site posted a series of blistering reviews from advance audience screenings. Day after day, excoriating takedowns appeared, many from hard-core Bat-fans who infused their prose with mocking disbelief.

The difference between the carping that went on over on forums like Mantle of the Bat and Knowles's extended crusade against the film was one of simple numbers. In May of 1997, Mantle of the Bat's hit counter—tracking the total number of visits the site had received since its launch—stood at 32,291. In that same month alone, Ain't It Cool News received over two million visits from nerds and normals alike.

A *New York Times* profile of Knowles that ran several months after

Batman and Robin premiered dubbed him "Hollywood's worst night-mare."

> The real threat is that Knowles's Web site . . . is starting to set the
> journalistic agenda in Hollywood. The advance buzz about a
> movie has an effect on stories and even reviews—and Knowles is
> affecting the buzz. "They printed a rumor that we were reshooting
> the ending of 'Batman and Robin,'" [Warners' head of film mar-
> keting Chris Pula] says. "Well, all of a sudden it was the buzz. Ev-
> eryone was calling. It was destructive. It was not true. And it woke
> me up to their influence."

In an interview with *People* magazine, the same Warners marketing
executive lamented the new state of affairs: "Now anybody with a computer is a newspaper. . . . One guy on the Internet could start enough of
a stir that causes a reactionary shift in the whole marketing program."
Within a month after giving these interviews, Pula was gone.

The film's promotional machine churned on, undaunted by the
souring buzz. The stars appeared on *Oprah, The Tonight Show*, and an
"exclusive E! *Batman and Robin* special."

When the already wounded film finally limped into theaters on June
20, reviews were universally negative. The *New York Times* mustered
some faint praise for Thurman's Poison Ivy but bemoaned the movie's
"nonstop glitter," while Siskel and Ebert called it a "tasteless bore" and
"dreary," respectively.[*]

But the only review nerds cared about was from Knowles, and what
it lacked in syntax and spelling it made up for in sheer frothing nerd-
fervor:

---

[*] Ebert betrayed his status as a true Batman nerd in his *Chicago Sun-Times*
piece, by taking a moment to stop midreview and dish about the Bat-jaw:
"Clooney has the best chin yet."

Then JOEL SHUMACHER's [sic] name falls upon the screen and the sounds of BOOS fill the theater. . . . BOOS for the director, I'm not familiar with this phenomenon. Has this happened before? Folks, I'm going to tell you to do something hideious [sic], something against my better judgement, but I simply have to tell you to see BATMAN & ROBIN. Why? After all my screams of agony, of pain, or mistrust of Joel Schumacher? Because no matter how bad you have heard this film is, nothing can prepare you for the sheer glorius [sic] travesty of the 200-megaton bomb of a film this is. This film is so bad, so awful, so vanity ridden with horrible over the top performances, that nothing I can say, can prepare you for it. This film will fill you with disbelief and rage if you are a long standing BATMAN fan, if you aren't, you'll be bored.

Over on Mantle of the Bat, "disbelief and rage" pretty much summed it up:

"You have got to be fucking kidding me. I hope they crucify Schumacher and hang him from the tallest building in Hollywood," wrote one poster.

"Schumaker [sic] you little piss ant!" said another. "Who the fuck gave you the right to direct anything remotely as cool as Batman! . . . [P]ick up a comic book you asinine fool? . . . What the fuck? And NIPPLES?"

Batman and Robin became the first Batman film not to break box-office records, coming in with the seventh-highest three-day opening take of $44 million—$10 million less than *Batman Forever*. The film suffered a precipitous 63 percent drop the following weekend and though it enjoyed considerable success overseas, with a total global take of $238 million, it only managed to muster a domestic take of $107 million.

Schumacher was convinced Ain't It Cool News had damned the film with its "yellow journalism" and in post-premiere interviews remained philosophical about the future. "I'd like to do one more, but I think we need to wait," he said before proceeding to invoke what was fast becoming his stock rationalization. "I feel I disappointed a lot of the older fans by being too conscious of the family aspect. I'd gotten tens of thousands of letters from parents asking for a film their children could go to."

"AN ANATOMICALLY CORRECT RUBBER SUIT PUTS *FIRE* IN A GIRL'S . . . LIPS!"

Let's note that Schumacher's version of "a film children could go to" is one in which a man is strapped to table, injected with poison, and turned into a monster; another man attempts to murder a woman by throwing her into glassware, only to be murdered himself; and a woman performs a striptease while offering up single entendres about her "honeypot" and being "slippery when wet."

The issue isn't the sex jokes or the violence. It's Schumacher's disingenuous insistence that what went wrong with the film was its need to cater to children, even as he defended the newly engorged nipples and crotches. "I will take responsibility for casting and glorifying beauty and sexuality," Schumacher later said. "That's part of the fun of a Batman comic book."

To place *Batman Forever* in context, let's allow that in its exuberant attempt to update the overblown camp sensibility of the 1966 Batman series, the film offers a take on Batman and his world that's as valid, as firmly grounded in the character's history, as any. A Batman who puts in appearances at gala fund-raisers and carries his own credit card must and should always stand shoulder to shoulder with the Batman who lurks in the grimy shadows of Gotham's warehouse district.

But the sheer overproduced excess of the film ignores the fact that the feather-boa camp of the sixties hardened into the gimlet-eyed irony of the eighties and nineties. Florid, scenery-chewing villainy and overripe puns no longer landed on audiences the way they had in 1966. The culture had embraced other, less noisy, less effortful ways to mock the things it loved—a sharper and more knowing species of sarcasm that

valued rigorousness and restraint, and that never wanted to be seen trying too hard. By doubling down on *Batman Forever* and infusing the
film with the swing-for-the-fences broadness, exaggeration, and Ka-
buki-like emotionalism that were the hallmarks of camp, Schumacher
hadn't updated the effortlessly hip '66 series. Instead, he'd produced a
film that seemed bloated and sweaty, frenetic yet inert, dated and stul-
tifyingly square.

CRYING FOR BLOOD

Despite its less-than-anticipated box office, *Batman and Robin* went
on to make the Warners marketing and licensing departments happy,
bringing in an estimated $125 million from toys, accessories, and cloth-
ing. Nerd-rage or no, they had no intention of ending the franchise.
They'd already hired Mark Protosevich to start work on the screenplay
for *Batman 5* (working title: *Batman Triumphant*), which was set to be
directed by Schumacher and fast-tracked for a summer 1999 release.
When the Internet wasn't hooting with derision at *Batman and Robin*, it
was buzzing with rumors about the next film's plot and casting.

Protosevich's screenplay saw Batman tangling with the Scarecrow
and the animated series' own Harley Quinn (presented here as the Joker's daughter, not his girlfriend), and included a scene in which Batman
hallucinates the return of the Joker. The tone was darker, grittier, the
scale smaller, closer in.

As the rumors caromed across cyberspace—Howard Stern as the
Scarecrow! Madonna as Harley Quinn!—the movie websites Coming
Attractions and Dark Horizons, which happily devoted huge swaths of
their bandwidths to publishing unsubstantiated claims from "industry
sources," got fed up with the flood and refused to post more *Batman 5*
news and speculation.

Meanwhile, online outrage at Joel Schumacher continued to fester, erupting into entire websites devoted, with single-minded purpose, to wresting the Batman franchise from the director's hands. The

matter-of-factly-named Anti-Schumacher Batman Website and Bring Me the Head of Joel Schumacher were places for aggrieved fans to gather, list Schumacher's manifold offenses against Bat-kind, make and defend their personal casting suggestions, lovingly describe scenes they ached to see on-screen, and hark back to the good old days of Tim Burton.

"Tim Burton, whether you think so or not, had the unique vision for Batman," said one poster to the Bat-boards. "Joel Schumacher (who I'd personally like to beat about the head & shoulders) wanted to turn it into the 60's T.V. show drugged with sexual inneudos [sic]. Thus, he DESTROYED the Batman franchise."

Those posters whose vitriol did not devolve into crypto-homophobic ranting about nipples and butts tended to rail instead against the film's positioning of their beloved character as a product in the marketplace.

"We grew up on Batman, and to see him exploited for the commercial marketing (which is just what is happening) is infuriating," read the home page of Bring Me the Head of Joel Schumacher.

And there was this, perhaps the most unambiguous expression of the nerd zeitgeist there is: "The problem is non-Batfans."

Just as the Bat-fans of 1966 looked with derisive suspicion at the masses who tuned into *Batman* for what they considered the wrong reasons, so the Bat-fans of 1997 ached to reclaim Batman as their own. The wider world had distorted their one true Dark Knight beyond recognition. It was time, in their view, for Batman to abandon the mass consciousness, retreat to the comics page where he belonged, and lick his wounds, if not his nipples.

This species of seething resentment has always lurked in the dark, insular heart of nerddom. For long years, the heedless enthusiasm nerds felt for their pursuits had marked them as the Other, and made them objects of scorn and mockery. So they turned inward.

But the nerds remembered. And made sure the normals did, too.

Nerd culture is often open and inclusive, when it is powered by the desire to seek out others who share common interests and enthusiasms.

But nerdish passion is strong and unmindful; its very nature is to obliterate dispassion, nuance, ambiguity, and push human experience to either edge of a binary extreme: *My thing is the best. Your thing is the worst.*

Moreover, if you do not love my thing in the same way, to the same degree, and for exactly the same reasons that I do, you are doing it wrong.

Even in 1997, at the dawning of the Internet age, fan discourse was already beginning to devolve to vociferously held positions shouted across networks.

ASSORTED ABORTED ATTEMPTS

When George Clooney announced his desire to move beyond the Batsuit, Warners officially scuttled *Batman Triumphant*. In the months and years that followed, Joss Whedon pitched a new Batman origin, and rumors swirled that the Wachowskis were approached to write a *Matrix*-y script, at a time when many *Matrix*-y scripts were circulating around Hollywood. There was also *Batman: The Musical*, a never-mounted Broadway extravaganza that was to be directed by Tim Burton himself.* Joel Schumacher was still hustling as well. In 1998 he pitched a smaller, darker, edgier take on Batman—an adaptation of *Batman: Year One*.

Warners didn't bite, as they were considering another, similarly dark Batman pitch called *Batman: DarKnight*, featuring an older Bruce Wayne who comes out of retirement when Batman is falsely accused of murder. Sensing Warners' ambivalence, Schumacher officially left the franchise in 1999. In 2000 the studio announced that they'd passed on *DarKnight* to consider two other possibilities: a live-action version of their Batman-of-the-future animated series *Batman Beyond*, and an

---

* It seems somehow important to note here that the Joker's big number contained the memorable lyric "Where does Abercrombie & Fitch get all those boys / And where does [Batman] get those wonderful toys?"

adaptation of *Batman: Year One* written by Frank Miller himself, to be directed by Darren Aronofsky.

The live-action *Batman Beyond* didn't get past the script stage, and a planned WB network series called *Bruce Wayne*, starring a teenaged Wayne as he travels the world to gain the skills he would later use as Batman, was sidetracked when Warners executives worried that it would conflict with Aronofsky's theatrical film.

There is little chance it would have, however, given what Aronofsky and Miller came up with. "My pitch was *Death Wish* or *The French Connection* meets Batman," Aronofsky told writer David Hughes in the book *Tales from Development Hell*.

Before it could gain traction with the studio, in 2001 a poster who claimed to have seen a copy of Miller's first draft published a scathing review on Ain't It Cool News. The studio denied the script in question was authentic, but the damage was done, and the project foundered for another year before being officially scuttled.

That same year, *Se7en* screenwriter Andrew Kevin Walker got the go-ahead on a screenplay for *Batman vs. Superman*, to be directed by Wolfgang Petersen. Walker's script adopted a kitchen-sink approach, as a returned-from-the-dead Joker kills Bruce Wayne's girlfriend, sending Batman on a mission of vengeance that only Superman (about to divorce Lois Lane) can hope to halt. Ultimately, however, the project collapsed when its chief sponsor left the studio.

THE EARTH MOVES

Meanwhile, the Dark Knight struggled to weather the ongoing comics bust. In a series of one-shot comics he'd dutifully teamed up with other publishers' more popular properties, basking in the reflected glory, and better sales numbers, of *Captain America, Judge Dredd, Aliens, Predators,* and others. In 1995 DC had added a fifth ongoing Batman title, the quarterly anthology *Batman Chronicles*, to its output, which meant that a new Batman comic now appeared on store shelves every single week.

The following year, the four-issue anthology miniseries *Batman: Black and White* commissioned the industry's top writers and artists to create stripped-down, stand-alone Batman stories rendered in pen and ink, freed of the shackles of continuity. The result was formally innovative and stylistically adventurous, attributes not associated with mainstream superhero comics of the day.

But in a yearly sales chart top-heavy with titles like *Spawn: The Impaler* and *Deathblow and Wolverine*—comics that routinely sold between 150,000 and 200,000 copies—the premiere issue of *Batman: Black and White* sold less than 60,000 issues and slunk in near the bottom, at number 166.

In December 1996 writer Jeph Loeb and artist Tim Sale launched the thirteen-issue miniseries *Batman: The Long Halloween*. This sprawling riff on *The Godfather* enriched the world of Gotham City by spotlighting its two rival mob families in ways that would later provide Christopher Nolan's films with narrative grist. It also offered an issue-by-issue whistle-stop tour of Batman's rogues' gallery. *Long Halloween* returned to the character's crime-pulp roots and was hailed by comics critics and fans alike; it spawned two sequels.

Batman's most high-profile comics success, however, came in the pages of writer Grant Morrison and artist Howard Porter's relaunched *Justice League of America* series. *JLA*, unlike other Batman titles, managed to break into the chart of the year's top-selling books, albeit at number sixty-seven. In it, Morrison threw a series of cosmic apocalypses at DC Comics' "Big Seven" characters, envisioning the publisher's best-known heroes as a pantheon of Greek gods, with Batman in the role of Hades. Morrison's firm grip on the character ensured that Batman's status as the sole nonpowered member of the JLA served the storytelling and turned him into the breakout star of this fevered eschatological riot of a book. In Morrison's hands, the Dark Knight became the World's Greatest Tactician, a laconic and ruthlessly effective team leader whose contingency plans came with their own contingency plans.

This characterization would prove hugely influential over the next few years, both within the comics and across other media, because the great wheel of Batman's narrative was once again turning.

Since his very first appearance, Batman had twice churned through a three-phase cycle: from Lone Avenger to Robin's Father to Head of an Extended Bat-Family, and then back to starting position. And now, as had happened in the fifties, and again in the seventies, Batman once again assumed the role of Bat-paterfamilias* to an extended and frequently fractious coterie of costumed crime fighters that included Robin, Nightwing, Huntress, Oracle, Catwoman, Azrael, and others.

He would very soon need every ally he could get. In the main Bat-books, editor Denny O'Neil and his writers were about to unleash another massive event that would keep Batman occupied for more than two years.

The seeds had been planted in a story line that stretched through twelve issues of the Bat-titles in March and April of 1966, when a virus ravages Gotham, causing the city to be quarantined. In a subsequent fourteen-issue story line, the virus mutates, sending Batman and his fellow crime fighters to trace it to its sinister source: Ra's al Ghul. Both story lines illustrated how easily Gotham City's entire infrastructure could descend into chaos.

This was followed, in March 1998, by chaos descending: in an impressive eighteen-chapter feat of editorial coordination, every Bat-title simultaneously depicted a massive 7.6 earthquake leveling Gotham City and obliterating both Wayne Manor and the Batcave. The ensuing yearlong story line "No Man's Land" features Batman and his allies struggling to keep the peace in a Gotham cut off from the mainland and abandoned by the American government and its people.

The story line provided editor Denny O'Neil with the literal realization of his long-held editorial desire to isolate Batman and his world from the rest of the DC Universe. Its emotional climax—a tense

---

* Baterfamilias?

stand-off between Batman and Jim Gordon, as the impassioned Dark Knight convinces Gordon not to take revenge on the Joker after the madman brutally murders Gordon's wife—reaffirmed O'Neil's vision of Batman as a hero who values justice over all. Thus, the final chapter of "No Man's Land" was the final chapter of O'Neil's term as Batman's most influential writer and editor. Having rescued the Dark Knight from near-oblivion, re-created him, and steadily navigated him through some of the choppiest waters the industry had ever seen, O'Neil retired, to be replaced as Bat-editor by Bob Schreck.

DAYS OF FUTURE BATS

One odd by-product of the black clouds that continued to gather over the comics industry was a tendency for creators to tell stories that pitched Batman far into the future, as if to save him from the encroaching doom. However, the futures depicted in these tales of Dark Knights yet to come seemed just as grim as the present, if not more so. In 1996, for example—the same year that Marvel Comics filed for bankruptcy in the face of staggering debts—Mark Waid and Alex Ross produced the four-issue miniseries *Kingdom Come*. Written as a comment on the nihilistic, amoral heroes who now dominated the sales charts, the comic chronicled an apocalyptic clash between an idealistic Superman who'd given up on the world, a villain-led faction of bloodthirsty superhumans, and the ruthlessly pragmatic Batman, playing both sides.

Three years later, in January 1999, a vision of Batman's future with a more millennial tinge premiered on the WB Network. *Batman Beyond*, created by the same team behind *Batman: The Animated Series*, was launched when network suits raised concerns that the older, critically acclaimed series was hitting the wrong demographic. Older viewers were tuning in, not the young children whom advertisers so prized. The decision was made to start over with a new concept: a teenaged version of Batman to attract the preteen audience. Bruce Timm and producer Glen Murakami, unwilling to abandon the core tenets of the character, devised a means to keep their Bruce Wayne in the mix. They set the series in a technologically advanced future, where an elderly, infirm Wayne recruits a hotheaded teen to be an all-new Batman.

They filled the show with gifts for the fans, making Barbara Gordon the police commissioner who distrusted Bruce Wayne for reasons kept tantalizingly undisclosed, and threw in plenty of oblique hints over the ultimate fates of familiar characters like Robin and Nightwing. Mostly, however, the series focused on young Terry McGinnis's fractious relationship with his stern and demanding mentor, and explored the combination of new, colorful foes and visually striking action that the science fiction setting permitted.

At first, nerds were skeptical of the show's direction, but it didn't take long for *Batman Beyond*'s combination of tight, punchy stories and dazzling visuals to win them over. This was not their one true Batman; gone were the familiar pulp affectations of noir and crime drama—but it was *a* Batman, albeit one tinged with a cyberpunk aesthetic. It soon became clear that the series' organizing principle—to attract younger viewers—wasn't working. The show's story lines were just as complex as they'd always been, its tone just as dark, and the viewership remained just as old and nerdy.

In fact, a 2000 direct-to-video feature called *Batman Beyond: Return of the Joker* proved so dark—involving flashback scenes of Robin being tortured by the Clown Prince of Crime—that the studio demanded a lengthy series of cuts and even went back in to digitally remove blood from several scenes before the film was released. The story of the aged Batman's final confrontation with his archnemesis, *Return of the Joker* offered fans who'd faithfully followed the animated series from its beginning a powerful emotional payoff. Small wonder that they petitioned Warners for a chance to see the producer's unadulterated version; in 2002 they got their wish, and an uncut version became the first animated Batman film to earn a PG-13 rating.

Millions tuned into *Batman Beyond* and its 2001 successor, *Justice League*, which deposited Batman on a team of DC's "Big Seven" heroes.

The characterization of Batman seen on this series, and its retooled follow-up, *Justice League Unlimited,* owed a great deal to the team dynamic Morrison had laid out in *JLA*: a headstrong, unflappable leader who seems to possess the superpower of always being right—and whose disposition introduced plenty of chewy personality conflicts.

But back in comics shops, it was Frank Miller's vision of a future Batman that sent the Dark Knight sailing back up to the top of the sales charts again.

Fifteen years after *The Dark Knight Returns,* in December 2001, Miller returned to Batman in the three-issue prestige-format miniseries *The Dark Knight Strikes Again,* or, as it became known to fans and pros alike, *DK2.* A sequel to his 1986 magnum opus that defined Batman for a generation, *DK2* once again featured the coloring of Lynn Varley. Instead of the subtle gouaches that had provided *The Dark Knight Returns* with its evocative visual aesthetic, Varley colored *DK2* digitally and intentionally garishly. The book's hues vibrantly clash and sizzle before the eye, producing an assault on the senses matched by Miller's rough, jittery line work and background-free layouts. The book has a rushed appearance that aims to evoke a feeling of urgency but succeeds ultimately in producing a sense of narrative chaos.

Miller's story is a faint and thready signal that only too willfully gets lost in the visual noise: following the events of *The Dark Knight Returns,* Batman resurfaces to free his fellow Justice Leaguers, who have been imprisoned under the dictatorial regime of Lex Luthor. The fate of Dick Grayson is finally revealed,* and Batman is presented as a military leader dedicated to the overthrow of the status quo and who is willing to see thousands, even millions, die in the pursuit of that goal.

But the story isn't the point. *DK2* was poorly reviewed in the comics press for what was perceived as its slapdash quality, which many critics

---

* He's become a genetically mutated, superhero-murdering shape-shifter/maniac. Naturally.

and fans read as Miller's cynical attempt to cut corners and run to the bank with his check. Perhaps anticipating the backlash, Miller talked to comics journalist Sean T. Collins as the first issue appeared in stores and laid out *DK2*'s mission statement:

> I'm not trying to do some Tennessee Williams play in costume. I mean, that's not what this material is. This is opera. It's got to be large. Superheroes don't become drunk drivers—they destroy planets. It's just a different scale. It's Wagnerian. You can play on themes that are very real in day-to-day life, but they all have to be translated into this larger-than-life mode. If I want to do naturalism, nobody's going to be wearing tights.

Ultimately, however, it's that Wagnerian impulse that blunts *DK2*'s impact. Miller's intent is once again broadly satiric—but here it's so broad that it seems to target everything and nothing at once. *The Dark Knight Returns* had offered a larger-than-life—but very specific and very considered—vision of Batman to engage and unsettle the wider world beyond the nerd ghetto. But *DK2* says nothing of note about Batman, or about superheroes, or about society.

And yet, *DK2* was a phenomenon of the kind comics shops hadn't seen in years. It became the top-selling comic of 2001 and the second-highest seller of 2002—accomplishments made more impressive when its $7.95-per-issue cover price is considered. The first issue sold over 187,000 copies—more than four times the number of copies the regular *Batman* comic sold in the same month. Poor reviews in the comics press could do nothing to slow the book's momentum. Neither could abysmal in-store word of mouth and such dispassionate online assessments as "This comic is so fuck-backwards retarded that almost every page has something on it that makes me want to pull my eyeballs from my head and throw them at Frank Miller." None of it mattered: nerds heard "Frank Miller's Batman" and they came, and they bought.

For the first time in a decade, the total number of comics sold in a given year inched up instead of plummeting down.

A STUDY IN CONTRASTS

The success of *The Dark Knight Strikes Again* speaks to the central role that nostalgia plays in the emotional life of nerds. The old saw that any nerd's favorite comics are whatever he or she was reading at age thirteen carries the weight of truth. A collective nostalgia for Miller's Batman had driven *DK2*'s surging sales. Nerds who'd come of age during the darkest years of the early-nineties comics boom, however, now found a twelve-issue story line targeted directly at them, which kicked off in the December 2002 issue of *Batman* (#608).

Written by Jeph Loeb, "Hush" closely followed the formula of his earlier *Long Halloween* miniseries, with its narrative switchbacks and red herrings, serial guest appearances by every major friend and foe of the Batman cast, and a climactic reveal of the mastermind behind the story line's credulity-straining schemes. But what truly made "Hush" the ripest and most pungent form of nerd-bait was its art, drawn by Jim Lee.

Jim Lee had been a central figure in the comics boom of the late eighties and early nineties—his steroidal men, with their grimaces and their puzzling superfluity of ammo pouches, and his women, with their ability to risk spinal torsion by simultaneously aiming their breasts and their buttocks at the reader, helped usher in the era's fashion for visual excess. His every page was a pinup, and the only body language his characters spoke fluently was that of the bodybuilder's pose-down.

"Hush" featured an endless series of Lee's signature go-for-broke splash pages. Nerds ate it up and asked for more: eight of the story arc's twelve chapters were number one sellers (the other four landed in second place), representing sales of over 150,000 copies per month, on average. Such numbers were fractions of those seen during the speculator-driven comics boom, of course, but their relative month-to-month consistency offered some hope that the comics industry's implosion was finding its level and stabilizing at last.

The comic series *Gotham Central*, which premiered in February 2003, was everything the slickly commercial "Hush" story line was not. A grounded, visceral, street-level police procedural, *Gotham Central* focused on the unglamorous day-to-day lives of the men and women of Gotham City's Major Crimes Unit. The genius of the book was its prosaic, process-oriented depiction of life in Gotham City, where outlandish psychopathic murderers lurk around every corner. Batman made only rare appearances in the book—many members of its cast looked on him with resentment—but a typical *Gotham Central* story arc found MCU detectives investigating the aftermath of a supervillain's confrontation with the Dark Knight and picking up the pieces of the lives that had been shattered in its wake.

Ed Brubaker and Greg Rucka split the writing duties, with Brubaker chronicling the GCPD's night shift and Rucka the day. They shared Michael Lark's heavy, claustrophobic, and decidedly unpretty line work, which underscored the book's status as the true spiritual successor to *Batman: Year One*.

Despite considerable critical acclaim, in a comics marketplace besotted by flashier, more pulchritudinous pursuits, *Gotham Central* struggled to find an audience.

KNIGHT VISIONS

The years of waiting for Batman to return to the big screen had passed fitfully for the nation's nerds. They didn't begrudge a few years to let the memetic field go fallow, but *Batman and Robin* was now six years gone. Finally the movie gossip sites began to toss around a new name: Christopher Nolan, whose 2000 film *Memento* offered a quirky central mystery couched in a meditation on memory and identity.

But nothing was confirmed, and nerd patience was wearing thin. Which is why, when special effects sculptor Sandy Collora screened his modest, $30,000 eight-minute short *Batman: Dead End* at San Diego Comic-Con on July 19, 2003, nerds and normals alike read about it the next day on Ain't It Cool News and dozens of other sites.

Collora, a protégé of special effects artist Stan Winston, outfitted a bodybuilder in an old-school, skintight gray tights/black trunks Batman outfit, painstakingly sculpted a cowl that vividly evoked the comics, and put this eerily realized Batman through a brutal, expertly choreographed back-alley brawl under pouring rain. The fact that Batman's opponents, in this fevered fanboy cinematic wet dream, were Punishers and Aliens made the whole affair seem more than a little goofy, but it certainly helped stoke nerdly passions.

Batman: Dead End was little more than a demo reel for Collora's directorial skills, but its attention to the essential visual elements of the Dark Knight tapped into the hard-core fan's thirst to see their hero in action again, stripped of the sundry baroque distractions Burton and Schumacher had so doggedly affixed to him.

As impressively iconic as Collora's Batman was, there was another version of the Dark Knight on comics stands that same summer that spoke even more eloquently to the character's enduring appeal. Well, versions, technically.

The crossover comic *Planetary/Batman: Night on Earth* seemed, on the surface, at least, like many of the cynically tossed-off team-up books in which the Dark Knight had put in a dutiful appearance. *Planetary*, a team book launched in 1999, followed a small group of super-humans on a multidimensional quest to uncover "the secret history of the world"—a task that put them face-to-face with analogues of Doc Savage, the Fantastic Four, Captain Marvel, and Batman himself.

Writer Warren Ellis and artist John Cassaday exploited the book's alternate-realities conceit to bring the Planetary team in contact with several different versions of Batman. As wave after wave of reality-altering energy surges through Gotham City, the Batman of 2003 morphs suddenly into the paunchy, civic-minded Adam West Batman, who subsequently transforms into the massive Frank Miller Dark Knight, who is replaced by the dynamic O'Neil/Adams Batman, who shifts into the original Bob Kane/Bill Finger Bat-Man.

Ellis's point—a controversial one among many of the most vocal adherents to the "badass Batman" school of fandom—is that all of these versions are Batman. They are all equally true, equally valid, because it's his motivation that matters, not his methods.

It's an argument Ellis drives home by closing the book on a brief speech delivered by the Dark Knight to John Black, a criminal whose parents were killed. The speech serves as an elegant summation and distillation of who Batman is, who Batman must always be, no matter the vicissitudes of his time and the changing tastes of his audience. It expresses the most important and enduring thing about him: the specific quality of hope, beaten but unbowed, by which he is both driven and defined:

BLACK: How do you cope?

BATMAN: Do you remember your parents?

BLACK: Yes.

BATMAN: Do you remember their smiles?

BLACK: Yes.

BATMAN: Do you remember the times when they made you feel safe?

BLACK: Yes.

BATMAN: That's what you hold on to. That's what you can do for other people. You can give them safety. You can show them they're not alone. That's how you make the world make sense. And if you can do that—you can stop the world from making people like us. And no one will have to be scared any more.

8

Trilogy of Terror (2005–2012)

Why so serious?

—THE JOKER, *THE DARK KNIGHT* (2008)

In the eight years that passed between the release of Joel Schumacher's *Batman and Robin* and the premiere of Christopher Nolan's *Batman Begins*, the world changed.

In the 1997 of *Batman and Robin*, the World Wide Web was still largely a place by nerds, for nerds, where early adopters gathered on message boards to debate and dissect their passions, often in a language deliberately constructed to be impenetrable to noobs.

It was a time before YouTube, Google, Facebook, and even MySpace, before the ascendance of blogs. Even the towering cultural milestone that would come to be known as the Hampster Dance lay still one year off in the Internet's golden, unimagined future. And while more normals visited the Web of 1997 than ever before, they did so to passively consume its content at the *New York Times*, *Salon*, or the just-launched *Drudge Report*, or simply to consume, via Amazon and eBay.

In 1997, only 37 percent of American homes had access to the Internet. But this figure was increasing by roughly five million homes annually. Just four years later, in fact, nearly 60 percent of American homes were wired. During this period, Web traffic soared and millions of pages were added to message boards and sites like Wikipedia, which launched in 2001, while the number and variety of URLs devoted entirely to niche interests and hobbies surged as well. Suddenly, a single click of a mouse could yield home-brewing tips, sewing patterns, poker strategies, porn, medieval agrarian history, focaccia recipes, porn, instructions for maintaining a saltwater aquarium, and porn. The once-prohibitively-high barriers to entry that had cordoned off specialized areas of interest like wine appreciation and the Batman canon began to crumble, their gatekeepers sent packing.

Now anyone could brief themselves on a previously arcane subject in minutes and, by connecting with others in like-minded forums, fan the flame of their interest into a blazing, all-consuming inferno. The time of passive cultural consumption was over, replaced by a new age when even the most idle curiosity could and would get chased down ever-branching rabbit holes of fact and opinion.

And with these changes came another, larger shift, specific to popular culture fandoms. Throughout modern history, the mostly male cohort of nerds had received a given narrative's characters and plot with deference and treated them as sacrosanct, inviolate, fixed in a permanent stasis. The flow of information ran downhill, from publisher to reader, filmmaker to moviegoer, and any subsequent thought experiments or disputes that arose among nerds came from their strict but competing interpretations of the text in question. "We know that Batman would beat Wolverine in a fight," one fan might say to another, "because in 2000's *JLA: Tower of Babel* it is revealed that Batman keeps extensive files on all heroes and that said files include information on how to neutralize their powers. QED."

The nerd derived a very specific breed of pleasure from this fetishization of narrative, which extended to the physical object as well. Comics and toys were now precious treasures intended not to be read or played with but preserved intact, unsullied by human hands. Hence the obsession with bagging, boarding, and chronologically cross-referencing every issue of *Batman Family*, and with proudly displaying mint-in-box Boba Fett on a high shelf away from children, pets, and direct sunlight.

A cottage industry arose whereby experts assigned comics issues a grade based upon their physical condition and then permanently encased them in slabs of Lucite to keep them from losing their value—a process that, symbolically enough, transformed them forever from stories loved by children to knickknacks coolly appraised by teams of adults.

But this was not and had never been the whole story. In the fanzines of the sixties and seventies, alongside the familiar nerd disputes, price guides, and exhaustive inventories of every Golden Age appearance of favorite characters, some contributors had begun to offer something new—something that displayed a subtly different attitude toward the characters they loved.

Instead of simply *receiving* stories about Captain Kirk, or The Doctor, or Batman, these contributors created their own. Within a few short years this movement had birthed a full-fledged genre with the blandly descriptive name of fan fiction.

Written by and for a predominantly female audience, these stories played with genre conventions as often as they slavishly re-created them, interrogated new narrative possibilities, and challenged the numerous implicit and previously unquestioned assumptions coded into characters' relationships, sexual and otherwise. The result was something the historically male nerd audience had never experienced: an ongoing interactive dialogue with beloved fictional characters. "The culture talks to [fan fiction writers]," novelist Lev Grossman would say in 2011, "and they talk back to the culture in its own language."

Such deconstructive dialogues had taken place in editorial offices among professional creators before, as when *Mad* magazine spoofed Superman or James Bond. But fan fiction was the work of unpaid amateurs, and satire was rarely its aim. Instead, fan fiction writers approached their craft with an unalloyed, deadly serious, achingly nerdy zeal and purpose. They longed to get their hands on the characters they loved and mix things up, to play and tweak and slyly subvert, to eschew the tidy taxonomies and rigid subcategorizations so rigorously policed by male nerds and get *messy*.

For more than three decades, fan fiction writers had shared their work in self-published zines purchased or traded through the mail or at cons. In the earliest days of the Internet, fanfic forums devoted to specific characters and properties flourished. In 1998 came the launch of FanFiction.net, a comprehensive host site that allowed fanfic writers from across many fandoms to upload their stories into a single search-able online archive that required no technical or coding expertise. By 2002, the site had become the public face of the burgeoning fan fiction community and the focus of lengthy profiles in *Time* and *USA Today*—coverage that drew even more contributors and readers to that site, and to the growing community.

Fittingly, the first Batman fanfic posted to the site, in April 1999, keyed off the existing comics' continuity to retell Batman's origin. Oth-ers quickly followed, some of which riffed on the relationship dynamics of the Bat-family, some of which retold classic story lines from a minor character's perspective, and many of which pitted Batman against in-congruous foes like Wonder Woman, Spider-Man, and the pilots from *Mobile Suit Gundam.*

In 2002, attendance at San Diego Comic-Con International swelled from 53,000 to 63,000—a figure that represented its largest-ever one-year jump in ticket sales. As attendance increased, so did the number and variety of attendees who walked the floor in elaborately designed costumes. Cosplay had been a part of cons since their very earliest days, but each year brought a fresh influx of more fantastic and painstakingly wrought costumes.

Here again, two separate strains emerged: a male-dominated con-tingent that prized the rigorous and exacting reproduction of costumes, props, and characters from established properties, and a weirder, queerer cosplay community that assumed a less demanding and more playful approach. The latter community of cosplayers instead views the canon-ical texts of a given fandom as mere jumping-off points. Enter: Pimp Vader, Gender-flipped Wonder Woman, and Steampunk Ghostbuster.

What these two very different approaches have in common is a sincere desire for participatory engagement, a wish to enter the story and forge a personal, intimate, and emotional connection to the character. Far more personal, more intimate, and more emotional, these cosplayers believe, than is achieved by passively consuming the story.

The division between cosplay that prizes exactitude and cosplay that prizes attitude extends into Gotham City as well. Most Batman cosplayers have historically sought to re-create, down to the most infinitesimal detail, the look and feel of the comics or the films. Yet there have always been those who use cosplay to challenge this nerdish rage for order, the normative drive to reduce the broad and endlessly mutable concept of Batman to a single grim, gritty "canonical" version.

The more adamantly that nerds—and DC Comics, for that matter—insisted that loner, badass Batman was somehow the one true Batman, the more they ensured that other iterations of the character would reassert themselves around the edges. This is why, year after year, the brooding Batman of the comics and films grudgingly shares the con floor with versions of himself and his colleagues that have been wiped from comics continuity or disavowed by hard-core fans: a portly man dressed as Victor Buono's King Tut from the sixties *Batman* television series poses for a photo op; a toddler dressed as Bat-Mite gazes in wonder around the PlayStation booth.

Fanfic and cosplay are fandom's twin release valves: they evince and encourage an inclusive playfulness that other aspects of nerd culture shun; they tease and interrogate fandom in ways that open it up and make it both more engaged and more engaging.

Batman's comic book publisher, DC Comics, has recently expended tremendous effort to attract new audiences by offering new story lines and one-shots touted as "great jumping-on points" and serially rebooting their entire narrative universe to dispose of history and continuity deemed complicated and off-putting. Their hard-core, predominantly male readership is aging—a 2012 industry report estimates the average age at thirty-eight years old—and DC Comics understandably seeks a more diverse consumer base.

It's instructive to look at how the nerd community changed between the 1997 of *Batman and Robin* and the 2005 of *Batman Begins*. It was during this time that fanfic and cosplay—and the playful, slyly subversive spirit they engender—began to truly infiltrate nerd culture. The homophobic outrage over Schumacher's Bat-nipples was a function of how monolithic the online Batman fan base looked at that time, but in 2005 there were more, and more varied, voices in the mix. Had *Batman and Robin* come out eight years later, the hard-core nerds would have hated it just as much as they had in 1997, but theirs would have been one reaction among many. The world had changed.

Warners didn't know this, however. Which is why, still stinging from *Batman and Robin*'s critical and commercial drubbing, they eagerly accepted Christopher Nolan's pitch to make a "serious, grounded" Batman film and, as they had in 1989, proceeded to target it squarely at the very hardest core of the hard-core Batman fan base.

BATMAN BEGINS BEGINS

David Goyer's comic book guy knew something was up.

The manager of Goyer's local comics shop in LA was on friendly terms with the screenwriter, so when, in the summer of 2003, he noticed Goyer buying a thick stack of Batman comics and graphic novels, he called him out. "You're writing a new Batman movie, aren't you?" he asked.

Goyer denied it and hurriedly left the store.

In fact, he'd been meeting with Christopher Nolan for weeks in the director's garage to hash out the story that would reintroduce Batman to the cinema. Nolan had sold his notion of a Batman film to Warners as a pitch, without a script.

Occasionally, the two men would go for a walk through nearby Griffith Park to Bronson Canyon—site of the cave mouth used as the entrance to the Batcave in the sixties series.

These oft-repeated anecdotes, among several others, were part of

Warner Bros.' concerted effort to establish the film's Batman bona fides among the hard-core fans. In publicity materials, licensing presentations, and press junket interviews, everyone involved in the production—Goyer, Nolan, the producers, and the assembled cast—hit the same talking points, again and again:

"I want to tell the origin with a certain degree of gravity, and in a more grounded way than what has been done before," Nolan said.

Exactly as DC Comics had done in 1970 in the wake of the Batman television series, Warners now set out on a mission of course correction. Their first priority was to publicly abjure Schumacher's garish and cartoony—and kinda gay—interpretation of the character and redirect the focus onto the comics themselves. This was no coincidence, as academic Will Brooker recounts in *Hunting the Dark Knight: Twenty-First Century Batman.*

"While the comic book industry may be the poor cousin to cinema in terms of cultural status and economic returns," Brooker writes, "film producers know that comic fans have a voice and power disproportionate to their number. There may not be many of them, but they're loud, and they can kick up a stink . . . the fans are respected, and courted, as a small but vocal pressure group."

The filmmakers began by seizing every available opportunity to tout the new screenplay's direct connection to the comics. Burton and Schumacher had famously rolled their eyes at the source material, but Nolan and Goyer swore undying fealty to Batman's comic book provenance. And not just any comics, but precisely those grim, gritty Batman comics the hard-core fan base prized so highly.

Batman Begins's first act follows the rough outline of a one-off story by Denny O'Neil and Dick Giordano published in 1989. That story, "The Man Who Falls," was, in turn, inspired by a scene in Frank Miller's *The Dark Knight Returns,* in which young Bruce falls into a well on the Wayne property and is terrorized by its resident bat. O'Neil uses this incident as the tale's central metaphor to explore the years Wayne spends traveling the world gaining his forensic training and martial arts skills. The film's first thirty minutes also introduce the villain Ra's al Ghul, who debuted in another O'Neil story from 1971, "Daughter of the Demon," with art by Neal Adams.

The second act, which finds Bruce returned to Gotham, borrowed from *Batman: Year One* both its bleak portrait of a scuzzily corrupt Gotham City and its depiction of the budding friendship between a young Jim Gordon and a still-nascent Dark Knight. The film's mob characters and crime-noir trappings were lifted from *Batman: The Long Halloween.*

Out of the thousands of Batman plotlines from which to draw inspiration, the filmmakers carefully chose four—each of which routinely appeared in online lists of favorite stories so lovingly curated by hardcore fans.

The film's muddled third act, however, which depends for its narrative suspense on a scheme involving the Scarecrow's fear toxin, a stolen microwave emitter, a hijacked train, and lots of municipal water department employees sitting around looking worried, was all Goyer and Nolan.

Nolan envisioned *Batman Begins* (or, as it was known for security reasons during production, "The Intimidation Game") as a realistic *French Connection*–style crime drama. And despite having over two decades of grim and gritty Batman comics as a model, if he hoped to turn the tale of a man who dresses up as a bat into gripping urban noir, he had some conceptual work to do.

First: that getup. The director felt Bruce Wayne's decision to adopt a bat disguise needed a firmer grounding in his childhood trauma. Previous Batman films had studiously ignored the reasoning behind Wayne's adoption of a bat costume, though the fervid *Batman Forever* had come closest, with a scene in which young Bruce discovers the Batcave. The oft-cited comic book explication—Bruce is interrupted while brooding in his study by a bat flying in an open window—was deemed too feathery, even vaguely supernatural, by Nolan, a loose end that didn't connect to any other element of the origin. As a filmmaker, Nolan prized rigorous, steel-trap plotting in which every element introduced into the narrative was expected to justify its existence and its utility—so he pulled an origin that suited him better.

By adding the "Little Brucie's Trapped in the Well!" incident from *The Dark Knight Returns*/"The Man Who Falls" into the film, Nolan established that the boy had been left psychologically scarred, with an enduring phobia of bats. It allowed the director to introduce the film's major theme—the power and purpose of fear—while lending Bruce's father Thomas Wayne enough screen time to register with the audience as a character.

Bruce's fear of bats promptly assumes a central importance to the film when the Waynes attend an opera at which performers in bat costumes unsettle the boy. Bruce convinces his parents to leave the theater early, whereupon they are mugged and murdered. Nolan and Goyer here inject a note of guilt into the origin; even their choice of venue nudges the inciting incident more closely in line with their somber vision. Most comic book accounts, after all, had the Waynes attending a Zorro film on that fateful night—a nod to the bold, swashbuckling sense of adventure embodied by O'Neil and Adams's Batman. But Nolan's Dark Knight would buckle no swashes; his was a darker, more operatically somber character.

Unlike his predecessors, Nolan set out to provide clear answers to the "why and how" of Batman: why the costume, why the obsession with justice, why he doesn't kill, and how he secures the equipment— all the baseline, unquestioned conventions of the superhero genre. Tim Burton—and Frank Miller before him—had answered the "why" questions with "because he's nuts" and waved away the "how" with "because he's rich." But Nolan and Goyer took pains to unpack the why of the bat persona by showing us Bruce working to overcome his phobia during his time with Ra's Al Ghul,* and—in the film's signature sequence—

---

* In the *Batman Begins* screenplay, unlike in the comics, the "Al" is capitalized.

standing triumphant as swarms of bats surround him in the newly discovered Batcave.

The film also shows us a young Bruce Wayne attempting to wreak
vengeance on his parents' murderer, only to be robbed of his chance to
do so by the mobster Carmine Falcone, who represents Gotham's moral
decay. Chastened, Bruce rejects the way of the gun, refusing to give in to
the corruption eating away at Gotham's heart, and resolves to do what
no one else can: to seek justice.

As for the how, Nolan had Goyer allot every piece of Bat-gadgetry a
passage of accompanying dialogue that establishes its plausible military
provenance. Each line is delivered in a clipped, hilariously macho cadence,
from the modern Bat-rope, described as "pneumatic. Magnetic grapple.
Monofilament tested to 350 pounds," to the suit, which we're informed is
"Kevlar bi-weave. Reinforced joints," and, especially, the Batmobile.

Or rather, the Tumbler—for the very word "Batmobile" was
deemed a relic of Batman's "campy," "ludicrous," and "outlandishly garish" cinematic past. The design of the Tumbler was the very first task
Nolan assigned the film's production designer, as he felt it would prove
emblematic of the new film's aesthetic. "Our entire approach to telling Batman's story could be found in the look and feel of that vehicle,"
Nolan said, urging the production team to aim always for "functional,
practical" utility and never introduce any design element whose purpose was "just to look good." The world he wanted to create was "gritty
and dirty and realistic."

Conscious of the historic tendency for Bat-villains to steal focus
from such a brooding, laconic hero, Goyer made sure that each of the
seven drafts the screenplay went through, with the help of Nolan's
brother Jonathan, kept a resolute focus on Bruce Wayne the man, par-
celing out the villains' screen time sparingly. He also chose to priori-
tize the martial artist aspect of Batman's ideological makeup. But this
required a trade-off. By emphasizing the physical training Bruce Wayne
receives, the finished film would effectively elide Bruce Wayne's status
as a master detective.

Despite this focus on combat tactics, Nolan did not skimp when it came to firmly delineating Wayne's moral injunction against taking a life—something Burton had ignored and Schumacher had winked at. The film does so by setting up a clear parallel between Bruce Wayne and Ra's Al Ghul. Having nearly completed his training among Ra's League of Shadows in a remote Bhutanese monastery, Bruce Wayne is told he must execute a local man who committed murder while engaged in an act of theft—a man very like the mugger who killed his parents. This is an important moment—one that allows the filmmakers to show us something essential about Batman. Here, he finally confronts and rejects vengeance completely, along with its practitioners, the League of Shadows itself. Nolan shows us the moment he resolves to go it alone and realizes that he must "become a symbol" not simply to strike fear into criminals' hearts, but to inspire the people of Gotham as an unstoppable, incorruptible, larger-than-life figure.

Eight actors auditioned for the part of Bruce Wayne, including Henry Cavill, Jake Gyllenhaal, and Cillian Murphy. In the end, despite narrow features and a jawline more triangular than square, the intense young actor Christian Bale secured the role. Although many improvements had been made to the Batsuit since the days of Burton and Schumacher,* the actor noted that the suit lent the wearer "this huge neck, like a Mike Tyson neck . . . it's more like a panther. It gives you this real feral look, as though you're going to pounce on someone any moment." The cowl was so tight as to give him a headache after wearing it for twenty minutes. Bale resolved to use both of these aspects in his performance, lending the character a distinctive, enraged growl that would provoke incredulous titters from audiences and more than a few bemused comments from critics.

Bale found in the character three separate roles and neatly delineated them over the course of *Batman Begins* and its sequels: the titular

---

* Read: Bale could actually turn his head while in costume.

costumed hero, all savage intensity and throttled rage; the private Bruce Wayne, forever searching for a path and a purpose; and the public pose of Bruce Wayne, a louche and smarmy dilettante who coasts through life in a cloud of smug self-satisfaction.

On March 4, 2004, Warner Bros. president Jeff Robinov announced that filming had begun in Iceland. In a highly unusual move on such a huge production, said filming was to be done without a second-unit director and crew: Nolan and his director of photography were going to handle it all themselves.

It was on this very same day that the filmmakers were handed a stinging reminder that the world had changed and the dawning of the Internet age would forever alter the way all films, but especially this one, got made.

The screenplay of *Batman Begins* leaked online.

A REACTION, PRE-"ACTION!"

It began with a script review at IGN.com. A column called "The Stax Report" offered a favorable appraisal of the screenplay, piously vowing not to spoil plot surprises: "I respect the filmmakers far too much to undermine their efforts. If anything I hope this review will only allay whatever fears some fans might still harbor about the project and to [sic] excite them even further about next summer's release." Immediately thereafter the author gleefully ticked off every story beat in excruciating, scene-by-scene detail, including the filmmakers' sundry deviations from, and additions to, what nerds considered Batman canon.

Nolan, Goyer, and the producers were acutely aware that the fan base was slavering for any information they could get and had instituted draconian security measures. Warner executives, for example, were never given copies of the screenplay but were forced to schlep out to Nolan's garage to read it over while Goyer or Nolan watched.

And yet, over the following weeks and months, more script reviews appeared on a host of sites, including SuperHeroHype and Ain't It Cool

News. What's more: buried in the comments sections beneath each of these reviews, URLs began to appear. Clicking on these links led to the famously secretive director's worst nightmare: temporary sites hosting scans of the film's entire screenplay, from opening shot to closing image.

Tellingly, however, despite the sundry tweaks that would have engendered sniffy outrage in a world that had never known a Schumacher, the hard-core fans ate it up.

"Just read through this," wrote a commenter on the Seriously! forums. "This movie is really sounding like it's going to kick ass."

Not all were glowing, of course. For example, a more dispassionate review that appeared in the forums of the screenwriting website Done Deal Pro read: "David Goyer's script for Batman: Begins [sic] is a collection of strong, absolutely INSPIRED moments surrounded by less-than-inspired bookend moments of 'nothing special' popcorn movie fluff that we've all seen before."

But most nerds possessed of sufficient zeal to chase down a script review and then spend long minutes poring over the full screenplay were sold. "This is going to be the best 'Batman' movie ever," avowed a poster on Moviehole.net, adding a gratuitous yet by now inevitable anti-Schumacher turn of the knife. "No butts about it."

The bat was out of the bag, and leaks would continue throughout production. While filming a scene of Batman looking out over the city from atop the Gotham courthouse (actually Chicago's Jewelers Building), a production assistant noticed a group of young men watching from a nearby parking garage. Their grainy video footage appeared online within hours.

Apart from location shooting in Iceland, London, and Chicago, most of the filming took place in an enormous abandoned dirigible hangar outside London, where the production team built entire city blocks of a grungy, rain-soaked Gotham City suffused in a dusky orange glow. The result looked nothing like Schumacher's much-derided urban-landscape-as-roller-disco mise-en-scène.

After 128 days of principal photography—a shooting schedule more than five times longer than any Nolan had experienced before—*Batman Begins* entered post-production. On July 28, 2004, Warners released a teaser trailer that offered only a glimpse of Bale in costume—but it was enough to generate grudging online excitement. "No endlessly focusing on the Batnipples," wrote Harry Knowles. "No smartass oneliners [*sic*]. No goofy looking villian [*sic*] dominating the trailer. . . . No sultry woman of the moment in tight leather . . . fuck me runnin' I must see this. Now. Well okay they can put a sultry woman of the moment in tight leather in it someplace but daaaamn if this ain't interesting looking."

By the beginning of 2005, a new, longer theatrical trailer and a poster of Batman against a sickly yellow sky kicked off a marketing push that saw every member of the cast and crew running to profess their love of the character and the comics.

It was a new world, one in which a respected director of small, cerebral indie films was now dutifully telling an endless succession of press junket interviewers that he hoped his movie would be "the cinematic equivalent to reading a great graphic novel." A world in which Christian Bale grew adept at listing his favorite Batman comics before roundtables of imperious comics journalists. A world in which publicists fawned over the actor's "Batman-like obsession," seriousness, and commitment to the role.

THE END OF THE BEGINNING

On June 15, 2005—a Wednesday—*Batman Begins* premiered in the nation's theaters and went on to a $73 million five-day opening-weekend take: an impressive showing, but short of the record-shattering blockbuster many had predicted. Crucially, however, studio tracking showed that the film had successfully widened its audience beyond the eighteen-to-thirty-four-year-old males who'd expressed the keenest interest in it.

Reviews were generally positive. Batman fan Roger Ebert said, "[It's] the Batman movie I've been waiting for." The *New York Times* grandiloquently declared that the film ushered Batman "into the kingdom of movie myth."

Variety, however, called it "dark and talky" and "drained of sheer childlike fun." The *Wall Street Journal* thought it "a ponderous story about a depressed hero who isn't much fun to be with."

As for the nerds? Nolan had granted them the very thing they craved: not simply a serious, badass Batman, though the film certainly delivered that. No, what *Batman Begins* offered them was something every fan who was ever shoved into a locker or shunned in a lunchroom secretly craves, however vociferously they may deny it: the acceptance and approval of the mainstream.

Nolan and Goyer had produced an assiduously faithful version of Batman that hard-core nerds prized so highly. Yet, normals loved it, too—they talked about it in office break rooms. They went back to see it again with their kids.

And this wasn't Tim Burton's stylized goth freak Batman or the straight-but-bent Batman of Joel Schumacher. This was the grim, butt-kicking Batman of fanboy dreams. They were, to put it mildly, on board:

"BATMAN BEGINS is the very best beginning to a superhero franchise I've ever seen," crowed Ain't It Cool. IGN agreed: "This is the Batman film you've been waiting for."

The collective "you" being addressed there, of course, was nerds, but the film's appeal proved significantly broader. Contrary to industry expectations, nearly half the audience (43 percent) was female, and over half (54 percent) were older than twenty-five. Further evidence that Nolan's film had reached a larger-than-expected female audience swiftly manifested on FanFiction.net, where the first tale set in the *Batman Begins* universe appeared as the movie opened. In the months that followed, new *Batman Begins* tales were being uploaded to the site at the rate of ten to twenty per month. Today, the fan stories that exist in Nolan's universe number in the thousands.

Professional critics and message board posters alike praised the film's sober, realistic approach, particularly in light of the character's most recent cinematic outings. A review from the website JoBlo.com follows a common pattern. After offering a nuanced poststructuralist critique of Katie Holmes's contributions ("great boobies"), the writer can't resist summoning the ghost of Schumacher: "Kudos also go out to director Christopher Nolan who was able to nix Joel Schumacher's disaster BATMAN scenarios, and present the world with something a lot closer to what we've been reading in the comics for years."

At this writing, over a decade has passed since *Batman Begins* opened in theaters, and the film has fully entered the popular-culture zeitgeist, though it has been overshadowed in the public mind by its sequel. To view it now is to be struck by how ruthlessly plotted this first movie seems, how meticulously and dispassionately Nolan introduces the conflicts that will thread themselves throughout the completed trilogy.

The movie isn't perfect—the *Wall Street Journal* and other critics who noted the film's lack of humor were onto something. What many mistook, in 2005, as a grim overcompensation for Akiva Goldsman's pun-besotted scripting now stands revealed for what it is: the dour and chilly aesthetic that typifies Nolan's work.

The film's structure serves it well, until suddenly it doesn't. Splitting the narrative into three tonally distinct genres—martial arts film, pulpy mob thriller, big dumb action movie—is an intriguing gambit for capturing discrete facets of Batman. But the movie's final act is marked by a kitchen-sink superfluity of fear gas, escaped inmates, a fire at Wayne Manor, a runaway train, and a microwave emitter/bomb, which only muddies the putative suspense.

It's true also that the film's dialogue, thick with solemn pronouncements about the nature of anger and the power of fear, if not some deadly combination of the two,* could have been markedly improved had Nolan simply instituted a moratorium on abstract nouns.

But these are quibbles. In *Batman Begins*, Nolan found a way to surgically implant the dark, brooding badass Batman that nerds loved

---

* "My anger outweighs my fear!"

into a gorgeous and notably cerebral film that left normals intrigued and wanting more.

DAWN OF *THE DARK KNIGHT*

Not that Nolan knew his next step, yet. Not exactly.

"It wasn't until *Batman Begins* was completely finished and we'd taken some time off that we got the chance to sit down and think, Okay, what exactly are we going to do with this?" he said.

He and Goyer had approached the first film with a vague, overarching three-part story in mind, though they didn't permit themselves to think of it as a trilogy. "We'd laid down the idea in *Batman Begins* that Bruce Wayne's plan in becoming Batman was to do what he could for a finite period of time. He had something like a five-year plan, a set amount of time he would spend setting Gotham straight, and then he would go off and do something else with his life . . .

"Then [in the next chapter] we would see Bruce getting deeper and deeper into his role as Batman. In a way, Batman himself would raise the extremity of behavior in Gotham, and would give rise to the Joker." Ultimately, in a third and final chapter, they envisioned bringing the Batman phase of Bruce's life to a permanent close.

This plan, of course, was much more than the sort of light tweaking they'd introduced in *Batman Begins* for the sake of tight cinematic plotting. This was an overhaul of major elements of the Batman legend.

The notion that Bruce Wayne's role as Batman was a temporary stint, no more than a "five-year plan"? Sacrilege. A direct contradiction of the original oath he swore in November 1939: "And I swear by the spirits of my parents to avenge their deaths *by spending the rest of my life* warring on all criminals" (emphasis mine).

The process of comics-to-film adaptation involves drastic culling and cutting, of necessity. By introducing the prospect that Bruce Wayne envisions his Dark Knight career as one he hopes to walk away from, Nolan and Goyer tether the larger-than-life superheroic ideal to the everyday. Bruce Wayne's motivation is clearer, more immediately palpable, more grounded in recognizable human psychology, and thus more acceptable to an audience of normals.

But in so doing, Nolan and Goyer sap from him the bold, grandiose, idealistic notion of his oath. They turn the powerful, impossible idea that drives him—his crusade—into something more believable but very much smaller. A temporary appointment. A posting. A gig.

They do this to raise the stakes, of course, and over the course of *The Dark Knight* he will learn that his original plan isn't sufficient to the enormity of his task. But in this one aspect of Batman's character, Nolan's passion for "hyperrealism" and believability leaches from his protagonist a significant measure of his pure, iconic power.

DOUBLING DOWN ON GRIM 'N' GRITTY

Nolan and his production team had been initially worried about how the stripped-down, antidecorative, utilitarian design aesthetic of *Batman Begins* would be received; the near-universal praise that met the film encouraged them to take it further on the next.

Where *Batman Begins* had rooted itself in the natural world of sweeping Arctic vistas and dark caverns, *The Dark Knight* would be a film of cityscapes, cold and sleek and modern, shot in a Chicago awash in fluorescent lighting and harsh daylight.

As for character arcs, they resolved that Batman himself wouldn't get one. At least not in the familiar Hollywood-screenplay sense of an emotional journey that leaves the protagonist utterly changed. He'd merely move a bit further down the path of accepting his mantle.

The film's true protagonist, Nolan and Goyer believed, would be Gotham's white knight, the crusading district attorney Harvey Dent. It would be Dent whose hubris would lead him down the path to tragedy and destruction, Dent whose mind and soul would get corrupted by the sinister influence of the Joker. And it would be Dent whose reputation Batman and Commissioner Gordon would desperately attempt to preserve, initiating a cover-up that would begin to fester in Gotham's heart at the film's conclusion.

The director wanted to steer his Joker away from the showboating hamminess of Jack Nicholson's portrayal for something smaller yet more terrifying. Ra's Al Ghul had been a calculating, coolly intellectual opponent. It was time for Batman to mix it up with a true psychopath, a violent and unpredictable terrorist who acted as a force of almost casual evil.

As for where the Joker came from and what motivated him—all the expository elements that Burton and Schumacher had lingered so lovingly over to establish their villains—Nolan wanted none of it. The bad guy's origin story was a cliché he was determined to avoid. What made the Joker interesting to Nolan was his effect on Batman—namely, how he served to sharpen and clarify why Gotham needed Batman, and his mission. So instead of offering one origin story, screenwriter Jonathan Nolan supplied him with two, asserted at different moments but with equal weight and both likely apocryphal—a narrative shell game the audience would never win.

Nolan's decision to dispense with the Joker's origin story generated the by-now-reflexive nerd outrage, but this was as nothing to the gleefully homophobic hand-wringing that attended his choice to slap some clown makeup on handsome young actor Heath Ledger. "I think he'll be a really gay Joker," offered one philosopher-poet on the SuperHero Hype.com forums, "[like] he was gay in that cowboy movie." Another said, "Heath blows in just about everything (and that wasn't a Broke Back [sic] Joke)."

CLOWN PRINCE

Principal photography on *The Dark Knight* (called "Rory's First Kiss" for security purposes) began in April 2007 in Chicago and concluded in November in Hong Kong.

The production continued to make use of the former dirigible hangar in Cardington near London, but this time out Nolan relied much more heavily on location shoots in and around Chicago, and devised more elaborate stunts. Many of these involved a new vehicle, the Bat-Pod, a custom motorcycle dreamed up by Nolan that proved perilously difficult for even highly skilled stunt drivers to operate.

The shoot was marred by the death of special effects camera operator Conway Wickliffe, killed when the vehicle he was riding in crashed into a tree while he filmed a car chase. During post-production, another blow: Heath Ledger, whose portrayal of the Joker was attracting industry attention even before it left Nolan's editing suite, was found dead of an accidental overdose in his Manhattan apartment on January 22, 2008. He was twenty-eight years old.

The Dark Knight's publicity campaign had commenced while the film was still being shot. A campaign website for Harvey Dent launched in May 2007, offering visitors the first photo of Heath Ledger's Joker in exchange for their e-mail address. At Comic-Con in July, "Jokerized" dollar bills—on which George Washington had been given dark eyes and a red smile—were handed out to attendees, advertising the website www.whysoserious.com. Visitors to the site were urged to become the Joker's henchmen by following clues; hundreds of fans in smeared Joker makeup caromed through the streets of the Gaslamp District on the scavenger hunt. On Halloween night, the website RorysDeathKiss .com instructed visitors to dress up as the Joker and upload photos of themselves visiting local landmarks.

Over the following months, marketers created a dense network of twenty fake websites (www.thegothamtimes.com, www.gothampolice .com, etc.), each laced with clues, games, and scavenger hunt instructions that would lead willing fans to more information. In some cases, that information was highly specialized—one site, a duck-shooting gallery, required visitors to shoot the ducks in a specific order procured by translating a previous clue into binary code—but fans who found the answers dutifully raced to online forums to share their strategies.

The company hired by Warners to create these exercises in "alternate reality gaming" calls these tactics an attempt to "reach people who are so media-saturated they block all attempts to get through." The approach deliberately and cannily exploits the hard-core nerd's love of arcana—and of knowing something before anyone else—by making them active participants in marketing to their less-obsessive peers. The company explains the marketing principle behind such viral campaigns simply: "Instead of shouting the message, hide it."

Shortly after Ledger's death, the film's viral campaign, which had focused on the Joker, began to revolve around Harvey Dent, with the company sending fake Harvey Dent campaign buses to various cities. Meanwhile, Warners had dispatched Goyer—the films' resident "comic book guy"—to hit the convention circuit and tease the rabid fan base and build excitement.

In May, *Dark Knight* roller coasters opened in two Six Flags theme parks, and a direct-to-DVD animated film *Batman: Gotham Knight*, comprising six connected stories set in Nolan's Batman universe by Japanese animators, was released ten days before *The Dark Knight* opened in theaters.

That opening took place at midnight on July 18, 2008, which kicked off a record-breaking opening weekend of over $158 million. The film went on to become the second movie in history to break $500 million in North America, and it did so in half the time it took *Titanic* to hit that mark. Its ultimate worldwide take of just over $1 billion put it in rare company, as only three films had accomplished that feat: *Titanic*, *The Return of the King*, and *Pirates of the Caribbean: Dead Man's Chest*.

Despite the company's heightened vigilance—including dispatching ushers with night-vision goggles to patrol theaters for camcorders—the first pirated copy of the complete film appeared on a file-sharing site the day after it opened. One media measurement firm estimates that over seven million illegal copies of the film were downloaded in 2008 alone.

The Dark Knight's critical reception was overwhelmingly positive, even soaring: "An ambitious, full-bodied crime epic," said *Variety*, while *Rolling Stone* was one of several outlets to praise Nolan's rejection of the kind of moral certainties superhero tales usually embody: "*The Dark Knight* creates a place where good and evil—expected to do battle—decide instead to get it on and dance."

Roger Ebert took this notion further, declaring, "Batman isn't a comic book anymore. Christopher Nolan's *The Dark Knight* is a haunted film that leaps beyond its origins and becomes an engrossing tragedy . . . Nolan has freed [Batman] to be a canvas for a broader scope of human emotions."

Critics boldly predicted that both the film and Nolan would be nominated for Oscars, and a widespread conviction emerged that Ledger would receive the first posthumous Oscar since Peter Finch in 1977.

This was everything the hard-core fans wanted. If they'd enjoyed the critical and popular success of *Batman Begins*, the unprecedented and nigh-unanimous acclaim for *The Dark Knight* sent them straight to their favorite forums to coo contentedly:

"Superb in every way . . . note perfect," wrote one Bat-forum poster. "Wow," said another. A poster in an Ain't It Cool News talkback enthused, "Saw it 6 hours ago and I can't stop thinking about it. Gonna see it again on Sunday and try to focus. I think I was just too damn excited about what was coming next to fully enjoy it." Just below that post, another forum denizen was more pithy. "Better than the second coming of Christ," he wrote.

SO SERIOUS

Given Heath Ledger's sudden, surprising death, it's perhaps inevitable that so much of the critical discussion revolved around the actor's performance. But his Joker is a unique and unforgettable cinematic creation, and it's that performance—Ledger's tiny, highly specific choices—that makes it that way. On paper, Nolan's Joker is "an absolute, an agent of chaos and anarchy," but on-screen such broad strokes fall away. Ledger's Joker is no force of nature but a person—a terrifying person, certainly, but one with a beating heart.

Most actors who assayed the role before him saw the Joker as a chewy, outsized character. God knows Cesar Romero aimed his girlish giggles at the back rows; Jack Nicholson's Joker was a creature of hammy, maniacal glee; in voicing the animated-series Joker, Mark Hamill fully embraced the flourish and theatricality of the role as well. But Ledger instead goes inward, a fascinating and inspired choice. It's unlikely anyone who's ever read the Joker in a comic would have imagined the flat, nasal, vaguely Midwestern vowels and diphthongs Ledger lends the character, as if this psychopathic killer clown were a carpet salesman from Cedar Rapids. Nor would they have imagined his pausing to lick his lips with distracted self-satisfaction as he threatens his latest victim. Instead of a cackling madman, his Joker seems, more than anything, bored by humanity and desperately impatient to turn over the tables.

"I'm not a schemerrrrr," the Joker tells Harvey Dent when he visits the man's hospital bed. "I just . . . do things." The script supplies Ledger, in this scene, with a somewhat lengthy monologue in which he explains his worldview, and his role as an agent of chaos, as he convinces Dent to abandon his moral code. This is perhaps the most important speech in the film, not because we learn anything about the Joker, but because, in this moment, as the Joker explains how he never plans, how he's just "a dog chasing cars," Ledger shows us what the script does not:

He's lying.

That's when we realize it—*everything* he says is a lie. Everything is part of his scheme, and Dent, Gordon, Batman, and all of Gotham are already caught up in it, doomed. It's the most terrifying moment in a film filled with unsettling imagery. We at last catch a momentary glimpse down to the depths of the character's soul, and find nothing there.

Fanfic writer and academic Leslie McMurtry notes that "the release of *The Dark Knight* in 2008 resulted in an almost instantaneous effusion of fanfiction . . . [most of which] analyzed, and, in many cases, eulogized, the Joker." The character would continue to fascinate and arouse writers of fanfic and makers of fan art years after Nolan's trilogy ended; Joker and Batman confrontations* set in the Nolan universe remain, at this writing, the eighth most popular subject on FanFiction.net.

---

* And/or romances.

Ledger would go on to win that posthumous Oscar for the role. But although *The Dark Knight* received seven other nominations in technical categories (and won for sound editing), neither the film itself, nor its director, was recognized by the Academy.

Within days of the nomination announcements, the critical community joined its voice to those of nerds apoplectic over *The Dark Knight*'s "Oscar snub." The *Guardian* weighed in first: "There remains the sneaking suspicion that many [Oscar] voters refrained from nominating *The Dark Knight* not because they did not believe it to be a great film, but because they did not believe it to be the right *sort* of great film."

Needless to say, the proprietors of the website DarkCampaign.com, "An Unofficial Grass-Roots Campaign to Support *The Dark Knight* for the 2008 Academy Awards," were put out. The day of the nominations, they posted quotes from several Hollywood filmmakers who'd expressed puzzlement that the film hadn't been nominated for best picture. The site's commenters ran to the barricades:

"I just made a Facebook group called Boycott The Oscars for snubbing *The Dark Knight* . . . everyone should join and spread the word . . . we need to make the oscars [*sic*] pay for this bullshit . . . ," wrote one.

"It was expected but this awards show has been irrelevant since *Citizen Kane* lost. But yeah this awards show can eat all the dicks," said another.

The following year, the Academy of Motion Picture Arts and Sciences doubled the size of the Best Picture category from five to ten. The expansion came to be known as "the *Dark Knight* Rule."

"BIGGER AND DARKER"

Despite the phenomenal success of *The Dark Knight*, and the entreaties of Warners executives, Nolan and his team weren't certain they had another Batman story to tell. They feared they wouldn't be able to top themselves.

And yet, they had ended *The Dark Knight* on an unresolved

dilemma: Batman and Gordon conspire to blame Harvey Dent's crimes on Batman, thereby preserving Dent's reputation as an incorruptible crusader for justice and ensuring that his many successful prosecutions won't be overturned. But it's a lie. The Joker has already successfully corrupted Dent's soul.

Nolan and Goyer had long envisaged a way to bring their tenure on Batman to its ultimate conclusion: a closing image of a young man stepping into the empty Batcave, inheriting Bruce Wayne's heroic legacy. "We came up with it several years ago," Nolan said later, "and everything had been building toward that conclusion."

Gradually, over the course of several discussions back in Nolan's garage, where it had all begun, they decided that the third and final film would deal with what happens when Batman and Gordon's cover-up is finally exposed. They envisioned a "bigger and darker" film in which Gotham City had cleaned up its act, inspired by Dent's shining example, unaware that "though things seem better, there is an evil beneath the surface that is going to bubble up."

Warners had assumed Nolan would conclude the trilogy with one or more of the more familiar villains—the Riddler, the Penguin—but Nolan and Goyer were determined to go in another direction.

The villains Batman had faced in Nolan's previous films—Scarecrow, Ra's Al Ghul, the Joker—were largely intellectual adversaries; now, they felt, it was time for something more physical.

The choice would astonish many nerd observers. The filmmakers chose Bane, a character born of the benighted nineties whose hopelessly hokey comic book shtick* seemed wildly out of sync with Nolan's fetishistic drive for groundedness. But he fit the bill: "We'd never had a physical monster as our villain," Nolan said. "Bane is a very well-conceived physical villain in the comics, but someone who has an incredible mind as well. And whereas the Joker's backstory was very obscure, Bane's is

---

* He's a 'roided-out criminal mastermind who dresses like a Mexican wrestler.

epic. We wanted to go the opposite way this time, using a villain with a very rich origin story."

That origin story would see significant retooling in the finished film, to better set up a major reveal in the third act. Nolan and Goyer decided to do away with the most extreme element of his comic book provenance: his addiction to the strength-bestowing drug known as Venom. And, by turning his mask into a mysterious apparatus of leather straps, motors, and metal tubes, the film's costumers managed to dial down the *luchador* and dial up the paramilitary mercenary.

Cowriter Jonathan Nolan, meanwhile, advocated tirelessly for the film to include Catwoman. Initially, Christopher Nolan and Goyer balked at the suggestion, imagining the highly sexualized, scenery-chewing Catwomen of yore. But once they imagined her as a representative of Gotham's underclass—a woman driven to burglary who assumes a variety of roles to infiltrate the lives of the wealthy—her role in the plot became clear.

For the film's plot, Nolan and Goyer borrowed liberally from two comics story lines of the nineties: Bane's takeover of an isolated and desperate Gotham was a nod to the "No Man's Land" story arc of 1999, while the film's midpoint turn—Bane breaking Batman's back—was inspired by the "Knightfall" crossover event in 1993–94. They were liberal adaptations, to be sure. By now Nolan's Batman films constituted their own, wholly separate and self-contained fictive universe that demanded its own resolution.

Which is likely why the film's once-heretical notion of a Batman who gives up his cape for good ruffled relatively few nerd feathers. Nolan and Goyer had introduced the idea in *The Dark Knight* by having Bruce Wayne come perilously close to revealing his secret to the world, ceding his role as Gotham's defender to Harvey Dent.

Such plot mechanics were pure Hollywood, and nerds recognized them as such. Nolan wasn't the first filmmaker to attempt to raise the stakes by having Bruce Wayne flirt with the possibility of giving up his role as Batman—Tim Burton and Joel Schumacher had trod the very same water, after all. But after two films that had earned their beloved character the acceptance of the mainstream, hard-core fans seemed to feel that Nolan had earned the right to end his story the way he wanted to, even if that meant his Batman did something their one true Batman never would.

The Dark Knight Rises (security code name: "Magnus Rex") began principal photography in May 2011 with a scene shot in a remote location near the India-Pakistan border. While the enormous Cardington hangar soundstage once again saw a great deal of use for the film's interior shots, Nolan filmed on location in Pittsburgh for most of its street scenes and exteriors—including the film's set piece, in which Bane causes an entire football field to collapse into the bowels of the earth.

Once again, the rise of the Internet threw a new and unforeseen set of challenges at the production. Shooting on public streets meant that passersby could and did blithely take cell phone pictures of props, sets, and—especially—vehicles, including a new, Nolanesque air assault vehicle called simply "the Bat." Producer Jordan Goldberg was mystified: "Due to the immediacy of Facebook and Twitter, the moment someone takes a picture, that picture is online. . . . . On the one hand, you're glad that people are excited enough about it to film that stuff, but on the other hand it ruins the illusion."

By the time production wrapped in November, hundreds of grainy cell phone photos of the Bat—and many photos of a climactic midday brawl between Batman and Bane shot on Wall Street in Lower Manhattan—could be found by even the most casual fan with access to Google.

The week before the film premiered, the website BoxOfficeMojo .com weighed its chances to break the opening-weekend record of $207 million set earlier that year by Marvel's *The Avengers*. As far as they were concerned, *DKR*'s chances looked good, for three reasons.

1. The promotional campaign ("The Legend Ends") made it clear that this would be the final installment: "Considering studios would prefer to milk a cash cow for as long as possible, this definitive ending is almost unheard-of for an original property. What makes it even more enticing is that audiences don't have the slightest idea how the story will end."

2. The conflict between Batman and Bane. "A hero is only as strong as his villain, and in this case Warner Bros. has done a nice job raising a B-level villain up close to A-level status."

3. Catwoman. "The gritty saga has to this point been very male-oriented . . . the campaign has given plenty of exposure to Hathaway's sexy, strong character, and it should go a long way to convincing the fairer sex to give this a shot."

FIRST REVIEW

But on July 16—four days before the film's official opening—the first review of the film appeared online, by syndicated critic Marshall Fine.

It . . . wasn't a rave.

"Nolan gets so caught up in creating an epic adventure that he hammers the 'epic' and neglects a crucial component: the adventure . . . There are things to admire and enjoy about *The Dark Knight*, but they ultimately get swept aside by the film's pretentious ambitions. . . . I'd say that anyone forecasting serious Oscar love for this lumpish, tedious film has been smoking too much of that potent, prescription California weed. *The Dark Knight Rises* rarely gets off the ground."

Within six hours of the review getting posted to the site Rotten Tomatoes.com, it had received some 460 comments from outraged fans—all of whom had yet to see the film themselves. One commenter envisioned putting Fine into a coma by pummeling him with a thick rubber hose. Another pithily urged him to "die in a fire." Several posters vowed to destroy Fine's website and briefly succeeded, when traffic temporarily crashed his servers.

AURORA

The Dark Knight Rises opened at midnight on Friday, July 20, 2012. At one of these midnight screenings, at the Century Aurora 16 multiplex in Aurora, Colorado, a young man named James Holmes seated himself in the front row. About twenty minutes into the film, he got up, exited the theater through an emergency door he left propped open, went to his car, changed into protective gear and a gas mask, and returned to the theater with tear gas grenades, a twelve-gauge shotgun, a semiautomatic rifle, and a handgun. At first, many in the theater thought he, like several other audience members, was wearing a costume. Minutes later, twelve people were dead and seventy others injured. Holmes was arrested outside the theater.

In the wake of this staggeringly senseless mass shooting, the country's nerves were frayed. Early reports that the young man had dyed his hair red and called himself the Joker became fodder for pundits and politicians. Security at many theaters was tightened in case of copycat shootings, and several ghoulish incidents—in San Jose, California, an unknown assailant threw a package into a theater showing the film and screamed that it was a bomb—were reported at movie houses across the country.

The nation's airwaves and op-ed pages grew thick with concerned voices decrying the role of film and video game violence on impressionable psyches, and parents, teachers, and government officials struggled vainly to find and elucidate reasons that might explain a horrifying act that had occurred in reason's absence.

Batman is a character who engages our darkest selves—the fear and violence we carry with us, the sudden desire for bloody vengeance that so easily seizes us when we get cut off in traffic or are put on hold by the cable company. That's why so many pundits were eager to draw connections between the character and the event; his status as an inkblot onto which we project our basest drives has always made it easy to mistake him for a creature of hatred, of darkness.

But though he lives *in* darkness, Batman is not *of* it. He was birthed in a senseless act of violence, but his mission, his life's work, is to prevent such acts from happening to others. That selflessness is why he's a hero, and it's why he has always represented not hatred but hope.

OUTRAGE INC.

The film went on to make $161 million on its opening weekend and ultimately grossed nearly $1.1 billion worldwide.

Critics generally praised the conclusion to Nolan's Batman trilogy—the word "satisfying" turned up in many reviews, as did, inevitably, the word "gloom," and once again the director's commitment to plumbing the ethical ambiguities of Batman's world earned plaudits.

Not every critic was smitten, however; the tone of even the most positive reviews was notably cooler than had been the case for *The Dark Knight*. Outright detractors emerged, complaining that the film's bombast seemed "overworked and ridiculously grim" (the *Chicago Tribune*) while others called it "dense and overlong" (the *New Yorker*). As more and more negative reviews appeared, threats like those received by Marshall Fine continued apace.

"Be prepared to have a bomb stuck up your asshole," began an e-mail to the critic Eric Snider, which continued, "Snider you are dead, now that I know where you live you are going down." An unfavorable review from the AP's Christy Lemire inspired a comment that read in its entirety, "Ms. Lemire: You're a stupid fucking bitch and I hope you die." Critic Devin Faraci of *Badass Digest*, noting that a colleague was getting deluged with outraged comments for giving the film only three out of four stars, expressed his frustration:

"These people have tied their identities and self-worth into Nolan's Batfilms so strongly that the smallest slight feels like a deep, personal attack. These sad, mentally unhygienic people lash out with fury. It's ugly and sad and makes me ashamed to be a nerd, to share a pop culture space with these people."

If the world had changed in the years between Schumacher and Nolan's respective takes on the Batman legend, nerds had changed with it, and in surprising ways. In 1997 fans had thronged to electronic bulletin boards and built websites for the sole purpose of flinging threats at Joel Schumacher. Fifteen years later, their vitriol was just as caustic, only now they spewed it in the opposite direction: not *at* Hollywood, but *from* it, or at least on its behalf, as if they felt themselves somehow deputized. The reason for this reversal: before the very first story meeting in Nolan's garage in 2002, Warners' marketing department had studiously groomed the filmmakers on how to genuflect before the altar of nerd-dom. Every statement that passed through the studio's publicity office was carefully positioned with this in mind, to ensure that Christopher Nolan wasn't seen as the co-opting outsider Schumacher had been. And despite the trilogy's many heretical deviations from canon, it worked. By 2012, Nolan was embraced as a suitably reverent acolyte to the Sacred Order of Bat-fans.

When it came to disparaging reviews from members of their own fraternity, like Ain't It Cool News's Harry Knowles, however, no concomitant backlash ensued. This is likely because they recognized something familiar in the timbre and specificity of Knowles's objections: "He's fucking BATMAN. BATMAN doesn't mope around his mansion unmotivated to participate in the fucking world." Knowles's nerd-frothing, and that of others like him, received no threats of boycott—or of physical harm—from hard-core Bat-nerds for a simple reason: game recognize game.

But the carefully (and professionally) nurtured goodwill nerds came to feel toward Nolan's efforts does not in itself explain why their response to negative reviews was so wildly disproportionate. Even mildly disappointed notices from professional critics were met with strident ad hominem, scorch-the-earth attacks. The few outright pans provoked threats of physical violence and death.

Over a *movie*.

We may intellectually accept that nerdy enthusiasms incline one to absolutism and self-righteousness. But it's impossible for the recipient of the performative online biliousness that has come to be known as trolling to gauge whether it originates from a place of petty malice or serious mental disturbance. The harm caused—the lingering atmosphere of disquiet and the lost sense of safety—is real, whether it was created by a dangerous sociopath or a bored, emotionally stunted nine-year-old availing himself of the anonymity of the Internet in the quick five minutes before leaving for soccer practice.

Assuming the nerds who threatened to harm movie critics for

daring to think *The Dark Knight Rises* less than thrilling were sincere, if piteous, adults, the vehemence of their reaction to criticism suggests a pervading sense of panic, even fear. Consider their position: The world had finally taken Batman seriously. This was no fad, no POW! ZAP! Batmania, no Bat-symbol as fashion statement. What's more, it was *their* Batman, the grim, badass avenger of the night. They didn't have to feel self-conscious about reading comic books or watching a children's animated series, and the love they felt for Batman was shared by billions of people around the world, people who took him—and, by extension, them—seriously.

Now, at last, Batman was a thing they could talk about publicly, proudly, with anyone. He was a lingua franca. He was *sports*.

Soon they would head into the theater once again, and bask in the reflected brilliance, and share their love with nerds and normals alike.

Unless.

It's no coincidence that Marshall Fine's review, which came out before the film opened in theaters, received the brunt of the most vicious attacks. The nerds who'd preemptively appointed themselves defenders of the film's reputation—like those who'd taken it upon themselves to advocate for *The Dark Knight*'s Oscar prospects, four years prior—were in a state of heightened vigilance. Fine's review was seen as a bellwether, something that might tip the critical balance against the film, unless action was taken. Thus the Bat-Signal was lit and hordes of thought vigilantes swooped down upon the evildoer before he could poison Gotham's water supply.

This is not to suggest that a handful of unhinged commenters represent Bat-fandom any more than the guy incoherently fulminating on a WOR call-in show represents all Mets fans. But the landscape of Bat-fandom had changed under the hard-core nerds' feet, and they struggled to recognize it.

In the seven years Nolan had been winning over the hearts and minds of Bat-nerds, the Internet, once a haven for like-minded Schumacher-loathing comics collectors, had filled up with the fans Nolan's films had wrought, including many younger fans who'd never picked up a Batman comic book in their lives. These nerds had come to their love of the character via Nolan's movies, the *Justice League* cartoons, *Batman Beyond*, reruns of *Batman: The Animated Series*, video games, their parents' old DVDs of *Batman Returns*, or even, to the hard-core Bat-nerds' abiding horror and disdain, from the thrice-daily showings of *Batman and Robin* on TBS.

And they weren't alone. Alongside these new voices were cosplayers, makers of fan art, and fanfic writers. The Internet provided a platform for a strain of hard-core comics readers who were smaller in number but who had been there from the beginning. These fans could throw down Bat-trivia, cite chapter and verse, and argue arcana with the best of them. They were inveterate, shameless nerds. They were also, not for nothing, women.

The website Sequential Tart had launched in 1999 with a simple mission statement:

> Maybe there are more women online who dig "boys' comics." Maybe other women get tired of seeing big-breasted bad girls every time they walk into a comics shop. Maybe they don't want to be told [what] they should or shouldn't like, whether it be horror or superhero, science fiction or fantasy. Maybe they want to make their own decisions, based on their own tastes instead of some preconceived notion. Maybe we could do something to make them feel that they aren't alone.

In 2004, former DC Comics editor Heidi MacDonald launched *The Beat*, a blog that curates comics industry news, which quickly became a daily destination for thousands who came to value MacDonald's sardonic, knowledgeable, and clear-eyed take on comics, and on the boy's-club atmosphere of comics publishing.

Women and girls had always read comics, of course, but the Internet supplied them new agency, new visibility, and a new means to

connect with others like them. The Batman fans among them contributed diverse perspectives on both the male and female characters
in and around Gotham. Writer Gail Simone was one such fan, who
created the website Women in Refrigerators* to decry the way superhero comics treated female characters as disposable. She would go on
to write the Gotham-based series *Birds of Prey*, in which long-sidelined
Bat-characters like Barbara Gordon assumed a central, ass-kicking role.

Of course, old-school fans, the ones convinced that the one true
Batman was now and had always been the one that existed between the
covers of comic books, hadn't gone anywhere. But even before Nolan
had started to work on his Dark Knight trilogy, the comic book Batman
began to undergo a series of shake-ups that would challenge the hard-
core fan base's most fervently held beliefs and leave their badass loner
Batman utterly changed.

Changed, and also, sort of, dead. Briefly.

---

* The title refers to a story line in *Green Lantern* wherein a supervillain chops
up the hero's girlfriend and stuffs her in their fridge for him to find.

9

The Unified Theory (2004–)

Darkness!
No parents!
Continued darkness!
More darkness!
Get it?
The opposite of light!

—LEGO BATMAN'S SELF-COMPOSED DEATH-METAL SONG,
THE LEGO MOVIE (2014)

In June 2004, *Batman Begins* was still a year away. Even as nerds rushed online to express their dissatisfaction with the casting of a pointy-chinned Welshman as Bruce Wayne, on the nation's comics shelves the "grim 'n' gritty" trend in superhero storytelling, begun some eighteen years before, finally reached its glum nadir.

In the seven-issue miniseries *Identity Crisis*, novelist Brad Meltzer and penciler Rags Morales conducted an exercise in retroactive continuity, or "retcon."

The basic impulse behind *Identity Crisis* was similar to Nolan's: a desire on Meltzer's part to tell a grounded, realistic story about superheroes—in this case, the Justice League of America. But where Nolan would manage to introduce a real-world physicality while preserving the larger, symbolic essence of Batman, *Identity Crisis* evinced a punishing and reductive literalism. Meltzer's chosen method for making superheroes seem more realistic was to depict the brutal murder of Sue Dibny—half of the Justice League's whimsical husband-and-wife detective team—and subsequently reveal that a classic JLA foe from the 1960s had once raped her. And he was just getting started: by the time *Identity Crisis* was over, more bodies had piled up, more dark secrets had come to light, and Meltzer had successfully dragged the larger-than-life heroes of the DC Universe out of the light and into the lurid darkness of an airport-bookstand potboiler.

As a hero with his roots in pulp novels, Batman was no stranger to stories in which the *implied* threat of rape served as a lazy plot device. But this was different: it was a stratagem to appropriate the bright, sunny JLA comics of the sixties and early seventies and turn them into risibly overwrought chronicles of spandex-clad murder and on-panel sexual violence.

Contemporary nerds proceeded to snatch the book up eagerly. Throughout its seven-month run, *Identity Crisis* hovered at the top of the sales charts, never dropping below the number three slot. DC Comics took note and ensured that the grim ramifications of *Identity Crisis* would redound through many of DC's story lines for years. The series' putative subject was good people forced to perform evil actions in the interest of justice. It was Meltzer's ham-fisted attempt to address the use of torture in the War on Terror, and it would cast a pall over the entire superhero genre that lingers still.

But it was a stand-alone Batman comic that debuted in July 2005— one month after Nolan's *Batman Begins* opened in theaters—that became a true phenomenon.

THE GODDAMN BATMAN

All-Star Batman & Robin, the Boy Wonder paired two giants of the industry—artist Jim Lee, mainstay of the nineties comics boom and bust, and Frank Miller. Miller had returned to Batman three times since his definitive and hugely influential *The Dark Knight Returns*, in *Batman: Year One*, *Spawn/Batman*, and *The Dark Knight Strikes Again*.

The events recounted in *All-Star Batman & Robin* take place in Miller's own, separate Dark Knight continuity, not long after the events of *Year One*. This time, Miller set for himself the task of telling the story of how Robin came to be Batman's partner.

The Batman that Miller gives to readers in the pages of *All-Star* is not the inexperienced crime fighter seen in *Year One*. Neither is he the crusty battle-scarred veteran of *The Dark Knight Returns* and its sequel. This is Batman at the very height of his powers, a creature of outsized, hypermasculine swagger. Who is also, Miller makes quite plain, completely nuts.

Over the course of the ten-issue series, Batman kidnaps Dick Grayson and proceeds to abuse the boy both verbally* and physically;† deliberately rams the Batmobile into police cruisers, killing the officers inside and critically injuring his girlfriend Vicki Vale in the process; and violently assaults Alfred for daring to supply young Grayson with food. Miller shows us the Dark Knight rationalizing these actions by claiming that the boy needs to be toughened up and Gotham cops are corrupt, but the characterization is deliberately extreme: his normally hard-boiled syntax goes full-on Tonto‡ and he laughs manically as he shatters his victims' bones.

The reader can sense Miller laughing, too—every page exudes the delight of a twelve-year-old boy getting away with something naughty. Miller clearly relishes tweaking what he has referred to as "the PC crowd": the series begins by ogling Vicki Vale in her lacy lingerie, lingers over the scantily clad Black Canary, and gleefully depicts Wonder Woman as a stereotypical man-hating shrew from "the isle of Lesbos." The cover of issue #5 is simply a tight shot of Wonder Woman's rump, drawn by Miller. Characters toss the words "retarded" and "queer" around lightly, and one issue had to be recalled when the letterer neglected to censor Miller's profanity-laden speech balloons.

---

* "Are you retarded or something? . . . I'm the goddamn Batman."

† Hauling him from a car by the neck and striking the boy across the face.

‡ "Dick Grayson. Aerialist. Twelve years old. Brave boy. Damn strong."

Miller wasn't writing for normals, as he had in 1986, but for that audience of hard-core nerds for whom the character of Batman represented a masculine ideal. With *All-Star Batman & Robin*, he gave his already turgid Dark Knight a steroid regimen.

If the series hadn't been beset by delays and ended after only ten issues, it's possible that *All-Star Batman & Robin* might have come eventually to its point: perhaps Miller was attempting to show that the Batman who existed before Robin came into his life was little more than a cruel, brutal, maniacal thug, and that it was caring for the boy that turned him into the hero he became. It may be that Miller hoped to paint a portrait of what his *Dark Knight Returns* Batman looked like back when he was completely under the sway of his schizophrenic ideation. But as with much about *All-Star Batman & Robin*, Miller's narrative purpose, whatever it might be, never quite manages to rise above the background noise of his crazy macho bullshit.

The first issue sold over 261,000 copies—more than twice the number of the second-best-selling comic that month—and went on to become the top-selling comic of 2005. But lengthy delays* and bad word of mouth† meant slipping sales, such that when the series was put on indefinite hiatus after its tenth issue appeared in August 2008, few noticed, and fewer cared.

TOWARD A UNIFIED THEORY OF BATMAN

What Miller was parodying, intentionally or not, was the Batman of the contemporary comic book era. Since the nineties, in a trend that began with Grant Morrison's JLA, comics writers had begun to emphasize an idea of Batman as a long-term strategic thinker, a master planner whose

---

* A full year passed between issues #4 and #5, for example.

† "I'm the goddamn Batman" became a much-mocked, and much-shared, Internet meme.

elaborate preparation gave him an edge over the criminal underworld and his fellow heroes. The "War Games" arc that ran through the Bat-books in 2004–05 turns on an elaborate contingency plan Batman had prepared in the event of a Gotham City gang war. The massive 2005–06 crossover event called *Infinite Crisis* involved the revelation that a dis-trustful Batman had built a spy satellite to collect information on all of Earth's villains and heroes.

The net result was a comic book Batman who'd ascended to a kind of untouchable narrative godhood. Gradually, writers came to write him, and readers to read him, as a man who was always six steps ahead of everyone else, a hero whose superpower was always being right, a champion who found no challenge particularly challenging.

Grant Morrison, who took over writing duties on the monthly *Batman* comic with issue #655 (September 2006), resolved to change that state of affairs and restore a sense of vulnerability to the character. Instead of raising the stakes by slaughtering Bruce's family and friends in a Meltzerian bloodbath, Morrison resolved to introduce a villain whose goal would be to break Batman emotionally, just as Bane had broken him physically in the nineties. Paired with artist Andy Kubert, Morrison concluded the very first issue of what would prove a hugely ambitious seven-year tenure with a shocking revelation: Batman had a ten-year-old illegitimate son.

To hard-core fans with long memories, this was not news. Back in 1987, writer Mike W. Barr and artist Jerry Bingham had produced the one-off hardcover graphic novel *Batman: Son of the Demon*, which de-picted Bruce Wayne fathering a child with Talia, daughter of his enemy Ra's al Ghul. But the book was a stand-alone story outside the continu-ity of the monthly comics and would eventually come to be considered an Elseworlds tale—DC Comics' umbrella term for alternate-reality versions of their heroes.

The return of Batman's son to comics' continuity was Morrison's first hint at what he had planned, which was nothing less than the utter rejection of the one true Batman so beloved by hard-core Bat-fans.

Morrison believed the fans' tendency to single out the somber-badass iteration of Batman was hopelessly out of step with the times. "I don't think it's appropriate—particularly in trying times—to present our fictional heroes as unsmiling vengeance machines," he told the comics site Newsarama as he began his run. "I'd rather Batman embodied the best that secular humanism has to offer—[after all,] a sour-faced, sexually-repressed, humorless, uptight, angry, and all-round grim 'n' gritty Batman would be more likely to join the Taliban surely?"

It wasn't just the reductive focus on grim-and-gritty Batman that he sought to change, but the whole notion of a reductive focus itself. To insist that one's favorite version of the Caped Crusader was somehow truer than others was the height of adolescent churlishness, in Morrison's view, and it was time to grow up. Batman the character may have been a chunk of intellectual property owned and fiercely protected by a corporation, but Batman the cultural idea transcended ownership and contained multitudes. "I want to see a Batman that combines the cynic, the scholar, the daredevil, the businessman, the superhero, the wit, the lateral thinker, the aristocrat," he said.

So Morrison built his massive, slowly unfolding meta-mega-narrative around a simple core concept: it was all true. Every story that had ever been written about Batman since 1939, even—especially—those that O'Neil and Adams had swept under the rug in 1970, all the "goofy" tales of spaceships and magic and interdimensional pests, even the sixties Batman show, had happened.

It was, *all* of it, Batman.

Kathy Kane, the glamorous Batwoman of 1956? She came back.

The 1956 *Detective Comics* tale that saw Bruce Wayne's father donning a bat costume for a masquerade party? It was back in canon, with a twist: a mysterious doctor named Simon Hurt donned the bat disguise and hinted that he might in fact be Bruce's father.

The trippy 1963 *Batman* story "Robin Dies at Dawn," which saw Batman subjecting himself to a scientific experiment designed to test the effects of isolation on the human mind, became the spine around which Morrison built his sprawling tale. Morrison combined elements of that story with imagery borrowed from the 1958 *Batman* story "The Super-Batman of Planet X!," which saw Batman transported to the distant planet Zur-En-Arrh to fight space crime.

With this alchemical storytelling mixture, Morrison proceeded to bring Batman lower than he'd ever been. An extended sequence depicted an amnesiac, emotionally shattered Dark Knight drugged out of his mind and pushing a shopping cart through Gotham's seedy underbelly. "I had fun doing a vulnerable Batman," Morrison said, "stumbling homeless through the streets on heroin, deranged and betrayed." But although Morrison could bend the rules, he knew that for Batman to retain his essential and abiding Batmanliness, he had to eventually outwit the foe and escape the death trap. Thus, with a little help from a hallucinatory Bat-Mite, Bruce Wayne reverts to a "backup personality" he's prepared in case of a mental attack like this one, recovers his sanity, and defeats the villain.

Morrison's ambitious plan could have easily misfired. Left to his own strange and sometimes psychotropic devices, his writerly tendency to litter the floor with obscure references and abstract ideas can seem smugly self-indulgent, like the friend only too eager to share the particulars of his mind-expanding peyote trip. But Morrison's doggedly myth-minded storytelling found powerful resonance in Batman and made the character, as a cultural concept, seem suddenly even bigger, more archetypal, more profound. He stared into the inkblot that is Batman and found something new.

Yet no sooner had Morrison accomplished his staggering feat of narrative synthesis, bringing together sixty-nine years of Batmen in a single, densely layered tale of epic heroism, than he killed Bruce Wayne.

Or rather, as was later revealed, he sent Bruce Wayne hurtling back through time to the ancient past, where he proceeded to struggle forward, era by era, assuming the personae of a shaman, a witch hunter, a pirate, a cowboy, and a gumshoe, even as his friends and colleagues in the present mourned him and went on with their lives. Because comics.

NEW DUO FOR A NEW ERA

Gotham may have been missing its Batman, but Robins, at least, were thick on the ground: Dick Grayson, the original Boy Wonder, had taken on the superheroic identity of Nightwing years before. Jason Todd, the second Robin, was suddenly back from the dead, through circumstances too byzantine to detail, and had adopted the name the Red Hood to become a murderous vigilante. Tim Drake was still the current Robin, but Bruce Wayne's son, Damian—insolent, ruthless, trained from birth by the League of Assassins—seethed impatiently in the wings.

In August 2009, in the pages of *Batman and Robin* #1, Dick Grayson stepped up to fill the power vacuum at the top of the Batman family. He assumed the role of Batman, and Damian Wayne stepped into Robin's red-breasted tunic. As for poor schlub Tim Drake, he for some reason chose to risk brand confusion by adopting the heroic code name Red Robin—a moniker ill-suited to inspiring fear in the hearts of criminals, unless they happened to be terrified by cheeseburgers.

Despite the hard-core nerds' abiding and oft-stated preference for a grim, lone-avenger Dark Knight, Morrison instead served them a caped-crusading Dynamic Duo, but—crucially—he inverted the dynamic. Dick Grayson's Batman was an easygoing, wisecracking mentor, while Damian Wayne's Robin was brooding and humorless.

Over the course of his run on the book, Morrison highlighted the pair's conflicting worldviews for comic effect, while showing Damian gradually coming to respect Dick for his compassion and humor. The tone was brighter and often unabashedly comic, and enjoyed healthy sales throughout Morrison's tenure, despite occasional delays.

But then, following a two-year absence, Bruce Wayne returned from his sojourn through time, flush with a new, entrepreneurial zeal. Wayne staged a press conference to announce the launch of "Batman Incorporated"—a Wayne-sponsored organization dedicated to taking Batman worldwide by franchising the Batman brand internationally. "Starting today," Wayne announces in *Batman Incorporated* #1 (January

2011), "we fight ideas with better ideas. The idea of crime with the idea of Batman. From today on, Batman will be everywhere it's dark. No place to hide."

Which is why, throughout 2011, two different but equal Batmen stalked the comics shelves. In *Batman Incorporated** Bruce Wayne trotted across the globe recruiting new Batmen for his worldwide initiative while still finding time to haunt the gothic spires of Gotham in the pages of *Batman: The Dark Knight.* Over in *Batman, Detective Comics,* and *Batman and Robin,* meanwhile, Dick Grayson wore the cowl.

It was a brief, bold experiment that effectively reversed the grand metafictional synthesis Morrison had achieved; like light passing through a prism, the idea of Batman now split into a tonal color spectrum, keyed to different tastes. It was all still Batman—the reader had only to pick from whichever section of the idiomatic salad bar she or he wished. While, for example, *Batman Incorporated* offered gleaming jet-set derring-do and a rapidly swelling cast as more international Batmen were added to the roster, in *Detective Comics,* writer Scott Snyder and artist Jock told a concurrent, unabashedly grim, and decidedly gritty tale in which Commissioner Gordon's adult son was revealed to be a sadistic murderer.

And so it went, for most of the year. Until September. At which point the whole gorgeous, messy experiment was abruptly ended by editorial fiat.

SOFT REBOOT: THE NEW 52

In 1986, DC Comics had started its characters and story lines over from scratch with the *Crisis on Infinite Earths* crossover event. In 1994, the *Zero Hour: Crisis in Time* miniseries again rebooted the established timeline, wiping many characters and previously established events out of existence. In 2006 the DC Universe took another metafictional

---

* Written by Morrison with art by Cameron Stewart.

mulligan, when the *Infinite Crisis* miniseries restored the network of parallel Earths collectively known as the Multiverse in a bid to erase the contradictions that arose in the wake of the previous *Crisis*. Just two years later, the misleadingly named *Final Crisis* event also threatened to end all of creation, until Superman, as is his wont, saved the day. Now, in 2011, DC announced that they would be starting over yet again—and this was to be no mere miniseries event. For the first time, the changes to the fictional DC Multiverse would be reflected by real-world changes to the comics that chronicled it. The end of 2011 would see a complete relaunch of the entire DC publishing line.

Every title was canceled, and fifty-two different comics were launched in November, with new creative teams and new numbering— all of them simultaneously starting with issue #1. Even *Detective Comics*, the company's flagship title and, after 883 issues, the longest-running comic book in existence, wasn't spared: November saw the launch of *Detective Comics* #1 (volume 2).

The reasoning behind this latest reboot was the same as that of those that had preceded it: an editorial conviction that comics story lines had grown too complicated and confusing to appeal to readers beyond the again-shrinking audience of hard-core nerds. A bold initiative like "the New 52" provided shiny new jumping-on points for new readers.

Batman had a long history of emerging from any given company-wide reboot more or less intact. He'd weathered the original *Crisis on Infinite Earths* without getting his ears bent, and apart from some ephemeral changes (now he was an urban legend, now suddenly he wasn't) he'd largely managed to rise above the tumultuous cycle of restarts and retcons that so often swallowed his fellow heroes.

But this time his luck had run out. The New 52 wiped away all of Morrison's playful narrative meta-shadings and Jungian synthesis to replace it with a broad-stroke, bullet-pointed Batman new readers would recognize.

In the pages of the four core titles—*Batman, Detective Comics, Batman: The Dark Knight,* and *Batman and Robin*—the classic status quo reasserted itself: Batman was now, and had always been, Bruce Wayne. Dick Grayson was Nightwing. Barbara Gordon, who'd spent the past twenty-three years in a wheelchair after the Joker's brutal attack in *The Killing Joke* . . . got better. And became Batgirl again.

In the New 52's sole surviving nod to Morrison's seven-year tenure, Bruce's son, Damian, was still the current Robin—for now.

SQUARE ONE, ONCE AGAIN

The New 52 books featured "younger, angrier, more brash, and more modern" versions of all DC heroes, according to the press release. And, in the case of Batman: grimmer, grittier, and broodier. Again.

The chief architect of the New 52 Batman was writer Scott Snyder, who moved from *Detective* to the main *Batman* title with the relaunch and proceeded to perform a bit of narrative bait-and-switch: *Batman* #1, predictably enough, featured the Dark Knight tangling with his familiar rogues' gallery of Arkham inmates. But over the course of the ensuing story arc, which would soon stretch across multiple Bat-books, Batman learns of a sinister cabal called the Court of Owls that has ruled Gotham City in secret for centuries.

The key set piece of the story line features Batman trapped for eight days in the Owls' massive underground maze, brought to the brink of insanity and beaten nearly to death by the court's enforcer. Artist Greg Capullo's innovative, inverted page layouts provide the reader intimate purchase on Batman's fracturing mind, and Snyder pushes the envelope further than even Morrison dared, depicting not one but two separate moments when Batman decides to give in and let death take him.

The first time, he finds the strength to go on at the last possible moment and inexplicably rallies, like Jason Voorhees in bat ears. The second occurs after he's made good his escape from the court's maze via the river, only to find himself trapped under its ice. What happens next is something never seen in seventy-five years of comics adventures:

Batman stops struggling and simply gives up, sinking to the bottom of Gotham River.

It's no cunning ploy, no deliberate feint to throw off his pursuers. Neither is he faking his death as he's so often done before, most memorably in *The Dark Knight Returns*. No, this was just as it seemed: the world overmatched him, and he let himself be claimed.

Here was a Batman robbed of agency, who had given in to despondency and actually surrendered to his fate. It was a risky move on Snyder's part—in some ways just as risky as Morrison's memetic metafictional myth making—to write a story in which the most doggedly and famously resourceful character in all of popular culture runs out of options.

Of course, Batman lives, though crucially not through any action of his own. In the next issue, we meet the deus ex machina du jour, and her trusty machina: a young woman with convenient access to a makeshift defibrillator.

Yet *Batman* #6 closes with a striking series of panels in which we watch Batman sink into despair. This is where Snyder, who in interviews has talked openly about his own struggles with depression, puts his mark on the character.

Superheroes, after all, are ideas that exist on a symbolic level; they express the essential truths of our emotional lives even as they reflect the tenor of the times we live in. In the Me Decade of the seventies, Denny O'Neil responded to the rise of pop psychology with a Batman who was obsessed. In the steroidal, action-movie eighties, Frank Miller wrote Batman as a violent sociopath. The War on Terror–era Batman of Brad Meltzer's *Identity Crisis*, and the comics that came hard in its wake, was distrustful, even paranoid. These characterizations were all attempts to humanize him and tie him to the given cultural moment, to have him find a psychological affinity with his readership and remind them that for all his wealth and skills and muscle and mind, he was just a man.

Snyder, just six issues into his New 52 run, showed us a Batman who had known actual defeat and who in his darkest moment surrendered to hopelessness. Thus his Batman added a new symbolic resonance to the character's emotional utility belt—beyond the willfulness of O'Neil, the rage of Miller, and the livid insecurity of Meltzer. Here was a Batman who could express an emotional state far more universal than any of those—one that touches the lives of nerd and normal alike with unlooked-for frequency: here was a Batman who represented depression.

It was unheard of. It was unprecedented. And to those who believe that superheroes exist to inspire, to lift us up, and that Batman in particular functions best as a parable of self-rescue, it was perhaps even unhealthy. But there's no denying it was something few expected to see manifest in the character's seventy-fifth year of existence: an entirely new emotional facet, attuned to the current zeitgeist.

LAST HURRAH

While Snyder was busy putting his own mopey mark on Batman, Grant Morrison briefly visited the New 52 DC Universe for a thirteen-issue run on the rebooted *Batman Incorporated*.* This run, which constitutes the second volume of the series, began in July 2012—fully half a year after the launch of the New 52 books forced the discontinuation of the previous *Batman Incorporated* series.

Morrison dutifully adapted to the new dictates of DC's New 52 reality—the series now starred Bruce Wayne and his son, Damian, as Batman and Robin—and he wasted little time signaling to his readers that his mad grand meta-experiment had come to an end, that both writer and comic would be toeing the company line. "Tell the others it's over, Alfred," says Bruce on the first page. "All of it. The madness is over."

Morrison, as ever, is holding crossed fingers behind his back here.

---

* One issue of which was not written by Morrison but by the series' artist Chris Burnham.

In this same issue, for example, Robin adopts a contaminated heifer from a slaughterhouse and christens it Bat-Cow.

These thirteen issues, which saw the Dynamic Duo facing off against a mysterious organization called Leviathan, were beset by delays that depressed sales. Despite Morrison's high-profile presence, only about fifty thousand copies of *Batman Incorporated* were sold month to month, roughly one-third that of the hugely successful flagship *Batman* title.

On February 27, 2013, issue #8 hit the stands. The cover depicted a ghostly silhouette of Robin's empty cape, with Robin's "R" insignia taking the place of the "R" in the acronym "RIP."

Seven years after his first appearance in the first issue of Morrison's *Batman* run, Damian Wayne was dead—killed by a Leviathan agent revealed to be one of his own clones. The issue was heavily promoted by DC publicists, and the news of Damian's death was spoiled by a story in the *New York Post* two days before the issue's release.

Morrison explained Robin's death as a function of the cyclical nature of the superhero narrative—and as efficient use of the Batcave's furniture: "It's about resetting Batman's status quo," he said. "For a long time Batman's had a dead Robin in the cave and it's always been a glass case with a costume in there . . . the one Robin that Batman couldn't save . . . it used to be Jason [Todd], but [now Jason's] come back to life—[yet Batman's] still got that case in the Batcave."

The entire line of DC's Bat-books mourned Damian's death—perhaps most movingly, an entirely wordless issue of *Detective Comics* written by Peter Tomasi and illustrated in stark, unsparing, and unsentimental detail by Patrick Gleason. This issue follows Batman as he sets out on patrol, finding reminders of Damian's presence everywhere.

Morrison wraps up his tenure on Batman with issue #13 of *Batman Incorporated* (September 2012). In the Batcave, Batman faces off against the leader of Leviathan—none other than Talia al Ghul, Damian's mother. In his book *The Anatomy of Zur-en-Arrh*, an issue-by-issue breakdown of Morrison's *Batman*, Cody Walker finds in this final confrontation a not-too-subtle sardonic benediction from Morrison himself:

Just before Talia's death, Morrison uses her final words as a commentary on the typical Batman story that the hero is going to return to.

"You with your jokers and riddlers, your evil doctors. All those grotesque mental patients you choose to 'match wits' with. You'll never rise above them. You'll play in the mud for the rest of your life." For a brief time, Batman rose above the criminals of Gotham City and became immersed in a world of spies, terrorism, and international superheroes. Now that's over and it's back to basics again.

Everything about Batman was returning to the way it had been before Morrison. DC Comics was in the Batman business: fully one-quarter of the publisher's comics now featured Batman. With that much riding on the bottom line, the era of Morrison's hyper-mega-meta Bat-God was over, replaced by a Batman far simpler, more familiar, and more accessible.

And less gay.

In the May 2012 issue of *Playboy* magazine, just as he set out wrapping up his story lines, Morrison offered a parting shot to the hard-core Bat-nerds who were only too happy to see him go.

"Gayness," he said, "is built into Batman. I'm not using gay in the pejorative sense, but Batman is very, very gay. There's just no denying it. Obviously as a fictional character he's intended to be heterosexual, but the basis of the whole concept is utterly gay. I think that's why people like it. All these women fancy him and they all wear fetish clothes and jump around rooftops to get to him. He doesn't care—he's more interested in hanging out with the old guy and the kid."

There would be no such glib trolling of the fanboys in the post-Morrison era. Instead, the books would now be dosed with heightened gore—Joker slicing his own face off, for example—to raise the stakes. And while the pervasive sense of gloom that now resettled over the books in the wake of Morrison's departure seemed par for the Bat-course, there was a new aspect to it. The death of Damian Wayne, followed soon after by the apparent-but-not-really death of Dick Grayson in still yet another crossover miniseries, introduced a new note of melancholy to Batman's perpetual brooding.

The classic three-stroke cycle of his existence, through which he'd dutifully churned for seventy-five years—lone avenger to father figure to head of an extended family, then back to the beginning—had now collapsed in on itself. Yes, he was still nominally the patriarch of a family of operatives, but in a sense he was more alone than ever: two of his sons were dead, and the rest of the family was keeping their distance.

Yet it worked, at least in the short term: since the New 52 relaunch, Snyder's *Batman* has remained one of the top-selling comics every month. At this writing, nearly four years since the New 52 Batman debuted, sales have begun to slip, but they are still well above their pre-relaunch levels. Whether the initiative has succeeded in securing those "new readers" the publisher so desperately seeks, however, remains unclear. The New 52 reality continues, and story lines inevitably twist and turn and double back upon themselves. Damian, for example, came back from the dead in late 2014. It's inevitable that the publisher will avail itself of the hard-reset button once again; the only real question is when.

But for now, the Batman of the comics—the Batman that the aging cohort of hard-core nerds claim as their own—looks a hell of a lot like he did ten years ago, and ten years before that, and ten years before that.

For seven deeply weird years, Grant Morrison had built a soaring avant-garde Bat-opera in which the dissonant instruments and atonal voices collected from across the character's entire history melded together to create something strange and new. Now, in its place, Scott Snyder and his fellow New 52 Batman creators are once again launching into Batman's familiar melody in a minor key. The result, while less soaringly ambitious, is solid, well-executed, and displays a deep understanding of the character's history.

Yet outside of the comics and their ever-aging, ever-shrinking readership, something odd happened—and is still happening—to Batman.

"LIGHTEN UP, FRANCIS"

The 1981 military comedy *Stripes* features an early scene in which the misfit members of a new army platoon introduce themselves to each other and to their drill instructor, Sergeant Hulka. One recruit, an intense young man with a piercing glare, begins.

PSYCHO: The name's Francis Soyer, but everybody calls me Psycho. Any of you guys call me Francis, and I'll kill you . . . And I don't like nobody touching my stuff. So just keep your meat-hooks off. If I catch any of you guys in my stuff, I'll kill you. Also, I don't like nobody touching me. Now any of you homos touch me, and I'll kill you.

SGT. HULKA: [*beat*] Lighten up, Francis.

The hard-core Batman nerds have gotten what they want at last. The Batman of the comics is a grim loner again, and the culture at large has embraced Nolan's dark, humorless, and hyperrealistic Batman. In fact, teaser trailers for Zack Snyder's *Batman v. Superman: Dawn of Justice* show us a grim, laconic Dark Knight squarely in the Nolan mode.*
And today, when the *New York Times* features coverage about comics in general and Batman in particular, the much-loathed words "POW!" and "ZAP!" feature in headlines only rarely.

The world has accepted hard-core fans' argument. Batman, this children's character who dresses up in a costume to effect the change he wishes to see in the world via face punching, is *serious*.

And *awesome*.

And definitely *not* gay.

And, most importantly, now and forever, *badass*.

This is the Batman narrative that now permeates the culture—the

---

* "Tell me, do you bleed?" An armor-suited Batman asks Superman as they shoot death stares at each other in the rain.

narrative that doesn't like nobody touching its stuff and doesn't want any of you homos touching it, neither.

But a counternarrative has steadily arisen, fueled by the Internet and its dogged tendency to challenge, provoke, and—when any idea asserts itself with such grave, self-serious portentousness—ridicule.

Notably, this ridicule is not powered by the "Careful, chum! Pedestrian safety!" camp of the 1960s television series, which made the abiding squareness of straight-and-narrow Batman the butt of the joke. Today, the comic targets are instead Batman's self-seriousness, his pomposity, his grimness, his performative intensity. What's more, it's this counternarrative that's gaining in strength, leaching into the wider culture from a host of different sources that all manage to say the same thing in a clear, unmistakable voice:

"Lighten up, Francis."

The 2005–06 animated series *Krypto the Superdog*—aimed squarely at a younger audience than previous small-screen DC projects—regularly featured appearances by none other than Ace the Bat-Hound. The masked German shepherd appropriated the grim, laconic mien of his owner, telling Krypto, "I'll bark if I need you. Which is unlikely."

The Web series *Hi, I'm a Marvel . . . and I'm a DC* parodied the Apple vs. PC ads of the mid-2000s, pitting the two comics publishers' flagship characters against one another. In it, Batman says, "You got that radioactive spider bite for free, that's not a bad deal. Boom, there's your powers right there. I had to get my powers by . . . oh, wait, that's right, I DON'T HAVE ANY POWERS."

The online series *How It Should Have Ended* features an animated Batman and Superman having coffee in a diner, relishing their respective cinematic successes. "I'm the hero Gotham DESERVES," Batman says. "But not the one it NEEDS. . . . It's . . . it's complicated, but . . . it's pretty awesome when you think about it."

On Tumblr, Facebook, Twitter, Instagram, and other social media platforms, a cottage industry has arisen around taking out-of-context panels from Batman comics and offering them up for comment. This can be done to highlight the character's gay subtext, as in a much-shared panel lifted from a 1966 *Justice League* comic, which was reproduced and shared without alteration and offers a master class in unintended comedy:

DR. BENDARION: Not only are YOU doomed . . . but so is everyone you have touched!

THE ATOM: (Jean Loring! I've signed her death warrant!)

THE FLASH: (I gave Iris West the kiss of death!)

GREEN LANTERN: (Carol Ferris . . . In deadly danger!)

BATMAN: (Robin! What have I done to you?)

The Internet also abounds with images that parody both the tragedy of Batman's origin and his dogged refusal to move beyond it, as in a panel from a 1965 issue of *World's Finest*, in which an alternate-reality Batman slaps Robin. In 2008, a poster to the site SWFChan posted that panel with the following dialogue and changed the text of Robin and Batman's speech balloons thusly:

ROBIN: Hey, Batman, what are your parents getting you for Christ—

BATMAN: MY PARENTS ARE DEEEEAAAAAD!

The image was widely shared, and in 2009 an enterprising programmer built a public macro generator site for the sole purpose of allowing users to replace the dialogue and share it with their networks. In 2012 a Canadian talk show uploaded a video entitled "Batman's Night Out" to YouTube, in which a man dressed as Batman walks the streets of Toronto shouting, "MY PARENTS ARE DEAD," to passersby. The video has been watched more than 2.5 million times.

The 2008 animated series *Batman: The Brave and the Bold* marked a major advance in the stealthy but steady progress of the Batman counternarrative. Essentially a bold, colorful, hugely imaginative expression of Grant Morrison's unified theory of Batman (minus the peyote), the show offered viewers a version of the Caped Crusader who looked an

awful lot like the way Dick Sprang used to draw him back in the fifties, with a simple, iconic costume and a cartoonishly square jawline.
By pairing Batman each week with a different character from the murk-
iest depths of DC Comics' deep bench, including Anthro, Klarion the
Witch Boy, and Prez, the series exultantly embraced a once-shunned
era of the Dark Knight's history—featuring spaceships, time travel,
magic, and monkeys.

Voiced with comically stoic gravitas by Diedrich Bader, the series'
Batman stood squarely at the center of the wildly whimsical goings-on
without being diminished by them. In fact, they served to better delineate the character and testified to his essential and abiding appeal. In
the series' tour-de-force finale, the producer's subtext became the series
text, as Bat-Mite visits a convention of truculent Batman fanboys and
takes a question from the floor.

FANBOY: I would say Batman was best suited in the role of gritty urban
    crime detective, but now you guys have him up against Santas? And
    EASTER BUNNIES? I'm sorry! That's not *my* Batman!
BAT-MITE: (reading from a card handed to him by the show's producers)
    "Batman's rich history allows him to be interpreted in a multitude of
    ways. To be sure, this is a lighter incarnation, but it's certainly no less
    valid and true to the character's roots as [sic] the tortured avenger cry-
    ing out for Mommy and Daddy."

Two months before *Batman: The Brave and the Bold* debuted on
Cartoon Network in 2008, Warners released an unrelated Batman video
game that embraced the same bright, whimsical, downright goofy aspects of the Batman character the animated series reveled in. In *Lego
Batman: The Videogame* and its sequels, players manipulate a comically
cute Batman avatar through a world of plastic bricks and fancy Bat-
gadgets. The all-ages nature of the game's design, its clever cooperative
gameplay, and the corny sense of humor of its creators made it a hugely
successful contribution to the character's legacy.

The LEGO games are outliers in the Caped Crusader's long video game history. For decades, games that allowed players to assume the persona of the Dark Knight featured poor graphics, confusing cameras, and repetitive gameplay. That shoddy legacy came to an end forever with 2009's *Batman: Arkham Asylum*, which offered players the ability to choose how they met a given level's objectives—they could take out armed thugs with gadgets, use stealth to overcome enemies silently, avail themselves of theatrics to terrify their prey, or launch a brutal suicide run using the game's deep and gratifyingly diverse combat engine.

The game's tone was familiarly grim, and the Arkham Asylum setting was suitably übergothic. But the ability to download a host of alternate costumes meant players could choose the kind of Batman they wanted to be—grim and gritty, or bold and bright, or any variation between. *Asylum*'s sequels have exported the game's excellent mechanics into the open-world environment of Gotham City itself, complete with side missions, new gadgets, new characters, and—crucially—costumes. One such costume, in a move that many found surprising, was the classic gray-tights-and-blue-satin Adam West number.

On January 15, 2014, news broke that the 1966–68 *Batman* television series would finally be released on home video. The announcement came not via a Warners press release, but in a manner that perfectly reflected the cultural ascendency of Batman's comical counternarrative: Conan O'Brien tweeted it.

For nearly fifty years, vendors had hawked bootlegs of the episodes at cons, but the series had never been officially released in any format. Legal wrangling between 20th Century Fox and DC Comics had rolled on for years, complicated by original contracts that made no provisions for home entertainment revenue. The show's surfeit of guest stars—or their estates—were all expecting some recompense as well.

And of course, as the UK's *Guardian* newspaper noted, "there was also the nagging feeling that DC Entertainment, who had spent decades repositioning Bruce Wayne's alter ego as a brooding, intimidating Dark

Knight, a process that reached its gloomy apotheosis with Christopher Nolan's blockbuster movie trilogy, might be slightly embarrassed by Batman's hinterland as a Batusi-dancing boy scout with shark-repellent Bat-spray to hand."

The first cracks in the Berlin Wall separating Adam West's Batman from the character whose image and reputation DC Entertainment so ruthlessly protected appeared in 2012, when DC licensed the rights to make action figures in the likeness of Adam West's Batman and Burt Ward's Robin to Mattel. In 2013, the toy company followed up with a scale replica of the 1966 Batmobile, one of which is now perched atop the pile of comics next to the computer on which I am typing these words and which is, in point of fact, pretty freaking sweet.

TUNE IN TOMORROW

And so we come to the Dark Knight today. The Batman asserted by his publisher in comics, and by Nolan on film, is a grim, dark, brooding, endlessly resourceful avenger who lurks in the urban shadows. This is Batman the Character, who was born in 1939 but did not truly come into himself until 1970, when he was created anew—by nerds, for nerds—just in time for comics' Great Inward Turn.

But Batman the Idea is different, because much to the dismay of intellectual-property attorneys, ideas like Batman don't stay on the page or the screen. They transcend their mediums and take up residence in the cultural ether, the global zeitgeist. This process changes them, fractures them, iterates them, and—most importantly—personalizes them. Nerds of the 1970s, for example, saw something familiar in Batman's newly obsessive characterization and found themselves drawn to it.

Today's nerds are just as obsessed and find the same resonances with Batman the Character that they always have. But the culture has changed around them; the wall between nerd and normal is now a thin, permeable membrane through which ideas like Batman flow freely back and forth.

The obsessed loner may be the most universally recognized aspect of Batman the Idea, but there are thousands more. To audiences who made *The Lego Movie* a blockbuster, he's a bluff, comically self-obsessed jerk voiced by Will Arnett. To artist Seamus Keane, who held a Batman-themed Vegas wedding, he's a role model. To writer Andrew Wheeler, editor of the website Comics Alliance, he's a fascinating gay icon:

> The concept of Batman may be open to endless reinvention, but any effort to make him less gay only adds layers upon layers to his gayness. Make him light and you emphasize his campness; make him dark and you emphasize his repression; give him a girlfriend or a female sidekick and you reaffirm his bachelorhood. He is both camp and butch; repressed and sexualized; erotically fetishistic and homoerotically anti-feminine.

And to comic book writer and artist Dean Trippe, he's a savior. In his 2013 Web comic *Something Terrible*, Trippe, a survivor of childhood sexual abuse, simply and movingly relates how important Batman was to him as a boy and remains to him as a parent. Bruce Wayne's dedication to justice represents an act of self-rescue that Trippe credits with saving his life. "Batman," he writes, "[is] the hero who taught me that even a child broken by tragedy and trauma could rebuild himself into someone useful to others."

This is Batman now: an idea that's been freed of its grim 'n' gritty moorings to absorb a host of meanings and resonances across the emotional spectrum. And at the core of every iteration, whether brightly comic or darkly serious, lies that childhood oath.

Not the costume, not the gadgets, not the car, not the money. Those are trappings. That selfless oath is what matters about Batman, and it is the reason he will continue to matter, whatever form he may take in the decades to come. Because Batman is the story every one of us, nerd and normal alike, tells ourselves when things seem at their worst. The story of someone dealt a savage, crushing blow that should wring the life from them but doesn't. Because they choose not to let it.

Instead, they resolve to go on. To stand up. To fight.

Pow.

Zap.

THE PHOTO OP

It was Saturday, my last day at San Diego Comic-Con. My flight back to DC was first thing in the morning, and the con floor was about to close; I made the rounds, hunting for back issues of *Batman Family* at a decent price.

The SDCC costume contest was a bit later that evening, but the cosplayers were already out in force. A battalion of Cybermen marched up and split ranks to stream past me.

A Christopher Nolan Batman trudged by, all black neoprene and bulky body armor, looking uncomfortable in the football-shaped cowl. They all did. This was easily the thirtieth Batman I'd seen rocking the Christian Bale look since the show opened three nights before. They were easy to spot on the crowded con floor; the black rubber seemed to absorb light. Amid the riot of color, they were bulky, officious black worker ants.

I smiled as he passed; he growled. Very Method. Good for him.

And then I turned, and saw Batman.

A different Batman, that is. A Batman who looked nothing like the Nolanesque hordes of pointy-eared SWAT team members I'd been seeing for days. A Batman whose complete and utter Batmannishness sent a delighted thrill through me like I was a tween in the presence of One Direction.

No, this was the Adam West Batman. And he was *perfect*.

Every detail was exact. The sheen of the blue satin trunks. The brilliant yellow of the utility belt, with its square, lidded compartments, just so. The smallness of the Bat symbol on his chest, which made it seem weirdly . . . *polite*, somehow? The wrinkles of the Bat–evening gloves. The cowl's hilarious, completely superfluous eyebrows, these twin little filigree elements that seemed more than a little fey, if not downright drag queeny.* And the paunch. God, the paunch.

It wasn't huge, but it was there, and it was perfect. I wondered if he'd trained for it, the way the dudes who were dressed as the Spartans from *300* had bench-pressed and guzzled Muscle Milk for months. I imagined a strict regimen of Schlitz and pasta buffets.

"Wow," I said to him. "That . . . that is perfect."

He looked up from the back-issue bin he was perusing. Smiled. "Thank you, citizen," he said. Perfect.

"I mean, everything," I said. "Down to the tiniest detail. Perfect. Amazing."

He stared at me. "Do you want a picture?"

I hadn't, particularly, but now I very much did. "Sure," I said.

He stepped away from the comic bins, out into the middle of the aisle. I fished out my phone and held it up.

"Shall I pose?" he asked.

"Sure, that'd be great," I said. "Do whatever. Up to you."

And that's when he brought his hands up to his face, palms out. He made two peace signs and peered out at me through the twin Vs between his index and middle fingers: the Batusi. Of course.

"How's this?" he asked.

"Perfect," I said, because it was.

---

* "Gayness is built into Batman," I thought. Also, onto him.

AFTERWORD

SINCE LAST WE LEFT OUR HERO

There is a scene in Zack Snyder's *Batman v. Superman: Dawn of Justice* that occurs near the top of the third act, shortly after an explosion in the U.S. Capitol kills hundreds of innocent people. In it, a morose Clark Kent, bundled snugly into thick winter gear, walks along a remote mountaintop and encounters his Earth-father, Jonathan Kent, who proceeds to deliver a brief monologue.

Never mind why Clark's trudging across said mountaintop. Or what he, a living solar battery impervious to cold, is doing swaddled in polar fleece. Or how it is that Jonathan Kent happens to find himself in that particular spot, at that particular moment, so as to impart the gravelly homespun wisdom he does—given that he, a Kansas farmer, is neither native to mountainous terrain nor, in point of fact, alive.

None of that's important—or at least important enough for Snyder's film to spend even a second of its two-and-a-half-hour running time on it. What's important to Snyder is the story the ghost/vision/ hallucination-brought-on-by-underdone-shrimp Jonathan Kent tells his son. That same story turns out to be as important to us here as well, because it neatly encapsulates everything that the film gets so wildly wrong about Batman, and Superman, and about the entire superhero genre.

It is a tale of Jonathan Kent as a boy, who, one night during a river flood, worked until dawn to help his father divert the onrushing wall of water, sparing their farm from destruction. The Kents were happy. They made the young boy a cake, and dubbed him a hero.

But later that day,

> . . . *we found out: we blocked the water all right, we sent it upstream. The whole Lang farm washed away. While I was eating my hero cake, their horses were drowning.*
>
> . . . *I used to hear them wailing in my sleep.*

Once again: "While I was eating my hero cake, their horses were drowning."

Reader, I giggled.

I sat there in my theater seat, and the sound bubbled up from my sternum and escaped my lips, high and disconcertingly musical. *Lilting*, even. In my defense, I wasn't alone: a few select members of the opening weekend crowd around me (the film hit theaters on March 25, 2016—just three days after this book was published) hooted at the leaden portentousness of those ludicrously bathetic lines, delivered in Kevin Costner's patented whisper-drawl.

That scene, it must be remembered, follows on the heels of another in which Martha Kent implores her son to turn his back on humanity: "You don't owe the world a thing," she says.

Which in turn follows a scene in which Batman, played with a permanent glowering pout by Ben Affleck, brands a bat-symbol onto the flesh of a captured criminal—the sight of which will, we learn, ensure that the man will be killed in prison.

Got all that? Because here's what it adds up to: Zack Snyder, the man charged with ushering the latest wave of DC heroes onto the movie screen, and thus into the wider cultural consciousness, does not believe in heroes. He's a Randian Objectivist tasked with bringing to cinematic life characters who are, at their essence, embodiments of a deep, fervent, and all-consuming altruism.

This is why the moral universe he creates around them is one in which the very notion of heroism, of selflessness, is unrealistic, even laughable, and ultimately futile.

A universe in which you can't save a farm without killing a bunch of horses.

BATMAN ON FILM: IT'S ALWAYS DARKEST BEFORE THE *DAWN OF JUSTICE*

If Batman continually cycles through phases of light and periods of darkness—and the preceding 300 or so pages have gamely attempted to show that he does—*Batman v Superman* finds him on a moonless night, at 4:00 a.m., in a cave, under a tarp. In every respect, this is the familiarly grim-and-gritty Batman of Frank Miller's *The Dark Knight Returns*: the filmmakers simply transcribed that book's central super-conflict onto the movie screen.

They had to make some adjustments, of course. They darkened the tone even further, leaving no room for the colorful, satisfyingly pulpy set pieces of the book. Mostly, they had to devise a new reason for Superman and Batman to come to blows. This proved easy enough on paper: *Man of Steel* famously ended with a Kryptonian battle royale that left thousands dead and Metropolis in rubble. *Batman v Superman* begins with that same scene of destruction viewed from ground level, through the (narrow, rage-filled) eyes of Bruce Wayne.

This sets up the narratively necessary Bruce vs. Clark antagonism simply enough, but the film can't manage to credibly sustain it. Sensing that its central conflict is built on a surface with the tensile strength of a crème brûlée crust, the film looks to Jesse Eisenberg's coked-up squirrel of a Lex Luthor, and his overcomplicated plot (which involves kidnapping, blackmail, Krypto-Terran genetic engineering, terrorism, Doomsday, and a jar of urine) to set the heroes against each other.

The film firmly establishes that Affleck's Batman is in the wrong—Alfred tells us this, Affleck's pout tells us this, as does the fact that he does Crossfit. And in the film's closing minutes, Batman does learn his lesson, albeit only over the cooling corpse of Superman.

Tellingly, on a press junket to promote the film, Affleck mentioned that he wouldn't allow his young son to see it. Because no film about a billionaire detective ninja and flying blue spaceman is suitable for kids.

The film had a huge opening weekend, earning $166 million in North America alone, the eighth-biggest opening weekend of all time. But bad word-of-mouth and sharply negative reviews—critics decried the film's dour tone, its operatic bloat, and its unintelligible plot— helped ensure that it experienced a staggering 69 percent drop in ticket sales on its second weekend.

A director's cut of the film released for home video, dubbed "The Ultimate Edition," clocks in at thirty minutes longer than the theatrical version. And while it dutifully fleshes out various aspects of the plot and provides basic and useful logistical information (by clearly establishing, for example, that Gotham and Metropolis are separated by a narrow bay), the extra scenes prove just as doleful and cynical as the rest of the film. It's precisely the same dim vision of super-humanity, just longer.

And that's the issue, because that gloomy tone was what had made *Man of Steel* so ponderous, three years before. Later, that same tone managed to infect *Suicide Squad*, a film released in August 2016, in which Affleck's Batman appears briefly. Like *Batman v Superman*, *Suicide Squad* enjoyed a hugely successful opening weekend, earning $133 million in North America. And like *Batman v Superman*, bad word of mouth and negative reviews drove its second weekend box office take down precipitously—by 67 percent.

The mess that is *Suicide Squad* cannot be laid directly at Zack Snyder's feet—it was directed by David Ayer—yet Snyder's influence is evident in every frame.

A pre-release trailer for *Suicide Squad* landed in theaters during the height of the critical backlash against *Batman v Superman*'s unrelieved grimness. That trailer ticked off the particulars—a group of DC Comics supervillains are forced to work covertly for the U.S. government—but it included every joke that had been shot. Warner's testing showed that audiences liked this lighter approach, and the studio ordered reshoots and additional scenes that would, theoretically at least, take the film in a more fun, freewheeling, and surprisingly un-Synderian direction.

The resulting film, perhaps inevitably, veers wildly in tone, collapses into narrative incoherence, and features a villain—Cara Delevingne's Enchantress—who evidently seeks to destroy the world through Voguing.

Suicide Squad's focus on antiheroes represents, in many ways, the purest expression of the cynicism that lies at the heart of Snyder's cinematic worldview—and the culmination of the grim-and-gritty approach that has been the default narrative tone in superhero comics since the late 1980s.

Antiheroes like those in *Suicide Squad* are embraced by a fan culture that, like Snyder, believes superheroes are naïve and (gasp! horror!) unrealistic things. This culture holds up moral ambiguity and ambivalence as inherently more interesting, more relevant and—crucially, as far as they are concerned—more sophisticated.

This is nonsense, as the role of superheroes is to be ideals, exemplars, absolutes—the stories we tell ourselves as we strive to follow their lead. As the culture has moved to embrace antiheroes like Deadpool, Wolverine, and Deathstroke, true heroes like Batman, who hold to a strict moral code and act out of a hopeful and sincere sense of altruism, are held up as uncool, outmoded, even downright hokey.

That kind of reflexive cynicism risks nothing, of course, which may be another reason it's become so pervasive. But there are encouraging indications that the unrelenting, monochromatic moodiness that has hung over DC cinematic universe for years may soon lift, or at least admit a bit of color.

A scene from the Zack Snyder's *Justice League* film, due in November 2017, was released at San Diego Comic-Con in 2016. In it, Affleck's Batman recruits Ezra Miller's Flash. Miller's performance is nervous and nebbishy. There are, in point of fact, actual *jokes.*

But perhaps the surest sign that the Great Wheel of Batman is once again about to turn from dark to light can be found in the fact that most screenings for *Batman v Superman* were preceded by a trailer for *Lego Batman: The Movie.*

In the preview, the tiny plastic Caped Crusader from 2014's *The*

Lego Movie, once again voiced by Will Arnett, remains a self-centered, boastful man-child. But now we see the world around him, which includes a scolding, long-suffering Alfred (voiced by Ralph Fiennes) and a hopelessly nerdy Robin (voiced by Michael Cera).

It's worth noting how thoroughly the long decades of monotonously grim-and-gritty Batman have changed the way we make fun of him. In the 1960s, the Adam West Batman was held up as the ultimate square: a milk-drinking, speed-limit-heeding do-gooder who represented everything the counterculture was striving to counter.

Today, we get Will Arnett's gruff, egotistical, emo Batman. The thing about him that makes him funny, in 2016, is that he takes himself too seriously.

BATMAN IN PRINT: VOLUMES, VOLUMES, VOLUMES

Writer Scott Snyder and artist Greg Capullo wrapped up their acclaimed run on *Batman* after 52 issues. Along the way, Snyder rounded the now-familiar bases that every writer with a long stint on a superhero comic book tends to hit:

1. Everything You Think You Know is Wrong
2. Origin: Retold!
3. Add New Villain
4. Kill the Hero (Temporarily)

But there was nothing rote in Snyder's writing, or in Capullo's kinetic and often unsettling art. Snyder continued to flesh out the sinister cabal that lurked in Gotham's shadows, and in an extended story arc weaving through every Bat-title, he had the Joker kidnap and threaten the entire extended Bat-family, while strongly implying that the Joker harbored romantic feelings for Batman. In a storyline called "Zero Year," he recounted young Batman's first, halting crimefighting attempts in a ruined Gotham, riffing on both *Year One* and "No Man's Land," and he contributed to a sprawling, year-long series called *Batman: Eternal* which offered a comprehensive portrait of Gotham's many layers.

He added characters to Batman's supporting cast, and, crucially, to his rogues' gallery as well. The mysterious mastermind Mr. Bloom, who appears to be some kind of sentient, anthropomorophic weed, is one Snyder/Capullo creation who makes for a chilling and memorable villain, equal parts Slender Man and Audrey II.

Most significantly, Snyder found a way to put a new spin on a "Death of Batman" storyline. He wiped Batman's memory, giving readers a chance to see who Bruce Wayne would have become, and the life he would have lived if his parents had never been murdered. During Bruce's brief angst-free idyll, Snyder and Capullo had Commissioner Gordon assume the role of Batman: dude got jacked, shaved his mustache, and donned a blue mecha-suit with long bat-ears to patrol the streets of Gotham, looking for all the world like a badass, anime Easter Bunny.

The disappearance of Batman was only one of the many comings and goings across the various Bat-titles in recent years. Batman's son, Damian, returned from the dead. Dick Grayson abandoned the role of Nightwing by faking his death and becoming a suave superspy. Barbara Gordon regained the use of her legs, gave herself a kicky costume makeover and moved to the hipster borough of Gotham. And following the destruction of both Arkham Asylum and the Wayne fortune, Batman's home temporarily served as a prison for his deadliest foes.

As part of an initiative called DC YOU, launched in 2015, the publisher attempted to broaden and diversify its output, including its Batman titles, which for generations had featured more white males than a Harold Bloom syllabus. The series *Gotham Academy* focused on a prestigious school filled with headstrong, racially diverse young women. And in the series *We Are Robin*, hordes of Gotham teens, including an African-American named Duke Thomas, formed a team of vigilantes who collectively assumed the role of Batman's faithful sidekick.

But as far as *permanent* changes to Batman's status quo . . . well. As this book has shown, there's no such thing.

"It's inevitable," I wrote in the last chapter of this book, "that [DC Comics] will avail itself of the hard-reset button once again; the only real question is when."

That real question now has a real answer: May 2016.

Yet this latest company-wide event, dubbed "Rebirth," wasn't truly another reset, reboot, or retcon. Rather it was a do-over, an opportunity to cast off most of the changes that had been brought about by the New 52, five years earlier: essentially, Rebirth is what it looks like when a publisher shrugs and says, "My bad."

The hype around the event focused on words like *hope, optimism, relationships,* and *legacy.* The New 52 had de-aged most DC characters and eliminated others completely; Rebirth was to be about restoring many of those abandoned connections and telling stories that inspire.

But Batman had weathered the changes wrought by the New 52 more or less intact, so his particular Rebirth has been less dramatic than other heroes in DC's stable. Dick Grayson has become Nightwing again. In the pages of *Detective Comics,* Batman has teamed up with Batwoman and Red Robin to train a new generation of Gotham guardians. And in the main *Batman* title, writer Tom King has fashioned what might, at first, seem yawningly familiar: a nearly infallible Batman at the top of his game. Crucially, however, he's also a Batman who is coming to term with his limitations, and worrying about his legacy.

King has also slyly amped up the book's humor: his Bruce is unafraid to crack wise, should the moment call for it, and his Alfred is so witheringly sarcastic he could have stepped out of a Wodehouse novel, morning coat and all.

BATMAN ON TV, SAME BAT-TIME

"I don't think Batman works well on TV," showrunner Bruno Heller told *Entertainment Weekly* in May 2014. "Frankly, all the superhero shows I've seen, I love them until they get into costume."

So that is exactly what he created in *Gotham,* which premiered on the CW on September 22 of that year: a Batman show, without Batman.

More specifically, a Snyderesque Batman show without Batman: the setting is underlit and grimy, the mood somber yet soapy, and the writing, particularly during the show's first season, is formulaic: the routine villain-of-the-week story structure soon palled, and producers quickly made adjustments to facilitate a more serialized format, with narrative arcs stretching over entire seasons.

The show's decision to focus on a young, headstrong James Gordon (Ben McKenzie) is a solid one, as it allows viewers to appreciate that Gotham's woes are simply too much for one good cop to tackle. The decision to begin the pilot with the murder of Thomas and Martha Wayne, however, proved far less effective, as the tableau of a tween Bruce (David Mazouz) kneeling over the bodies of his parents has become pop-cultural wallpaper—so ingrained in our collective memory it has lost the emotional power that it once possessed.

Gotham is a wildly uneven, and thus frustrating, property. As young Bruce, Mazouz is quite good—haunted and sensitive—but spends most of his screen time cordoned off from the rest of the show's characters, who themselves seem scattered across several tonally—and totally— different shows. There is the gritty cop procedural, in which Gordon and his partner fight corruption at every level of Gotham society, only to get chewed out by their superiors weekly. There is the straight-ahead crime show, in which mob families battle for control of the city in ruthless and frequently grisly ways. And there's the campy soap opera, filled with winking nods to the Bat-canon and scenery-chewing performances from Jada Pinkett Smith and Carol Kane.

As a main character, the square-jawed Gordon has difficulty holding our interest; his one-man war on corruption is also one-note. It didn't take long for producers—and viewers—to realize that the true heart of the show lies in Robin Lord Taylor's Penguin. Taylor's performance is nuanced and deeply emotive; he's so effective that he can even make the show's thuddingly expository dialogue work—dialogue which, as in so many superhero shows, leans too hard on abstract nouns like "justice," "power," "crime," "fear," "good," "evil," and, especially, maddeningly, "this city."

(If showrunners simply issued an edict against abstract nouns in dialogue, *Gotham* would immediately improve in quality by 25 percent.)

. . . though each episode would get 50% shorter.

Several direct-to-home-video animated Batman films have been released since this book first went to press. Two are particularly notable, in that they are based on two of the most important and influential Batman comics ever made: *The Dark Knight Returns*, and *The Killing Joke*.

Of the two, the animated *Dark Knight Returns* proves less interesting, as it's simply a doggedly faithful page-to-screen adaptation of the comic. Using the original book as storyboard, and getting some excellent performances from Peter Weller as Batman, Michael Emerson as the Joker (not to mention Conan O'Brien as a doomed, David Letterman-esque talk show host) produces a perfectly solid two-part Bat-adventure, yet one that seems inevitably smaller, more prosaic, than the groundbreaking book upon which it was based.

The animated adaptation of *The Killing Joke*, on the other hand, is far more ambitious—and a fascinating failure because of it.

Fans of *Batman: The Animated Series* likely assumed the project was in good hands—Bruce Timm and Alan Burnett were among *The Killing Joke*'s producers, and Kevin Conroy and Mark Hamill returned to voice Batman and the Joker, respectively.

Brian Azzarello wrote the screenplay, and correctly identified the original comic's key narrative weakness—the offhand way it positions the violent and possibly sexual assault of a woman (in this case, Barbara Gordon) as nothing but a triggering action for the hero's story. Azzarello and the producers were determined to make Barbara a fleshed-out character, adding an extended prologue dealing with her last days as Batgirl.

On paper, a good idea. In practice, cringeworthy. Because, in a woefully misguided attempt to raise the emotional stakes, *The Killing Joke* includes a scene in which Batgirl and Batman have sex.

In (and at least partially out of) costume.

On a grimy Gotham rooftop.

It was meant to be shocking, of course, and it was—and not for the fetish-porn visual element, though that was . . . potent. The film never adequately establishes, let alone justifies, why Barbara Gordon would make a move on a man who is so clearly a father figure to her. It feels labored, contrived. *Wrong.*

Which is interesting, given that the Batman-Robin partnership has accrued decades of coy and largely unintended sexual subtext; a scene in which the two of *them* go at it would be jaw-dropping of course, but it would also feel, in a strange way, inevitable, even *earned.*

The sex scene is one thing, but there's the rest of the film to contend with, with its brutal, exploitative violence against Barbara and Commissioner Gordon. A scene in which the Joker delivers a long monologue to Gordon while the poor schmuck is trapped on a funhouse ride is lifted straight from the comic—but collapses completely in the film. On the page, it works, barely. But once spoken aloud, even by an actor with Hamill's gifts, the monologue in question reveals itself as wildly overwritten, ham-fisted, and clunky: thick clots of abstractions about the nature of sanity that bring the proceedings to a dead halt.

The film ends with a post-credits coda showing Barbara Gordon, in a wheelchair, setting out to fight crime as Oracle. It's a good impulse, meant to leave the viewer with an empowered version of Barbara, but it's incapable of dispelling the grave disservice the preceding seventy minutes have done to the character.

Both *The Dark Knight Returns* and *The Killing Joke* were hugely important when they appeared in the 1980s. They remain milestones.

But the thing about a milestone is that, over the long years it spends exposed to the elements, it inevitably erodes.

ONE LAST THING

I am typing these words on the morning of October 11, 2016. This afterword was due to my editor yesterday, but I'm cheating the deadline a bit because I wanted to make sure I got to write about one particular animated Batman movie—the one that was released just today. The one I got up at four in the morning to watch.

It is called *Batman: Return of the Caped Crusaders.*

It is set in the world of the 1966 Batman television series. It features the voices of Adam West, Burt Ward, and Julie Newmar.

I mean . . . right? Deadline, schmeadline.

When I first began researching this book and talking to scores of Bat-fans about their devotion to the character, it struck me how few of them shared my love of the 1966 series. Or at least, how few would admit it. Some furtively copped to enjoying it—one guy insisted he liked it, "but only ironically"—a statement which seemed somehow to defeat itself. This was not long ago, only three years or so, but the series hadn't yet made it to Blu-ray. For most of the men and women I spoke to, regardless of their age, the series was a pop-culture artifact about which they'd heard a great deal, or a cluster of memories bound up in nostalgia and emotion. What it was not, to them, was a *show*.

All of that changed in 2014, when the entire series was released to home video, and later to streaming services. Now love for the show has come out of the closet where it belongs. The comic book series by Jeff Parker, set in the show's trippy, Pop-art fictional universe, nails its singular tone without seeming like mere pastiche. A wave of Batman '66 merch—toys, games, t-shirts, posters. and pajamas—has crested in Targets across the land. And the Twitter account, @BatLabels, which posts screenshots of the show's meticulous and exhaustive expository signage, has gathered nearly 40,000 followers in less than one year.

And now, this. And now, *Batman: Return of the Caped Crusaders.*

It's a loving and profoundly nerdy homage to the '60s series, bursting with color, energy, and Bat-labels on every damn thing. Clever nods abound to the show's love of alliteration ("I call it Batnip—one scratch, and that mass of muscles will be mine to manipulate!"), absurdity (the teensy li'l Bat-ears on the helmet of Batman's space-suit, for example), deathtraps (Batman and Robin are nearly cooked as a giant frozen dinner), and squareness (Robin gets a good talking-to about jaywalking), plus there's plenty of plain old good jokes, as when Batman boasts of his Bat-Analyzer:

BATMAN: This machine contains the information of TWO SETS of encyclopedias! It'll be able to collect and analyze data in MERE SECONDS!
ROBIN: HOLY EINSTEIN!

The thing truly comes alive in the performances, however: Voice actor Jeff Bergman nails both William Dozier's stentorian narration, and Cesar Romero's distinctive Mid-Atlantic accent. West, Ward, and Newmar gamely return to form, clearly having a ball. Newmar hasn't lost a step, and if Ward today sounds less like a Boy Wonder than an Uncle-With-a-Timeshare-in-Tampa Wonder, his enthusiasm shines through. West remains a national treasure, with a voice still capable of snaking through a line like "A blimp! Unorthodox, but *diabolical!*" to wring the utmost from it.

The plot, happily, is pure silliness: Catwoman, Joker, Riddler, and Penguin team up to steal a duplication ray. When Catwoman turns Batman evil with a magic potion, he makes duplicates of himself to take over Gotham.

But it's the many meta-textual winks to eight decades of Bat-history that truly delight. Batman and Robin ride Whirly-bats; Batman appears on variety show called *Gotham Palace* (an homage to West's 1966 appearance, in costume, on the variety show *Hollywood Palace* where he sang "Orange-Colored Sky"); a camera filming a Bat-fight duly tilts 45 degrees to the right; when Batman punches one crook, the sound effect that ensues is SPRANG!—a salute to Dick Sprang.

(I wondered briefly if we'd see a similar homage to Bill Finger, but once I took that thought to its logical conclusion I decided it's probably okay that they didn't.)

Of course, the effect of Catwoman's potion over the course of the film, as he slowly but steadily transforms from clean-cut goody-two-shoes to a violent, brutal Batman who distances himself from Robin and strikes out on his own, cannot help but read as a not-terribly-sly echo of the character's evolution from the '60s to the grim-and-gritty '80s and beyond.

But perhaps the purest joy *Return of the Caped Crusaders* provides is a scene in which it neatly rehabilitates the character of Aunt Harriet—and steers directly into the homoerotic skid. Aunt Harriet sees Bruce and Dick dashing off to answer the Batphone and—flighty, dithering matron no more!—sidles up to Alfred.

AUNT HARRIET: Can you *believe* the lengths those two go to keep their little secret?

ALFRED: . . . Secret, ma'am?

AUNT HARRIET: (*Knowing*) Why, Alfred. You *really* don't see it?

The fact that this scene is preceded by one in which young Dick practices his ballet pliés, and is immediately followed by Alfred excusing himself from the conversation by mentioning that "the upstairs doorknobs need polishing" feels like nothing less than a gift; one long overdue, perhaps, but one freely—and, it must be said, fabulously—given.

GHW
Washington, DC
October 11, 2016

BIBLIOGRAPHY

BOOKS

Beard, Jim, ed. *Gotham City 14 Miles: 14 Essays on Why the 1960s Batman TV Series Matters*. Edwardsville, IL: Sequart Research & Literacy Organization, 2010.

> A varied and variously entertaining collection of perspectives on the sixties series. After its cancellation, the show spent years exiled from the public consciousness and from the hearts of the very nerds who grew up loving it. Its recent return to favored status has been a long, slow road; this book was an important mile marker along the way.

Beatty, Scott. *Batman: The Ultimate Guide to the Dark Knight*. New York: DK Publishing, 2001.

> This kid-friendly coffee-table dossier on the comic book Dark Knight captures him as he was at the turn of the millennium. To read it now is to see the character frozen in four-color amber, hovering between the last days of the Age of Schumacher and the dawning of the Era of Nolan.

Bongco, Mila. *Reading Comics: Language, Culture, and the Concept of the Superhero in Comic Books*. New York: Routledge, 2000.

Chewy, thoughtful academic take on superheroes and the language we use to talk about them.

Brooker, Will. *Batman Unmasked: Analyzing a Cultural Icon.* New York: Continuum, 2001.

Hugely insightful and well-argued cultural history of Batman that neatly dissects many long-held but provably false bits of received wisdom about the character and about comics history. Brooker's approach is academic and exacting, which can't help but leach into the book's occasionally dry tone. (You up on your post-structuralist semiotics? Then you'll be fine.) But he's particularly good on the gay readings of Batman—and the gay panic of Batman fans.

Brooker, Will. *Hunting the Dark Knight: Twenty-First Century Batman.* London: I.B. Tauris, 2012.

Another helping of intellectually rigorous and agreeably tweedy analysis from Brooker, this time focused on the Nolan films and their sociopolitical themes. He defaults to academic jargon less often here than he did in *Unmasked*, making for a leaner, more energetic examination of what the character has come to stand for at the dawn of the twenty-first century.

Burke, Liam. *Fan Phenomena: Batman.* Bristol, UK: Intellect Books, 2013.

Burke collects essays on Batman fandom, written by both the superfans themselves (cosplayers, fanfic writers, comics store clerks) and those who study fandom and publish about it. A mixed bag, with some excellent writing on fanfic, the marketing of the Nolan films, and their online reception.

Collinson, Gary. *Holy Franchise, Batman!: Bringing the Caped Crusader to the Screen.* London: Robert Hale Limited, 2012.

Hokay, well, let's stipulate: terrible title. But a handy guide to the many noncomics incarnations of Batman. There's not a lot of information here you don't also find in Scivally, below, but Collinson's got a good eye for the illustrative anecdote and turns what might otherwise be colorless production details into engaging narratives.

Coswil, Alan, et al. *DC Comics Year by Year: A Visual Chronicle.* New York: DK Publishing, 2010.

A handsome year-by-year chronicle of DC Comics' first seventy-five years. Extremely useful for getting the view from thirty thousand feet, with its at-a-glance summations of concurrent developments across DC's superhero books, year by year. Provides great context, though the prose tends to get a bit booster-y.

Couch, N. C. Christopher. *Jerry Robinson: Ambassador of Comics.* New York: Abrams Comics Arts, 2010.

Overdue appreciation of Robinson, with plenty of archival images and material to help earn his many contributions to comics—and his unstinting advocacy for poorly recompensed comics creators—their rightful place in history.

Daniels, Les. *Batman: The Complete History.* New York: DC Comics, 1999.

The definitive guide to the Dark Knight's first sixty years, this lavishly illustrated coffee table book lays out Batman's major developments and sundry transformations in a clear and colorful style.

Dini, Paul, and Chip Kidd. *Batman: Animated.* New York: HarperEntertainment, 1998.

> Lots of information on the conceptualization, development, and execution of the animated series, all lovingly laid out in pages designed by Bat-fan Chip Kidd. His devotion shows: this is a fantastic-looking book.

Eisner, Joel. *The Official Batman Batbook.* New York: Contemporary Books, 1986.

> An episode-by-episode guide to the sixties series that's more a just-the-facts celebration than analysis or commentary. Plenty of (black-and-white) photos and random factoids, including a comprehensive listing of every "Holy ____!" Robin uttered in the series' run. Loved this book as a teen and have held on to it since. Which is just as well, as the production quality of the revised 2008 edition is pretty lousy.

Eury, Michael, and Michael Kronenberg. *The Batcave Companion.* Raleigh: TwoMorrows Publishing, 2009.

> Hugely helpful deep dive into the Bronze Age Batman. Interviews with creators (whose recollections differ on many key points) give us a clear look at the personalities behind some of the greatest moments and images of that era. Neal Adams, in particular, emerges as the kind of guy my mom would call "a real character." Eury and Kronenberg cram the book with all manner of factoids, sidebars, and analyses that provide a comprehensive understanding of how the O'Neil/Adams Batman changed everything.

Feiffer, Jules. *The Great Comic Book Heroes.* New York: Dial Press, 1965.

Cartoonist Feiffer was a tender thirty-six years old when he wrote this hilariously crotchety remembrance of the comics of his youth—dollars to donuts the guy was shaking his fists at clouds when he was still in knee-pants. But he was one of the first writers of note to tackle comics-as-literature (albeit "junk" literature, as far as Feiffer's concerned), and this book remains an irascible hoot. I first read it at the age of seven, as it served as the preface to a 1965 volume of reprints of Golden Age super-hero comics, which I picked up on a remainder table at a B. Dalton at Exton Square Mall in 1975. Feiffer's hard-nosed prose, and those weirdly dark, violent comics, awoke something in me. I still have this book and thumb through it at least once a month, not least because the Golden Age Hawkman is, as we critics say, a hot piece.

Fleisher, Michael L. *The Encyclopedia of Comic Book Heroes, Volume I: Batman.* New York: Collier Books, 1976.

This is an astonishing, and astonishingly nerdy, achievement in scholarship: Fleischer cataloged every character, story line, and Bat-gadget in the first thirty years of Batman's comic book adventures and turned them into this weighty encyclopedia. But he brought more than on-the-spectrum obsessiveness to the task; his entries on Bruce Wayne's romantic life and moti-vation, for example, evince deep and supple thought. I read this cover-to-cover as a kid, though it got a bit repetitive (just about every entry describes Batman defeating an enemy "through an elaborate ruse," which—yeah, okay, fair). But every work of Bat-scholarship that has followed this massive tome is built upon it.

Gabilliet, Jean-Paul. *Of Comics and Men: A Cultural History of American Comic Books.* Jackson, MS: University Press of Mississippi, 2005.

The prose gets a bit dusty, but Gabilliet provides important cultural context for many of the developments I write about in chapters 2 and 3.

Greenberger, Robert. *The Essential Batman Encyclopedia*. New York: Del Rey Books, 2008.

A backbreaking update and expansion of Fleischer's 1976 Batman encyclopedia (see above).

Hajdu, David. *The Ten-Cent Plague: The Great Comic Book Scare and How It Changed America*. New York: Picador, 2008.

A thorough, energetically written dissection of the Wertham era and its lasting repercussions.

Hughes, David. *Tales from Development Hell: The Greatest Movies Never Made?* London: Titan Books, 2012.

Main source of information about the aborted Aronofsky Batman film I cover in chapter 7.

Jacobs, Will, and Gerard Jones. *The Comic Book Heroes: From the Silver Age to the Present*. New York: Crown Publishers, 1985.

Breezy whistle-stop tour of the sea change(s) superhero comics underwent in the sixties and seventies. Better on Marvel than on DC, but lots of good information about the aging of comics readership during this turbulent era.

Jesser, Jody Duncan, and Janine Pourroy. *The Art and Making of the Dark Knight Trilogy*. New York: Abrams, 2012.

A beautifully designed (Bat-fan Chip Kidd strikes again) coffee table book filled with photos, profiles, and production details from Nolan's Batman films. Thorough, impressive, and if the writing gets a bit reverent and solemn now and then, well, I mean: consider the subject.

Jones, Gerard. *Men of Tomorrow: Geeks, Gangsters and the Birth of the Comic Book.* New York: Basic Books, 2005.

Excellent, well-researched accounting of the very early, and sleazy, days of comics publishing.

Kane, Bob, and Tom Andrae. *Batman and Me.* Forestville, CA: Eclipse Books, 1990.

Kane's self-hagiography. This pitched attempt to erase Bill Finger's contributions from history makes for enervating reading.

Kidd, Chip, and Geoff Spear. *Batman: Collected.* New York: Watson-Guptill Publications, 2001.

Sumptuously and lovingly photographed compendium of all manner of Bat-merch over the years.

Legman, Gershon. *Love and Death.* New York: Hacker Art Books, 1963.

A passionate treatise decrying sexual censorship, including a chapter that attacks the violent imagery of comic books with trademark Legman gusto.

Levitz, Paul. *75 Years of DC Comics: The Art of Modern Mythmaking.* Los Angeles: Taschen, 2010.

Weighing in at sixteen pounds, this is a coffee table book that could serve as a coffee table. Truly a book meant to be mounted on a sturdy lectern in the center of a room and track-lit. Levitz walks the reader through DC Comics' history aided by lots of beautiful, exquisitely reproduced comics art. Comes with its own carrying case, complete with handle. Look, it's a big, big book, is my point here.

Morrison, Grant. *Supergods*. New York: Spiegel & Grau, 2011.

Morrison shares the thinking behind his approach to Batman and other heroes—and shares lots of drug trip stories as well. The former are fascinating insights, the latter are drug trip stories.

Nobleman, Marc Tyler. *Bill the Boy Wonder: The Secret Co-Creator of Batman*. Watertown, MA: Charlesbridge, 2012.

Nobleman fights the good fight here, shining a much-needed spotlight on Bill Finger's role in Batman's creation for an all-ages audience. Amusing, well researched, important.

O'Neil, Dennis, ed. *Batman Unauthorized: Vigilantes, Jokers, and Heroes in Gotham City*. Dallas, TX: Benbella Books, 2008.

Editor O'Neil brings a varied assortment of voices together to ruminate on disparate aspects of Batman. As an organizing principle for a series of essays, "Batman" is a bit loose, but the collection manages to hang together.

Pearson, Roberta E., and William Uricchio, eds. *The Many Lives of the Batman*. New York: Routledge, 1991.

A great collection of essays on Batman, including one that digs into the numbers over the years—not just sales, but how the demographics of comics readership changed—which I consulted throughout. Shame about that cover, though. Yow.

Rosenberg, Robin S. *What's the Matter with Batman?* Lexington: Robin S. Rosenberg, 2012.

Psychiatrist Rosenberg puts the Caped Crusader on the couch, citing many psychiatric sources, and concludes (spoiler) that Batman does not suffer from any major mental disorders. Riiiiiight.

Rovin, Jeff. *The Encyclopedia of Superheroes.* New York: Facts on File, 1985.

Another work of nerd scholarship for which I was grateful as a teenager. Led me to many heroes I'd never heard of—my abiding love for the Flaming Carrot is all Rovin's fault—and served as an inspirational example of writing that distilled big, goofy ideas like superheroes into clear, pithy prose.

Salkowitz, Rob. *Comic-Con and the Business of Pop Culture.* New York: McGraw-Hill, 2012.

Salkowitz is a business writer and a nerd, and he asks big questions in this book about the future of nerd culture that he proceeds to tackle with rigor, acumen, and humor. Lays out what's going on now and what he expects the coming years will bring with practiced, clear-eyed business savvy.

Schwartz, Julius, and Brian M. Thomsen. *Man of Two Worlds: My Life in Science Fiction and Comics.* Jefferson, NC: McFarland, 2008.

Autobiography of Silver Age editor/ur-nerd Schwartz, who brought superheroes back from the brink of oblivion and whose love of ape covers is the stuff of legend.

Scivally, Bruce. *Billion Dollar Batman: A History of the Caped Crusader on Film, Radio and Television, from Ten-Cent Comic Book to Global Icon.* Wilmette, IL: Henry Gray Publishing, 2011.

I was familiar with Scivally's work, especially his exhaustive-ness in tracking down the tiniest production detail, from his book on the Man of Steel's multimedia exploits, which was my bosom companion while I wrote my Superman book. This was like going home—the same comprehensive approach, this time directed at the Caped Crusader's adventures outside the comics page. Everything you need to know. In fact, way way more.

Simon, Joe, and Jim Simon. *The Comic Book Makers.* Lebanon, NJ: The Comic Book Makers, 2003.

Joe Simon was there on the front lines in the Golden Age, and in this book (written with his son) he combines personal mem-oir with industry analysis.

Van Hise, James. *Batmania II.* Las Vegas: Pioneer Books, 1992.

Gleeful celebration of the POW! ZAP! Batman, including in-terviews with producers, writers, and actors.

Vaz, Mark Cotta. *Tales of the Dark Knight: Batman's First Fifty Years, 1939–1989.* New York: Ballantine Books, 1989.

A well-illustrated overview of Batman's first half century, clearly written while the first wave of grim-and-gritty comics was cresting. Vaz seems ashamed of the Silver Age Batman, *really* hates the sixties TV series, and waves away any gay readings of the character as ridiculous. I didn't agree with Vaz's take when I read this book at twenty-one, and I don't agree with him now, but it's a fascinating document of the time, and the nature of post–*Dark Knight* Bat-fandom.

Walker, Cody. *The Anatomy of Zur-En-Arrh: Understanding Grant Morrison's Batman*. Edwardsville, IL: Sequart Organization, 2014.

Engaging and informative analysis of Morrison's Batman run that never devolves into musty academe-speak. Clearly the work of a thoughtful, engaged, yet critical fan.

Wertham, Fredric. *Seduction of the Innocent*. Port Washington, NY: Kennikat Press, 1972.

Here it is, the Book That Ate Comics, in all its great and terrible glory. It's a surprisingly quick read, well worth the time of anyone with any interest in comics and comics culture. I've always been struck by the disconnect between what Wertham actually says and what the comics cognoscenti claim he does.

Wright, Bradford W. *Comic Book Nation: The Transformation of Youth Culture in America*. Baltimore: Johns Hopkins University Press, 2001.

Wright covers some of the same ground Hajdu and Jones cover above, with an approach that's slightly more American studies/ broadly sociocultural in scope.

York, Chris, and Rafiel York, eds. *Comic Books and the Cold War, 1946–1962: Essays on Graphic Treatment of Communism, the Code and Social Concerns*. Jefferson, NC: McFarland & Company, Inc., 2012.

Excellent examination of the prevailing mood of the country that Wertham keyed into/cannily exploited.

COMICS

All citations provided in the book's main text.

COMICS COLLECTIONS AND GRAPHIC NOVELS

Johns, Geoff. *Batman: Earth One*. New York: DC Comics, 2012.

Miller, Frank. *Batman: The Dark Knight Returns*. New York: DC Comics, 1997.

———. *Batman: The Dark Knight Strikes Again*. New York: DC Comics, 2004.

Moore, Alan. *Batman: The Killing Joke*. New York: DC Comics, 1988.

Morrison, Grant. *Arkham Asylum: A Serious House on Serious Earth*. New York: DC Comics, 1989.

———. *Batman Incorporated: Demon Star*. New York: DC Comics, 2013.

———. *Batman Incorporated: Gotham's Most Wanted*. New York: DC Comics, 2013.

Slott, Dan. *Arkham Asylum: Living Hell*. New York: DC Comics, 2003.

Snyder, Scott. *Batman: The Black Mirror*. New York: DC Comics, 2011.

————. *Batman: The Court of Owls*. New York: DC Comics, 2012.

————. *Batman: The City of Owls*. New York: DC Comics, 2013.

————. *Batman: Death of the Family*. New York: DC Comics, 2013.

————. *Batman: Zero Year—Secret City*. New York: DC Comics, 2014.

Snyder, Scott, et al. *Batman: Night of the Owls*. New York: DC Comics, 2013.

Starlin, Jim. *Batman: A Death in the Family*. New York: DC Comics, 1988.

————. *Batman: The Cult*. New York: DC Comics, 1988.

Tomasi, Peter J. *Batman and Robin: Born to Kill*. New York: DC Comics, 2012.

————. *Batman and Robin: Pearl*. New York: DC Comics, 2013.

————. *Batman and Robin: Death of the Family*. New York: DC Comics, 2013.

————. *Batman and Robin: Requiem for Damian*. New York: DC Comics, 2014.

Waid, Mark. *Kingdom Come*. New York: DC Comics, 1997.

Wolfman, Marv, et al. *Batman: A Lonely Place of Dying*. New York: DC Comics, 1990.

MAGAZINES

Alter Ego: One of the main superhero fanzines of the sixties, revived in 1999. Source of many of the interviews with creators I've excerpted in the book.

Amazing Heroes: A favorite magazine of my youth, published by Fantagraphics from 1981 to 1992. Focused on superhero comics: interviews, profiles, industry gossip. A fascinating, first-draft-of-history chronicle of the comics boom and bust.

Amazing World of DC Comics: Published by DC Comics themselves from 1974–78, this neither-fish-nor-fowl periodical assumed the tone of a fanzine but was clearly written by DC's marketing department.

Batmania: Biljo White's seminal sixties Bat-fanzine. Twenty-one issues are archived online at comicbookplus.com/?cid=746.

Comics Buyer's Guide: Influential and massively informative comics magazine; launched in 1971 and ceased publication in 2013, making it the longest-running English-language comics-focused periodical. Edited for years by Don and Maggie Thompson, and by Maggie after Don's death in 1994, *CBG* helped launch the career of many excellent writers and helped move mainstream press coverage past the "POW! ZAP! COMICS AREN'T JUST FOR KIDS ANYMORE!" era.

The Comics Journal: In its day, featured some of the finest comics criticism around; now an online publication supplemented by gorgeous, massive semiannual print editions.

Comics Scene: Intermittently published comics news magazine that flourished in the eighties, published by Starlog. Featured several entertainingly apoplectic letters from readers outraged by Michael Keaton's Bat-casting.

Life: The March 11, 1966, issue featured Adam West's Batman on the cover and an in-depth (for *Life*, anyway) profile of the burgeoning phenomenon that would come to be called Batmania.

REPRINTS/ANTHOLOGIES

Batman: A Celebration of 75 Years. New York: DC Comics, 2014.

The Batman Chronicles. Vols. 1–6. New York: DC Comics, 2005, 2006, 2007.

Batman in the Eighties. New York: DC Comics, 2004.

Batman in the Fifties. New York: DC Comics, 2002.

Batman in the Forties. New York: DC Comics, 2004.

Batman in the Seventies. New York: DC Comics, 1999.

Batman in the Sixties. New York: DC Comics, 1999.

The Greatest Batman Stories Ever Told. Vols. 1 and 2. New York: DC Comics, 1988, 1992.

The Joker: A Celebration of 75 Years. New York: DC Comics, 2014.

The Joker: The Greatest Stories Ever Told. New York: DC Comics, 2008.

Superman/Batman: The Greatest Stories Ever Told. New York: DC Comics, 2007.

WEBSITES

Ain't It Cool News, www.aintitcool.com: Übergeek Harry Knowles's too-passionate-for-copyediting website and forum, whose history is bound up with the Bat-franchise. Knowles's pitched loathing of Schumacher's take on the character had WB executives worried, and the script for *Batman Begins* leaked online via the AICN message boards, among other places.

The Beat, www.comicsbeat.com: Essential daily check-in for comics-related news and analysis.

Comic Book Resources, www.comicbookresources.com: Comics news site focused on superheroes; features Brian Cronin's "Comics Should Be Good" and its regular feature "Comic Book Legends Revealed," an excellent source that led me to several excellent sources.

ComicsAlliance, www.comicsalliance.com: Of all the comics news sites out there, CA comes at the comics industry and its fans with a refreshingly enlightened take on issues of sex, race, and sexuality. Smart, passionate writing.

Comics Chronicles, www.comichron.com: Absolutely indispensible archive of comics sales charts over the decades, accompanied by deep and engaging analysis from site proprietor John Jackson Miller. Easily the site I consulted most often. Hugely useful.

The Comics Journal, www.tcj.com: The online home of *The Comics Journal*, a resource for excellent criticism and profiles touching on the entire comics medium.

The Comics Reporter, www.comicsreporter.com: News, interviews, and insightful reviews from Tom Spurgeon.

Dial B for Blog, www.dialbforblog.com: DC's Silver Age comics are lovingly and irreverently profiled by writer "Robby Reed." I'm indebted to
him for his assiduous chronicling of Bob Kane's many "swipes" from
other sources.

Internet Archive Wayback Machine, archive.org/web/: The Bat-
historian's best friend. Though the actual URLs are long defunct, all
the frothing nerd-dudgeon once found on sites like Mantle of the Bat:
The Bat-Boards, Bring Me the Head of Joel Schumacher, the Anti-
Schumacher Batman Website, and many more can be called up with a
few keystrokes from the mist-shrouded (and spittle-flecked) depths of
the Internet.

Newsarama, www.newsarama.com: General comics news site.

News From ME, www.newsfromme.com: Comics writer and historian
Mark Evanier's garrulous, entertaining, and highly informative blog.

Sequential Tart, www.sequentialtart.com: A site by and for women who
love comics—and also for anyone who wants to read excellent comics
writing without the toxic sludge of casual misogyny and homophobia
that still clings to much of fandom.

Women in Refrigerators, lby3.com/wir/: Writer Gail Simone chronicled the grim-'n'-gritty nineties in real time. She launched this site listing
the many, many women characters who were being used as chattel by
male writers—brutally attacked, raped, or killed off simply to raise the
stakes for male superheroes. Still relevant, more's the pity.

ACKNOWLEDGMENTS

I talked to many fans and creators for this book, but I am more disorganized and lousier at note-taking than someone in my position has any right to be, so I will shamefully overlook many people who helped.

The world's leading Batmanologist, Chris Sims, talked to me at length, which is good because there's no way I could've written this book if he hadn't. In said discussions I only elicited two "Glen, here's why you're wrong"s. Counting that as a victory. Dean Trippe is a passionate and charming authority on all things Batman, and you really need to read his *Something Terrible* like, yesterday. I cornered lots of folks at cons and online to talk Bat-stuff, and they all helped shape my thinking: John Jackson Miller, Mark Evanier, Batton Lash, Lea Hernandez, Graeme McMillan, Scott Aukerman, Ali Arikan, Scott Snyder, Steve Rebarcak, Alan Scherstuhl, Rob Salkowitz, Brad Ricca, Tim Beyers, Alexander Chee, Mark Protosevich, John Suintres, and really lots and lots of other smart, funny, wonderful people I don't remember; see above, in re: my terribleness.

Jeff Reid was a huge help, tirelessly chasing down sources and resources and generally being a thoughtful and agreeable sounding board throughout the writing process. Marc Tyler Nobleman's an excellent writer and historian and an authority on Bill Finger; I'm deeply grateful he agreed to read over the first chapter and offer his thoughts. Egregiously heterosexual pal-for-life Chris Klimek read the whole damn thing and gave me his take; he's what my Dad used to call a good egg.

Need any of your nits picked with verve and élan? Have you met the great and good Maggie Thompson, indefatigable authority on comics, and grammar, and life in general? You should get on that. Maggie read an early draft and sent me a string of enthusiastically remonstrative text-message corrections for days. Any mistakes you find in this book are only there because I hubristically ignored Maggie's advice like a chump.

Eric Nelson got this book off the ground, Sydelle Kramer kept it flying, and my tenacious and insightful editors, Brit Hvide and Julianna Haubner, brought it home safely, for which I am profoundly grateful. Aja Pollock and Jonathan Evans copyedited the sprawling thing with vim and a profoundly nerdy, it-getting sagacity. An early draft of the introduction was what got me the Amtrak Residency for Writers, and I revised the book on the Empire Builder and Coast Starlight, an unforgettable, once-in-a-lifetime experience. Friends and family offered emotional support and red wine throughout the process, and made plenty of "So what's next? Aquaman?" jokes, but don't hold that against them. After fifteen years, Faustino Nunez became my husband over the course of this book's life; he continues to make me a better man simply by association—only now he does so legally.

INDEX

IMAGE CREDITS

1. From *Detective Comics* volume 1, #27 (May 1939). Art: Bob Kane. Script: Bill Finger.

2. From *Detective Comics* volume 1, #33 (November 1939). Art: Bob Kane. Script: Bill Finger.

3. From *Batman* volume 1, #1 (June 1940). Art: Jerry Robinson, Bob Kane. Script: Bill Finger.

4. From *Detective Comics* volume 1, #475 (February 1978). Art: Marshall Rogers, Terry Austin. Script: Steve Englehart.

5. and 6. From *Detective Comics* volume 1, #38, (April 1940). Art: Jerry Robinson, Bob Kane. Story: Bill Finger.

7. From *World's Finest Comics* volume 1, #30 (September–October 1947). Art: Bob Kane, Jack Burnley. Script: Bill Finger.

8. From *Batman* volume 1, #92 (June 1955). Art: Sheldon Moldoff, Stan Kaye. Script: Bill Finger.

9. From *Detective Comics* volume 1, #233 (July 1956). Art: Sheldon Moldoff, Stan Kaye. Script: Edmond Hamilton.

10. From *Detective Comics* volume 1, #341 (July 1965). Art: Carmine Infantino, Joe Giella. Script: John Broome.

11. From *Detective Comics* volume 1, #395 (January 1970). Art: Neal Adams, Dick Giordano. Script: Denny O'Neil.

12. and 13. From *Batman: The Dark Knight Returns* #1 (February 1986). Art: Frank Miller, Klaus Janson. Script: Frank Miller.

14. From *Batman* volume 1, #405 (March 1987). Art: David Mazzuchelli. Script: Frank Miller.

15. From *Batman: The Killing Joke* (May 1988). Art: Brian Bolland. Script: Alan Moore.

16. From *Batman* volume 1, #427 (December 1988).

17. From *Planetary/Batman: Night on Earth* (August 2003). Art: John Cassaday. Script: Warren Ellis.

18. From *Batman* volume 2, #7 (May 2012). Art: Greg Capullo, Jonathan Glapion. Script: Scott Snyder.

ABOUT THE AUTHOR

Glen Weldon has been a theater critic, a science writer, an oral historian, a writing teacher, a bookstore clerk, a movie usher, a winery tour guide, a PR flack, a spectacularly inept marine biologist, and a slightly-better-than-ept competitive swimmer. His work has appeared in *The New York Times*, *The Washington Post*, *The New Republic*, *Slate*, *The Atlantic*, *The Village Voice*, *The Philadelphia Inquirer*, and many other places. He is a panelist on NPR's *Pop Culture Happy Hour* and reviews books and comic books for NPR.org. The author of *Superman: The Unauthorized Biography*, he lives in Washington, D.C.